RETHINKING INCLUSIVE EDUCATION: THE PHILOSOPHERS
OF DIFFERENCE IN PRACTICE

Inclusive Education: Cross Cultural Perspectives

VOLUME 5.

SCOPE OF THE SERIES

This series is concerned with exploring the meaning and function of inclusive education in a world characterised by rapid social, economic and political change. The question of inclusion and exclusion will be viewed as a human rights issue, in which concerns over issues of equity, social justice and participation will be of central significance. The series will provide an inter-disciplinary approach and draw on research and ideas that will contribute to an awareness and understanding of cross-cultural insights and questions. Dominant assumptions and practices will be critically analysed thereby encouraging debate and dialogue over such fundamentally important values and concerns.

The titles published in this series are listed at the end of this volume

Rethinking Inclusive Education: The Philosophers of Difference in Practice

By

JULIE ALLAN
University of Stirling, Scotland, UK

 Springer

A C.I.P. Catalogue record for this book is available from the Library of Congress.

ISBN 978-1-4020-6092-2 (HB)
ISBN 978-1-4020-6093-9 (e-book)

Published by Springer,
P.O. Box 17, 3300 AA Dordrecht, The Netherlands.

www.springer.com

Printed on acid-free paper

CONTENTS

FOREWORD

One of the important responsibilities that advocates of inclusion need to continually practise is that of self-criticism. This includes examining and re-examining the assumptions informing our perspectives, the concepts that we use including 'inclusive education' and our intentions, especially in relation to the question of change. We need to beware of the danger of unexamined orthodoxies, the possibilities of adopting inclusive language with little, if any, changes in our thinking and practice and a sterile and insensitive position with regard to the pursuit of new or alternative ideas.

In this very important book, Allan powerfully reminds us of the necessity and centrality of these concerns and provides a direct, perceptive and thoughtful, examination and critique of the varied barriers to the task of how to make inclusion happen. Allan challenges the reader to step back and re-examine the rationale for inclusion through an alternative mindset. She challenges the varied attacks upon inclusion including those in the education business to stop using economic (it costs too much) and pedagogical (it is bad for the other children in the class and traumatic for the disabled children) and social (just too much for the teacher's workload) reasons for closing the door and doing the right thing, and those who argue that inclusion was an experiment that did not work.

The book draws on a wealth of research material covering theoretical, conceptual, practical and policy-based issues. Points of connection, and contradictions are drawn out and illustrated contextually, providing some serious criticisms and questions. It both provides a valuable resource and suggests ways in which the struggle for inclusion can move forward.

This book is not an easy read, in that it draws on authors and ideas we may not be familiar with, introduces alternative conceptions and ways of covering and engaging with key issues and challenging questions and thus provides a thought-provoking, unsettling and disturbing analysis.

By drawing on what she calls the philosophy of difference, Deleuze and Guattari, Derrida and Foucault, Allan explains how their ideas can possibly contribute to innovatory ways of conceiving and engaging with the question of inclusion. Through the introduction and application of new concepts such as 'rhizome,' 'deterritorialization' and 'transgression', the emphasis is on active 'experimentation', 'playing', 'inverting' and 'stuttering' over ideas, issues and innovatory concerns such as the question of uncertainty in the process of transformative change. Allan confirms the impact of these approaches on her own perspective and understanding which, she maintains, has provided her with more optimism and insights into the conditions under which inclusion might become more possible.

Allan brings children and young people and their families into the mix not to address inclusion as a problem but to understand it in the context of how to move forward. She is seeking an answer to what is 'good inclusion' rather than what is 'effective inclusion' and to do that she goes, as she says, to those who are most affected to tell us what it means.

Importantly, the book is not just a theoretical examination of the ways the ideas of the philosophers of 'difference', Allan introduces, can be brought to bear on inclusion. The final chapters provide practical suggestions for applying those ideas: ideas about the relationships of teachers and children; ideas about reshaping teacher education; disability arts in the schools; the question of the nature and process of inclusive research and the challenges of a political engagement with inclusion.

We are delighted to include this book in our series and hopefully it will contribute to preventing the ossification of ideas and to a more open, serious dialogue between interested parties over what constitutes fundamentally important issues and questions.

Len Barton
Marcia Rioux
August 2007

ACKNOWLEDGEMENTS

This book spent much of its early life in Whitby, North Yorkshire, and whilst it is more fitting to pay tribute to people, rather than places, I remain indebted to this eccentric space and its endless supply of fish.

Len Barton and Marcia Rioux, series editors, gave me very detailed and constructive feedback on the draft manuscript and John I'Anson offered advice on sections of the book, worked on the project on children's rights, in which some of the Deleuzian ideas were developed and, importantly, helped to come up with the title for the book. Maria Jonckheere, of Springer, was warmly enthusiastic and encouraging.

Other individuals were part of discussions in which I tried out some of the ideas contained within the book and I am grateful to John Field, Linda Ware, Dora Bjarnason, Heather Lynch, Peter Cope, Roger Slee, Susan Peters, Joan Forbes, Walter Humes, Joron Pijl and Anne-Lise Arnason. I am fortunate to have supervised a number of Doctoral students who have put some of the ideas of the philosophers of difference to work on their own projects on art, social welfare and nursing and the work of Dr Fiona Dean, Dr Ralston McKay and Dr Kevin Dawson has been inspirational. John Field kept my 'to do' lists for the book topped up with silly ideas and I am grateful for the vigilance this inspired.

My greatest gratitude is reserved for the students I have encountered over recent years, who have challenged my understandings and exposed my ignorance, of inclusion and exclusion. Raschida and Alistair (pseudonyms of course) in particular and the children and young people involved in events more generally provoked this project and I sincerely hope it responds – and does justice – to some of the challenges they have issued.

INTRODUCTION

The strain imposed by social inclusion in some of our schools is in danger of becoming a time bomb waiting to explode unless properly resourced . . . we all want inclusion for all young people in Scotland, including asylum seeker children, so that they to can look forward positively to the future. However, that future inclusion which all politicians are happy to sign up to and pay lip service to comes at a price. And in too many schools at the present time that price is the health and well-being of Scottish teachers . . . disruptive pupils may be a minority, but they are a growing minority. Now is the time to say enough is enough. This trend must be reversed. These pupils will not be included in mainstream provision unless their behaviour can be guaranteed. All schools must be given the ability to exclude the disruptive. (Douglas Mackie, Educational Institute of Scotland Presidential Address, 2004)

Total inclusion is a form of child abuse, especially if the child is in the completely wrong environment for their educational needs. (National Association of Schoolmasters Union of Women Teachers in the UK, 2001)

The recent commentaries from teachers unions identify the continuing – and troubling – presence of certain children, particularly those identified with behavioural difficulties as a serious threat to the emotional wellbeing of teachers. Questions raised by teachers unions about whether inclusion can realistically be achieved have emanated from concerns about teachers being unprepared (Macmillan et al, 2002; Edmunds 2003) and concerns that inclusion is placing unnecessary pressures on teachers and adding to their existing stress. The Canadian Unions have expressed concern about 'the physical and psychological strain teachers suffer from students who are verbally and physically abusive to teachers' (Crawford and Porter, 1992, p. 15) and more recently about teachers' capacities to keep up with the demands of inclusion (Edmunds, 2003). In 2002, the Nova Scotia teachers union voted unanimously to withdraw its support for inclusion, pronouncing the teaching of disabled children in regular classrooms a 'nightmare' (CSIE, 2002), although this was contested on legal grounds. In the US, attention has been drawn to the 'collision course' between high stakes testing programmes and inclusion (National Association of Education, 2005) and a wave against inclusion has been discerned within Scandinavia (Persson, 2006). Dismissing inclusion as 'a costly disaster'

1

(Shakespeare, 2005), both the National Association of Schoolmasters and Union of Women Teachers and the National Union of Teachers (Shakespeare, 2005; Macbeath et al, 2006) have expressed concerns about the cost of inclusion for other pupils in the school, particularly where there is disruptive or violent behaviour from disabled pupils. This concern was echoed by a teacher, writing anonymously, who argued that the price of inclusion was too high:

> Teachers just cannot spread themselves equally amongst their pupils . . . Classrooms were never about learning, they are about social interaction and building confidence and about pupils becoming 'whole' people. No-one would wish to exclude any child from being part of this experience but at what cost to others when the problems are such that the learning environment is destroyed and everyone pays a price? (Primary teacher, General Teaching Council Scotland, 2004, p. 13).

Researchers report that teachers are increasingly talking about inclusion as an impossibility in the current climate (Croll and Moses, 2000; Ballard 2003a; Thomas and Vaughan, 2004), lacking confidence in their own competence to deliver inclusion with existing resources (Mittler, 2000; Hanko, 2005). In research undertaken by Macbeath et al (2006), there was a general positive regard for inclusion, with teachers seeing the benefits for all pupils, yet they expressed concern about whether mainstream schools were able to provide a suitable education for children with complex emotional needs. They also questioned whether alternative, special provision might better serve children with complex special needs. Harvey-Koelpin (2006) reports that well-meaning and dedicated teachers in the US, who were previously willing to include disabled children in their classroom, have begun to refuse them because of concerns that their low test scores would have a negative effect on their own school careers.

Even Mary Warnock, hailed as the 'architect of inclusion' (CSIE, 2005a), has changed her mind. In a pamphlet published by the Philosophy of Education Society of Great Britain (Warnock, 2005) she argues that the move towards inclusion was a big mistake. She claims that there is a 'body of evidence' (p. 35) which suggests that the experience of disabled children in mainstream school is generally 'traumatic' (p. 43). Without offering this evidence, and without reference to the extensive publications by disabled people supporting inclusion (Barton, 2005), she contends that exclusion is inevitable even if it begins well in the primary school:

> Young children can be very accommodating to the idiosyncracies of others, and teachers tend on the whole to stay with their class, and thus get to know their pupils and be known by them. The environment is simply less daunting than that of the secondary school. In secondary schools, however, the problems become acute. Adolescents form and need strong friendships, from which a Down's Syndrome girl, for example, who may have been an amiable enough companion when she was younger, will now be excluded; her contemporaries having grown out of her reach. The obsessive eccentricities of the Asperger's boy will no longer be tolerated and he will be bullied and teased, or at best simply neglected (p. 35).

The media responded to Warnock's dramatic u-turn with a predictable search for cases of children who had been 'damaged' by inclusion (Warnock, 2005, p. 35) and offered sombre reports of personal tragedy. Melanie Phillips (2005), writing in the *Daily Mail*, remarks 'Now she tells us!' but points out that this is not the first u-turn by this influential individual and cites previous changes of mind in relation to euthanasia and human cloning. Phillips argues that inclusion has 'caused chaos and misery for countless thousands of children and their teachers and had made many schools all but ungovernable' and asks:

> Is it not deeply alarming that a person who has played such a seminal role in literally changing the culture of this country should turn out to be such a flake? (Phillips, n.d.)

Barton (2005), while elegantly dismissing Warnock's pronouncements as ignorant and offensive, also expresses some concern about her 'naïve and politically reactionary demand' (p. 4) for acceptance that 'even if inclusion is an ideal for society in general, it may not always be an ideal for school' (Warnock, 2005, p. 43). He warns that such thinking, if realised in practice, 'will contribute to the building up of serious individual and socially divisive problems for the future'. (Barton, 2005, p. 4). There was much relief and delight, however, among the supporters of special schools who viewed Warnock's words as a reprieve and as evidence that 'the tide is turning on SEN provision' (Gloucestershire Special Schools Protection League, 2005) although there was some regret that 'it took her 30 years to discover inclusion was going wrong' (ibid). David Cameron, speaking at the time as a lowly Conservative MP, told the House of Commons that Warnock had issued a 'stunning recantation' and recommended that the House took notice of 'such a significant report by a respected figure' (Hansard, 22 June, 2005, Col 825).

Parents have become increasingly concerned about the unwillingness of schools to accept their child (Audit Commission, 2002; Ofsted, 2004) and have experienced considerable pain and anguish in the 'long road to statementing' and in the 'struggle to get a child with special needs everything it needed to be fully included' (Macbeath et al, 2006, pp. 59–60). Their experiences in the role as 'consumer' and 'partner' (Vincent, 2000, p. 2) appear to be negative and exclusionary. For those parents whose children have made it into mainstream, there have been concerns about the schools' reluctance to embrace full inclusion (DisabilityResources.org, n.d.; National Council on Disability, 1994) and worries that the teachers are ill prepared to give their children the support they need (Eason, 2004; Macbeth et al, 2006). Mark Vaughan of the Centre for Studies in Inclusive Education, insisting that 'Inclusion is working', argues that those parents unlucky enough to encounter negative attitudes within mainstream schools are 'victims of half-hearted integration, not inclusion' (CSIE, 2005b), but this may not reassure parents who feel 'betrayed as their children's educational needs went unmet' (Halpin, 2006).

Inclusion appears to be in something of a sorry state, characterised by confusion, frustration, guilt and exhaustion. Disabled commentator Tom Shakespeare (2005) suggests that there is also a measure of 'hysteria,' 'moral panic' and an 'alarming backlash against the principle of inclusion'. Questions about *how* we should include appear to be displaced by questions about *why* we should include and under what conditions. The exclusion of certain children from mainstream schools has become legitimate and acceptable, especially if it can be argued that they would have a potentially negative effect on the majority of children within the mainstream.

This book is an attempt to understand how inclusion has become such an impossibility and seeks to find a way to go on with inclusion in ways that are acceptable to children and young people and their families. It does this by attempting to reframe the 'problem' of inclusion as an ongoing struggle, involving those affected most directly in finding 'solutions'. The book uses some of the ideas of the philosophers of difference – Deleuze and Guattari, Derrida and Foucault – and puts them to work on the inclusion 'problem'. The result is a series of tentative propositions about how inclusion might be reworked into a different kind of task for all those involved – including children and young people and their families. These require a leap of imagination, but not faith, and necessitate the engagement with undecidability and the impossible, in an attempt to 'draw a line of creation out of a speeding line of annihilation' (Haghighi, 2002, p. 144).

The book is divided into three parts. Part one is concerned with *The state of inclusion* and Chapter 1 discusses the *territories of failure,* inhabited by inclusion and examines the frustration, guilt and exhaustion experienced by those attempting – and failing – to include. It considers how teacher education, instead of preparing beginning and experienced teachers to at least want to include, seems to exacerbate the problem. Chapter 2, *The repetition of exclusion in policy and legislation,* asks why exclusion is so impossible to resist and explores how exclusion is repeatedly reinscribed in policy and legislation. The recent Scottish Additional Support Needs legislation, replacing the troublesome and exclusionary system of statementing with something far more exclusionary, and the House of Commons Education and Skills Select Committee's (2006) Inquiry into special educational needs which endorsed segregated schooling provide bleak illustrations. In Chapter 3, the problems caused by *excluding research* are considered. The inability of the research to produce better understanding of inclusion and the failure of researchers to make any material difference to the lives of disabled people, and the frustration and pain that this has caused, is examined.

The three chapters in Part two, *Putting the philosophers of difference to work on inclusion,* set out the key ideas of three philosophers of difference which might be put to work to reframe the inclusion project. Chapter 4, *Deleuze and Guattari's smooth spaces* begins with a discussion of why philosophy, as active experimentation, could offer an escape route for challenging some of the closure in educational practice and then sets out four aspects of Deleuze and Guattari's work – the rhizome, deterritorializations, difference and becoming – which appear to be of relevance to the project of inclusion. Chapter 5, *Derrida and the (im)possibilities of justice,* considers the role of deconstruction, a 'philosophy of hesitation' (Critchley, 1999, p. 41), in identifying closure and injustice within texts. Chapter 6, *Foucault and the practice of transgression,* explores briefly the conceptual tools relating to power and knowledge, but focuses mainly on the strand of Foucault's work concerned with ethics and considers the potential of transgression to challenge exclusion.

The final part of this book, *Rethinking inclusion?* contains some practical suggestions for putting the ideas of the philosophers of difference to work on inclusion. Chapter 7, *Teachers and children: subverting, subtracting, inventing,* sets out the work upon the relationships between teachers and children which could create better prospects for inclusion and some examples of experimentation are offered. Chapter 8, *Nomadic learning to teach,* offers some suggestions for reshaping teacher education and continuing professional development. Chapter 9, *Performing inclusion: instructive arts experiences,* considers how the explicitly political nature of disability arts might be used within schools to provide students with opportunities for embodied and rhizomic learning and to promote inclusion and social justice. Chapter 10, *Inclusive research* explores some of the new problematics which emerge from the implication of the philosophers of difference in research practices. The nature and scope of a more ethically responsible research agenda for inclusion is sketched, with consideration of the kinds of questions which might be addressed, a reframing of research relations, and the implications for analytical work and writing. The final chapter, *Inclusion politics,* ponders the question of why we should struggle for inclusion and attempts to come up with some answers to this. In calling for a more politicised engagement with inclusion, I speculate on the conditions under which inclusion might be a more realistic possibility. The inclusion 'problem', as will be seen, is hugely complex, contentious and potentially overwhelming. The ideas of the philosophers of difference which surface provide a fresh take on the kind of challenges involved in inclusion. Putting them to work on it offers an escape route out of abandonment and defeat. It is at least worth a try.

PART ONE: THE STATE OF INCLUSION

1. TERRITORIES OF FAILURE

Inclusion has been attacked from a number of directions, making it seem an even greater impossibility than ever before. As well as the complaints from the teachers unions about the physical and psychological strain on teachers and the damage done to children and young people by inclusion, it has also been assaulted by special educationists who have dismissed it as ideological and an unproven bandwagon (Kauffman and Hallahan, 1995; Kavale and Mostert, 2004). Parents have expressed concern about the adequacy of support received by their children in mainstream schools and even parents of 'other' children have questioned the impact of inclusion policies, especially where there are disruptive children. Now Warnock's denunciation of the whole idea of inclusion threatens to see it off. There is little doubt that inclusion has a troubled existence and that it is being written off, at least in some quarters, as an abject failure. This chapter considers the territories of failure associated with inclusion – the confusion, frustration, guilt and exhaustion – and examines the doubts raised about whether inclusion will ever become a reality.

CONFUSION

The first territory of failure concerns the confusion which reigns over the inclusion 'project' and what it is supposed to do. The intention that inclusion should replace integration, brought in with the *Warnock Report* (Department of Education and Science, 1978) and the subsequent legislation, was welcomed by those who were critical that integration had been little more than calculus of equity (Slee, 2001a), concerned with measuring the extent of a student's disability, with a view to calculating the resource loading to accompany that student into school. Slee describes the crude mathematical formula which is used: Equity [E] is achieved when you add Additional Resources [AR] to the Disabled Student [D], thus $E = AR + D$. Inclusion, formalised and to an extent mandated by the Salamanca statement, was supposed to be about more than placement in mainstream schools and was presented as the twofold activity of increasing participation and removing barriers (Barton, 1997). Suspicions have been voiced, however that inclusion is no better than integration and has merely replicated exclusionary special education practices

9

(Slee, 1993; 2001a; Slee and Allan, 2001). Dyson (2001) suggests that tensions within the inclusion movement have led to a 'recalibration' (p. 27) of inclusion which amount to pleas for 'old fashioned integration' (ibid).

There appears, however, to be deep uncertainty about how to create inclusive environments within schools and about how to teach inclusively. The failure to consult with children and young people and their families means that there is little notion of the kind of inclusive practices that are acceptable to them. Whilst we continue to be ignorant about the features of *good* inclusion, we are assailed with advice about *effective* inclusion, all of which is appallingly meaningless and likely to entrench the sense of failure among teachers. As Booth et al (2003a) note, inclusion is understood differently by scholars, or at least they start from different positions, and as Garcia and Metcalf (2005) point out, there is a continuous invention of new terminology and nomenclature, aimed at being more neutral than what previously existed. The attempt by Booth and his colleagues (2003a) to produce a composite view of inclusion from contributors to their edited collection seems only to add further confusion. By their own admission, their composite definition 'glosses over differences of view' (p. 167), but it also plunges us into essentialism and distracts us from concerns about what inclusion might *do* for individuals and their families. Inclusive education, the preferred epithet for some, is used without recognising its oxymoronic nature and without considering that schools were never meant to be for everyone (Slee, 2003) and must, in order to function, position some individuals as failures.

According to Warnock (2005), who has *come out* against inclusion, the confusion is one of which 'children are the casualties' (p. 14). She acknowledges her own part in creating confusion and admits that the 1981 legislation 'contained the seeds of confusion which, I fear, can be traced back to the 1978 Report of the Committee of Inquiry' (p. 20). Although she never argued, in that report, that all children and young people should be educated in mainstream and indeed maintained that there would continue to be a place for some special schools, the report came to stand for mainstreaming. In what has been received as a dramatic about turn, she pronounces inclusion, to be 'the most disastrous legacy of the 1978 report' (Warnock, 2005, p. 22) and one which she now regards as difficult, if not impossible, to challenge:

> Like an inheritance that grows and becomes more productive from one generation to another, this concept has gained a remarkable foothold in our society (p. 22).

In her defence she claims that two major 'warnings' (p. 25) were given to the Warnock committee by the Department for Education. The first was that dyslexic students should not be taken into account by the Committee, since at the time this was 'barrred from the civil service vocabulary' (p. 26). The second warning concerned social deprivation and the Committee was urged to exclude children in such circumstances, including those for whom English was a second language, from its deliberations. Warnock claims this 'embargo' (p. 27) set up much of the confusion about inclusion which reigns today. This may well be the case, but her solution of reinventing special schools, 'based on a new concept of inclusion' (p. 14) to house vulnerable children, particularly those with communication difficulties, but also children in care, is baffling. These schools, she argues, would remove children from the terrible trauma associated with mainstreaming, where bullying is inevitable, and allow them to specialise in the Performing Arts or IT in an environment where 'inclusion is thus assured' (p. 48). Warnock's remedy, together with her deeply offensive language, describing, for example, 'children suffering from autism' (p. 14), 'a Down's Syndrome girl' (p. 35) and the 'obsessive eccentricities of the Asperger's boy' (ibid), suggests that her own confusion is considerable.

Parents' confusion over inclusion arises from being denied basic information about provision for disabled youngsters and from being generally discouraged from challenging education authorities and schools when they have concerns about provision. Although there has been a growth in the number of parents challenging the refusal of a place in mainstream schools through the tribunal process, this still represents a small proportion of the population of parents with disabled children. The Audit Commission (2002) reported on the stress experienced by parents in England and Wales who had to fight to get a statement for their child, even though this was no guarantee of a mainstream placement. The UK's Independent Panel for Special Education Advice noted, in its submission to the Education and Skills Select Committee Inquiry into Special Education Needs (House of Commons Education and Skills Select Committee, 2006), the difficult role in which parents of disabled youngsters were placed within the Code of Practice for Special Education:

> There is no acknowledgement in the Code that parents are obliged to police their [Local Education Authority], in order to ensure that their child receives the provision which their needs call for, nor that most parents will need considerable support to be able to fulfil this role (p. 22).

They point out that special education legislation does not, in itself, place a burden on parents, but Local Education Authorities breaking the law, and the absence of an enforcement agency, does:

> And, it is a burden which less able and/or less confident parents simply cannot cope with. The consequence is that children with sen whose parents are less able and/or less confident end up being the least likely of all the children with sen to receive the provision they need (p. 22).

For black and ethnic minority parents, restricted information on schooling options are commonplace and the impression is often given that special schooling is the only option. Research undertaken for the voluntary organisation *Parents for Inclusion* (Broomfield, 2004) reported that some disabled black children were placed in a mainstream setting without any support and their parents were then placed under intense pressure to remove them and to pursue a segregated placement.

In the US, the National Council on Disability (2000), an independent agency that advises Congress and the President on disability policy, claimed that school districts were using tax dollars to fund 'expensive and time-consuming litigation' against parents and 'even parents with significant resources are hard-pressed to prevail over local education agencies when these agencies and/or their publicly financed attorneys choose to be recalcitrant' (Disability Resource.com, n.d.). In an attempt to ensure a 'level playing field' for their child within mainstream US Advocacy groups, such as Children and Adults with Attention Deficit Disorder (CHADD), have begun turning to the Rehabilitation Act of 1973 (an anti-discrimination civil rights statute for handicapped persons) and its *Section 504*. This provision has been deemed necessary to 'assure attention and co-operation by a teacher or a school' (New Horizons for Learning, n.d).

Instead of inclusion being a source of debate among researchers and scholars, it has become a curious, highly emotive, and somewhat irrational space of confrontation. On the one side, there are the so-called 'inclusionists', advocating to have children educated in mainstream schools and who see this as 'consciously putting into action values based on equity, entitlement, community, participation and respect for diversity (Booth et al, 2003b). On the other side, the special educationists argue for the retention of special education and have dismissed inclusion as a particularly dangerous 'bandwagon':

> Discriminative disability often leads to the creation of *bandwagons* defined as a cause that attracts an increasing number of adherents, amassing power by its timeliness, showmanship, or momentum. Bandwagons provide a communal sense of purpose, an energizing camaraderie, and a collective voice whose power exceeds its importance. Bandwagons are used to champion a cause, engage in sweeping yet attractive rhetoric, and generally to promise far more than they ever have hope of delivering while simultaneously downplaying or ignoring the negative aspects of their edicts (Kavale and Mostert, 2004, p. 232).

The special educationists' contention has been that inclusion does much harm to children and they have demanded empirical evidence to the contrary:

> . . . there is almost no empirical evidence attesting to the efficacy of full inclusion . . . the inclusive bandwagon continues without supportive evidence primarily because it is presumed that morally and ethically "It's the right thing to do" (Kavale and Mostert, 2004, p. 234).

Ideology has become the 'weapon' with which both sides berate each other. The fight, however, resembles a form of handbagging, with one side smacking the other with the accusation that the other is being 'merely' ideological. Whilst ideology is itself much misunderstood and misrecognised there could be something in the truism that ideology is like sweat – you can't smell your own.

Brantlinger (1997) can be credited with initiating the first of a series of challenges to the 'attackers of inclusion' (p. 426), and their claims that inclusion was being used as an ideological weapon with which to beat special education. She made the point that inclusion was, of course, ideological, as indeed were the attempts to defend the special education empire. She and others have been rewarded with vitriolic attacks which Danforth and Morris (2006) have analysed, using the sociological literature of 'heresy' (p. 135). Brantlinger (2004a). however, has remained puzzled that her values orientation, has met with such hostility. Such inept and crass confrontation, in which the opponents trade insults and talk past one another (Gallagher, 1998) ensure that inclusion continues to be seen as little more than a threat to the wellbeing and safety of particular children.

Warnock (2005) also swings her ideology handbag in her disavowal of inclusion and denounces the damaging effects of 'ideology of inclusion' (p. 23). She suggests that inclusion 'springs from hearts in the right place', but, as an ideology it 'dictates', (p. 39), 'entails' (ibid) and leads to 'SEN children' (p. 40) being 'lumped together indiscriminately, as though they share a common right to be educated in mainstream schools' (p. 40). According to Warnock, it is, of course, the children who suffer from the effects of ideology:

> The fact is that, if educated in mainstream schools, many such children are not included at all. They suffer all the pains of the permanent outsider. No political ideology should impose this on them (p. 45).

The special education scholars such as Fuchs and Fuchs (1994) and Kauffman and Hallahan (1995) have a particularly powerful influence within the US, within Higher Education Institutions (HEIs) and on editorial boards of journals. These individuals have, to an extent, controlled the flow of the 'debate' and ensured that any discussions of the possibilities for inclusion have been confrontational and non-productive and that confusion has continued to reign. These authors offer their own brand of sophisticated analysis, by distinguishing between *special* education and special *education* and produce evidence of the latter's efficacy over the former. Special *education* (adapting and modifying instruction) can, they claim, 'sometimes' (Kauffman and Hallahan, 1995, p. 228) be 20 times more effective than *special* education (interventions, including medication). They declare that the 'inclusion philosophy, because it does not focus exclusively on students with disabilities, really seeks to alter not special education but general education' (p. 183). This is a good illustration of the confusion which surrounds inclusion and the superficiality which characterises much of the discussion about it. Special educationists are in a less powerful position outside the US, in both their HEIs and in the journals, but this is because, as Slee (2001b) notes, many of them have reinvented themselves as inclusionists, continuing to preach special education to students under a more publicly acceptable guise and with more judicious language:

> Traditional special educators demonstrate a remarkable resilience through linguistic dexterity. While they use a contemporary lexicon of inclusion, the cosmetic amendments to practices and procedures reflect assumptions about pathological defect and normality based upon a disposition of calibration and exclusion (p. 167).

Slee (2001b) has also noted an 'astonishing lack of reflexivity by some special education researchers' (p. 120) about the nature of their research and their 'appalling ignorance of the scope of inclusive education' (ibid). He includes in his critique those who are 'passing' as inclusionists, but who still appear to hold to the values and practices of special education and to the pathologies of students. Whilst the special educationists have continued to create considerable damage, those who do appear genuinely to be advocates of inclusion could also be charged with failing to understand the position of the special educationists and making little effort to clear up some of the confusion associated with inclusion to generate more substantive and meaningful debates.

FRUSTRATION

In her Reith Lectures in 2002, Onora O'Neill observed that the accountability we now experience was aimed at 'ever more perfect control over institutional and professional life'. The web of accountability in which teachers are caught is characterised by a 'tyranny of transparency' (Strathearn, 2000, p. 309), which emphasises proving rather than improving (Ball, 2000) and forces the fabrication of success. The pressures this creates take away the teacher's soul (Locke, as cited in Ballard, 2003b) and with each new policy and each new initiative:

> to the old "teacher musts" and "teacher shoulds", new collections of impera-
> tives are simply added. Even when contradictory positions are posed, the text
> simply expands to incorporate them (Cormack and Comber, 1996, p. 121;
> original emphasis).

These imperatives contribute to an 'intensification' (Smyth et al, 2004, p. 144) of teachers' work which undermines their professionalism:

> They are harassed by the burdens of time with insufficient time to complete
> all their work tasks in ways that give satisfaction. They have to cut corners in
> the work by doing essential things first, including a host of administrative and
> other non-teaching duties, at the expense of creative work like preparation.
> They face the potential atrophy of teaching skills through lack of opportunity
> for engagement with teachers in professional development and participation
> in collaborative networks (Smyth et al, 2000, p. 144).

Teachers are complicit in these intensifications through their own 'strong work cultures and considerable loyalty and dedication to the education service' (Menter et al, 1997, p. 132). As Booth (2003) notes, teachers' work is characterised by fear of, and obsession with, what is demanded by the 'centre':

> Work in many schools is dominated by a continuous fear of inspection and an
> obsession with meeting centrally set targets so that the balance of the cur-
> riculum is disrupted and education can become the incessant process of
> preparing for the tests and being tested (p. 36).

Elliot (2001) suggests that 'colonisation through audit fosters pathologies of creative compliance in the form of gamesmanship around an indicator culture' (p. 202) and creates substantial distrust. As Codd (1999) points out 'trust breeds more trust and conversely distrust breeds more distrust' (p. 50) and our only relations become contractual because 'writing down what is to be done is the only way we can 'trust' it will be done' (Ballard, 2003b, p. 18; original emphasis). This is profoundly exclusionary.

Inclusion is constructed within accountability regimes as some kind of final destination for certain students, but the limited understanding of what inclusion means to the recipients has led to the establishment of quite unimaginative and inept 'outcomes', which are merely concerned with physical presence in mainstream schools and not with the quality of the school experience. The accountability culture creates closures, but also catches everyone – policymakers, teacher educators, researchers, teachers, parents and students – in a performance, forcing them to enact a version of inclusion which is merely about the tolerance and the management of presence and difference. Tolerance, as Slee (2003) reminds us, is the language of oppression and he cites a disabled colleague who told him that 'if anyone else inferentially told him that they would tolerate him and others like him he would *kick their fucking head in!*' (p. 216; original emphasis). This response highlights the damage which the careless and unreflexive language of inclusion does to those at whom it is directed.

The culture of accountability has been read as working against and undermining inclusion, preventing teachers from working inclusively (Dyson et al, 2004; Ballard, 2003b) and as Barton (2004) notes, teachers have become 'scapegoats' (p. 65) for all kinds of failures over which they have no control and the 'target of a sustained and systematic attack by the tabloid press, politicians, industrialists and parents' (ibid). The frustration expressed by teachers and their union representatives, who contend that they cannot achieve inclusion in the present climate, is hardly surprising even if it is disconcerting.

Disruptive students, or those with behavioural difficulties appear to have increased teachers' frustration with inclusion and have pushed some beyond their limits. Warnock is clear that it is disruptive youngsters who create the biggest problem for schools:

> Since 2002, heads and governors have been liable to a criminal charge if they exclude a disruptive child from a mainstream school against the wishes of the parent. Yet it seems clear that disruptive children frequently hinder teaching and learning (ibid, p. 14).

The House of Commons Education and Skills Select Committee (2006) also noted the frustration caused to everyone by the growing number of children with problem behaviour in mainstream schools:

> The Warnock SEN framework is struggling to remain fit for purpose and where significant cracks are developing in the system – most starkly demonstrated by the failure of the system to cope with the rising number of children with autism and social, emotional or behavioural difficulties (SEBD) – this is causing high levels of frustration to parents, children, teachers and local authorities (p. 12).

There is particular frustration for teachers regarding the 'diagnosis' of Attention Deficit Hyperactivity Disorder (ADHD) which has increasingly been applied to youngsters with behavioural problems, with estimates of prevalence ranging from one to six percent of children (Lloyd, 2003). Teachers have expressed doubts about the extent to which they feel they can contain these medicated and often violent youngsters within ordinary classrooms. Some suspicion has been cast upon the extent to which the category of ADHD 'actually' exists and on the role of drug companies in encouraging teachers and parents to pursue a diagnosis and subsequent medication (Cohen, 2006). There is little doubt that those children who have acquired this label, whether medicated or not, present their teachers with enormous anxieties about how to ensure effective support and safety. It is also apparent that the rapid move in many countries towards discussing children's behaviour within a medical discourse (Stead et al, 2006) offers little help that is of value.

For parents of disabled children, the lack of information about provision options and schools' and education authorities' apparent unwillingness to accept their children in mainstream create frustration and often intense pain. One parent described her particular 'horror story' of her child's experience in mainstream:

> In the second year with the public school district, my daughter was bitten twice, and sent home repeatedly "sick," when she was not. I learned later that some kids were sent home "sick" due to the fact that if the aides or teacher called in sick, there was no one to cover . . . In the third year with the same school district, I thought things were going to be better. The [school] program had gone through 4 teachers within my daughter's two years in that class. I was finally impressed with her new teacher, but one month later she quit and moved away. Last year, her teacher was much nicer and experienced BUT my daughter didn't get to finish the year without having a bad accident. She was propped up against a bar in a big metal spaceship on the playground. She was not spotted (my daughter can bear weight on her legs but cannot stand on her own). She fell back and split her head open. This resulted in her getting 3 staples put in her head (Special Child, n.d).

Another parent spoke of the hurt caused by her young son's exclusion from significant amounts of school life:

> He was excluded from some activities at school because they refused to allow him to attend unless someone else was there. In a lot of cases we weren't told they were actually on. We were told he wasn't able to attend on those days. Those things still hurt. It was as if we were being excluded ourselves. The whole family (Barkkman, 2002, p. 91).

A parent who refused to apologise for her son and 'his right to be in school' (Barkkman, p. 78) spoke of the reactions from teachers to her: 'every now and then you'd get a teacher who would think, "The mother's a lunatic" ' (Barkkman, 2002, p. 79). For some parents, the attitudes of professionals provoked rage and, for others, led to a mental breakdown:

> The principal put forward this report which was so damming and I looked across at Jeremy and I've never seen it before, and I've never seen it since, but Jeremy was about to kill him (Barkkman, 2002, p. 37).

> I had this thing about him being at a special school, and that's why I finally cracked up, I suppose, I didn't want him in that setting . . . but I couldn't articulate it at the time. I didn't know what it was . . . I can see how I wound up to melting down . . . I just hit the wall. I used to smoke and drink which covered

a lot of the hurt and grief, and then I decided to quit smoking and drinking and
all that repressed emotion came out in one almighty tidal wave (Barkkman,
2002, p. 161).

Black and ethnic minority disabled youngsters are far more likely to be placed in a
segregated setting than their white counterparts (Broomfield, 2004). They are also
more likely to be poorer, have fewer of their social, educational and health needs met,
and to face a bleak future segregated from the rest of society with limited independence and employment opportunities. Although this creates high levels of frustration
for black and ethnic minority parents, it appears that few feel able to challenge
schools or education authorities.

The frustration experienced by teachers and by parents at the apparent impossibility of inclusion has an intensity and depth which is disturbing, especially where it
appears to lead to significant personal costs.

GUILT

The difficulty in embracing full inclusion has produced, as well as a sense of failure,
considerable guilt about the youngsters who, it is felt, are being let down. One
teacher described her upset at the prospects of one violent youngster being 'ruined'
by inclusion:

> It's enough to make you cry, and I do cry sometimes. I don't want to see this
> young boy's life ruined. I don't want him not to get an education but we are
> losing him in this school. He shouldn't be here. I look at him and wonder if
> he won't one day kill himself or someone else. I'm scared of him and scared
> for him. He is so young but he is also so badly mentally disturbed. The pol-
> icy of inclusion is finishing this child off – not saving him (Sunday Herald, 16
> January, 2005, p. 1).

A teacher in Harvey-Koelpin's (2006) study conveyed a strong sense of guilt that inclusion was not possible because 'it takes more human hands than are available' (p. 138),
while another, although more forthright in refusing to teach disabled children, recognised it as undermining motives for becoming a teacher in the first place:

> Teachers don't want them. If my job depends on their test scores and they are
> reading at a first- or second-grade level and I am teaching fourth grade . . .
> I don't want those kids. I do because I am a teacher and went into teaching to
> help kids. But if my job depends on it . . . my care payments depend on it . . .
> my apartment payment depends on it . . . I don't want those kids (p. 140).

Inclusion becomes a 'headache that won't go away' (Baker, 2002, p. 697) and this
seems particularly the case for students with behavioural difficulties. Inclusion for
these children appears elusive, a ghostly presence that can never quite be achieved.
These inclusion 'ghosts', fuelled by guilt that inclusion is *not yet there*, turn nasty:

> It is crawling with them . . . shrouds, errant souls, clanking of chains in the
> night, groanings, chilling bursts of laughter, and all those heads, so many

invisible heads that look at us, the greatest concentration of all specters in the
history of humanity (Derrida, 1979, p. 150).

Attempts to control these ghosts and deal with the guilt lead to a 'critical problematisation' (ibid, p. 153) of inclusion, by erecting a 'shield, an armor, a rampart' (ibid,
p. 153) against the process. Teachers have done this in the only ways open to them,
through defensive statements such as those voiced by the teachers unions, or by the
othering of particular children as beyond the capabilities of *ordinary* teachers. Policy
documents contain a critical problematisation of inclusion, albeit in a more subtle
way. This takes the form of language shifts, part of a widespread pattern of what JK
Galbraith (2004) calls 'innocent fraud' (p. 11), the renaming of troublesome concepts with terms which are 'benign and without meaning' (p. 14). These include the
substitution of full inclusion with such phrases as 'working towards inclusion'
(CSIE, 2001). The subtle and not so subtle language shifts enacted in policy discourse are examined in more detail in Chapter 2. The critical problematisation of
inclusion by teachers and in their more subtle forms within policies seeks to minimise guilt and enables responsibility to be evaded.

EXHAUSTION

There appears to be an exhaustion among those attempting to cope with the pressures
of inclusion, which Deleuze (1998) suggests creates closure and defeat:

> Being exhausted is much more than being tired . . . The tired person no longer has
> any (subjective) possibility at his disposal; he therefore cannot realize the slight-
> est (objective) possibility . . . The tired person has merely exhausted the realiza-
> tion, whereas the exhausted person exhausts the whole of the possible. The tired
> person can no longer realise, but the exhausted person can no longer possibilize
> . . . He exhausts himself in exhausting the possible, and vice-versa. He exhausts
> that which, in the possible, *is not realized*. He has had done with the possible,
> beyond all tiredness, "in order to end yet again." (p. 152; original emphasis).

The increasing talk of inclusion as an insurmountable challenge, whose possibilities
have been exhausted, is cause for concern. What is perhaps more alarming is that the
exhaustion with the struggle for inclusion leads to a search for approaches which are
simpler or less intensive or have fewer costs associated with them. This kind of
search, notes Gregoriou (2004), citing Lyotard (1993), is a demand which:

> Threatens to totalize experience, to reduce language to Newspeak, to rob
> thinking of its childhood and pedagogy of its philosophical moment. It is the
> 'demand' for reality (for unity, simplicity, communicability) and remedy:
> remedy for the parcelling and virutalization of culture, for the fragmentation
> of the life world and its derealization into idioms, *petits recits,* and language
> games (p. 233; original emphasis).

Some of the material resources for teachers, in the form of packages of advice and
support, appear to offer remedies to the 'problem' of inclusion. The plethora of
handbooks, promising such goodies as '60 research-based teaching strategies that

help special learners succeed' (McNary, 2005) or 'commonsense methods for children with special educational needs' (Westwood, 2002), construct inclusion as a technical matter and assail teachers with advice about *effective* inclusion. This amounts to lists of conditions required for inclusion, recommendations about strong leadership or assertions that 'Inclusive schools will certainly be aiming for the highest possible levels of performance across the school' (HMIe, 2004). These mantras reduce inclusion to a problem to be managed with techniques and methods (Sebba and Sachdev, 1997; Farrell and Ainscow, 2002). Whilst these might offer comfort and the prospect of a practical way forward for teachers, they are meaningless and are likely to entrench teachers' sense of failure in the long term. The absence of any discussion of values in these resources for teachers is alarming and furthermore, these guides miss the point that inclusion *is and should be* a struggle and allow institutions and teachers to evade responsibility for making more significant cultural and political changes in practice and thinking.

TEACHER EDUCATION AND SUPPORT: CONFOUNDING THE PROBLEM?

Student teachers will encounter some elements of inclusion and special needs during their initial teacher education and indeed have to demonstrate competence in this area. What this amounts to, however, is a perfunctory rehearsal of the mantras of inclusion and a tour of the range of children's deficits they are likely to see in the classroom. Student teachers are encouraged to pursue knowledge about children's pathologies in order to 'fix the world concretely and reductively' (Brantlinger, 2004b, p. 497). This form of 'training', rather than educating, arms them with 'recipes . . . [for] those kinds of kids' (Ware, 2003a, p. 158) but with little understanding about how to teach inclusively. It also lays the foundations for confusion, frustration, guilt and exhaustion by ensuring that student teachers feel that they do not know enough to respond effectively to children's needs. The ADHD 'epidemic', which as Lloyd (2003) points out that we had not heard of 15 years ago, is an example of the panic experienced by new teachers and a fear that children with such a diagnosis will be beyond their control. Beginning teachers' sense of themselves as incompetent is entrenched by their trepidation about the full range of pathologies that will present themselves in their classrooms and by their reluctance to seek help from senior colleagues in case they reveal their inadequacy.

As Brantlinger (2004b) has observed, education policy has replaced theory as a source of guidance for practitioners and this forms the content of much of teacher education. These policies consist mainly of bland platitudes about students who are 'different', but also contain some subtle manipulation of meaning and of the children caught up in this. The dependency on the 'big glossies' (Brantlinger, 2006a), special educational textbooks by teacher educators, may offer convenience and reassurance, but as Brantlinger (2006a) notes in her survey of US textbooks, they function as 'authoritative purveyors of technical knowledge' (p. 67) and portray idealised versions of classroom life and of children benefiting from interventions. When inclusion is covered, it is in 'odd forms' (ibid, p. 62), as a list of technical strategies for

managing the learning of disabled children. The absence of any critical interrogation
of these texts ensures that complex thinking is denied (Britzman, 1998; Pinar, 2002)
and that the values associated with difference, inclusion and justice are given little
attention. The school contexts in which student teachers do their placements are
experienced as bewildering and frightening and, of course, bear no resemblance to
the texts the student teachers have read. Student teachers are understandably concerned with their own plausibility and acceptance in these settings. Yet, because
student teachers are not taught to read these contexts critically, they remain ignorant
and ill at ease within them. Slee (2001b) has noted the perpetuation of the 'teacher
training imperative' (p. 173), purveyed by special educators. These individuals are
unlikely to invite questioning from student teachers about values or about how to
create the necessary conditions for inclusion.

At the same time as student teachers are required to buy into a version of teaching which encourages them to control students' behaviours by modifying their own,
they are kept under a veil of uncertainty about whether they will 'make it' as teachers, by ensuring that their knowledge of teaching is always partial:

> Incompleteness, often valorized in textual politics as ambiguity which exposes
> the limits of the metaphysics of voice, in the discourse of corporate training
> (which in a way has colonized the discourse of education) becomes another
> tactics of control in human resource management (Gregoriou, 2001, p. 230).

Student teachers, not having yet proved themselves competent as teachers, remain
'in debt' (Deleuze, 1992a, p. 4) and controlled through training:

> Many young people strangely boast of being "motivated"; they re-request
> apprenticeships and permanent training. It's up to them to discover what
> they're being made to serve, just as their elders discovered, not without diffi-
> culty, the telos of the disciplines. The coils of a serpent are even more com-
> plex than the burrows of a molehill (pp. 5–6).

At the same time, the notion of a teacher as expert persists and forces beginning
teachers to feign confidence in an effort to convince onlookers of their competence:

> The view of the teacher as expert also tends to reinforce the image of the
> teacher as an autonomous individual. As a possession, knowledge also implies
> territorial rights, which become naturalized by the compartmentalization of the
> curriculum. The cultural myth of teachers as experts, then, contributes to the
> reification of both knowledge and the knower (Britzman, 1986, pp. 450–451).

The standards which new teachers must achieve before they are accorded the status
of qualified status envelop the student teacher within rigid stratifications (Roy, 2003)
which deny complex thinking and firmly entrench their novice and incompetent identities. The standards have been recognised as invalid indicators of good teaching
generally (Smyth and Shacklock, 1998; Mahoney and Hextall, 2000) and as part of
the 'struggle over the teacher's soul' (Ball, 2003, p. 217); when the standards have
been applied to inclusion and participation, the effects have been sinister, pushing the
new teacher towards the management of, rather than engagement with, difference.

Within Scotland, the *Standard for Full Registration* (GTC Scotland, 2002a), to which beginning teachers have to aspire, includes working co-operatively with other professionals and adults. To meet this particular element teachers merely have to demonstrate that they can 'create and sustain appropriate working relationships with other teachers, support staff and visiting professionals'. Such low expectations in relation to inter-professional practice, together with the scarce mention of other professionals, and even then only as generalised others, inevitably leaves the beginning teacher surmising that a lack of importance is given to this work and encourages a focus on the more singular aspects of professional practice. This othering of professionals with whom teachers are supposed to engage 'appropriately', seen in the *Standard for Full Registration*, is continued in the *Standard for Chartered Teacher* (GTC Scotland, 2002b). However in order to gain this enhanced status, teachers are expected to exert an 'influence' on these generalised others. The influence does not appear to be a benign one.

The 'standardization' of inclusion and participation has reterritorialized difference as problematic to the new teacher. The Standards for England and Wales, for example, require teachers to 'recognise and respond effectively to equal opportunities issues as they arise in the classroom' (TTA, 2002). The Scottish Standard for Full Registration indicates that teachers must 'value and promote fairness and justice, and adopt anti-discrimination practices in all regards, including . . . disability' (GTC Scotland, 2002a). The Australian Professional Standards require teachers to 'design and implement learning experiences that . . . recognise and celebrate difference' (Education Queensland, 2002) and to understand the 'impact on learning of the full range of diversity in the school and broader community' (ibid). In the US, the distinction between teachers of 'exceptional children' and generalist teachers is maintained in separate standards. The former group must display 'a substantial knowledge base about how disabilities manifest themselves in young people [and] an extensive range of skills to address the instructional issues such disabilities pose' (National Board for Professional Teaching Standards, 1999). Accomplished generalist teachers have to show that they can:

> address issues of diversity proactively to promote equity and to ensure that their students – regardless of race, nationality, ethnicity, religion, exceptionalities, primary spoken language, socioeconomic status, sexual orientation, body image, or gender – receive equal opportunities to participate in, enjoy, and benefit from instructional activities and resources (National Board for Professional Teaching Standards, 2001).

The problem with these standards is that they create a problem and a spectacle of difference, to be managed and tolerated by the beginning teacher. The standards relating to inclusion merely have to be performed without necessarily committing to the values associated with them. And since there has been little attempt to specify what inclusive teaching might look like, it is inevitable that scrutiny of these standards will be light compared with the attention given to the more visible aspects of teaching such as classroom management.

The Higher Education Institutions in which teacher education takes place are driven by the standards agenda and managerialism and are themselves hardly models of inclusiveness (Allan, 2003a; Booth, 2003). Colleagues from Booth's English HEI point to the contradiction of inclusion being imposed on a 'framework which has been traditionally hierarchically competitive' (Booth, 2003, p. 39) while Ballard (2003a) notes that the New Right libertarian ideology of individualism that has shaped economic, education and social policies in New Zealand 'is not a context that is supportive of inclusion' (p. 59). The exclusion and injustices which student teachers encounter during their training is clearly not lost on them and Booth et al (2003a) ask if this could make them question the value of creating inclusive cultures in the schools they go to work in.

Teachers who opt to specialise in learning support are encouraged to acquire an identity as experts on children's deficits. Specialist postgraduate training consolidates this expert identity and whilst they are expected to address whole school issues and collaboration, they are also encouraged to pursue interests in particular impairments such as dyslexia. Attempts to persuade their colleagues to adopt more inclusive practices are often pursued as an act of conversion, but are met with resistance or, worse still, apathy. Consequently, learning support teachers experience their own particular frustration and adopt the demeanour of an inverted u shape, as one teacher described it (Allan et al, 1991), bending over backwards to respond to colleagues' demands for their presence in class, or resemble very ineffective butter, spread so thinly across the school that there is little impact. They can never give enough and are offered scant guidance on their uphill struggle.

Continuing Professional Development (CPD) offers little to teachers to assuage their frustration, confusion, guilt or exhaustion over inclusion. Teachers are required to undertake CPD but inclusion is rarely the focus of their efforts; instead, the content is often determined by the 'the need to respond to government requirements within an increasingly centralised system' (Booth et al, 2003b, p. 6). Much of CPD is driven by imperatives for 'joined up working', thrusting teachers together with professionals from health and social work and forcing them to search for common understandings, but with little common sense of what the point of this might be and how it might benefit children and young people.

IF WE SHOULD FAIL

The confusion, frustration, guilt and exhaustion associated with inclusion has made Warnock's comments extremely timely and welcome in some quarters. She may offer vindication for those believing that inclusion was, and still is, wrong headed, but, as I have suggested, also adds another layer of confusion, especially in the recommendation to relaunch special schools as inclusive special schools. A Government Working Group on special schools reported in 2003 that on the basis of the trends, full inclusion would be achieved by 2058 and that some English local authorities, including Manchester, parts of London (Wandsworth, Lambeth and Lewisham) and Brighton and Hove, would take 100 years (DfES, 2003). Warnock's declarations may slow this process still further.

The conditions under which teachers are supposed to struggle for inclusion are somewhat bleak. They have to do so in a legislative and policy context in which attempts to create inclusion appear consistently to fail. As Lady Macbeth counselled her husband, failure could be avoided 'if you screw your courage to the sticking place' and this book is an attempt to help locate the sticking place. But first, it is necessary to consider in more detail how the repetition of exclusion seems to be irresistible.

2. THE REPETITION OF EXCLUSION IN POLICY AND LEGISLATION

Special educational needs will be a thing of the past (Her Majesty's Inspector of Education Mike Gibson, Addressing the National Association of Special Educational Needs Conference, 2004).

The proud announcement of the demise of special needs, made by a member of Her Majesty's Inspectorate in Scotland, might have heartened those who have identified the special needs paradigm as a major contributor to exclusion (Booth and Ainscow, 1998; Ballard, 1999; Slee and Allan, 2001). It was, of course, wishful thinking that such a formidable component of the educational lexicon could be announced away, its demise assured by the authority of HMI. In one sense, the Inspector was merely signalling that the new legislation, introduced in Scotland in 2004, removed special educational needs from the statutory language and replaced it with the term additional support needs. The disappearance of special educational needs would, however, demand more effective conjuring skills than those bestowed on Her Majesty's Inspectors, talented though they are.

This chapter considers the processes within policy and legislation through which the point about inclusion continues to be missed in the search for the calculable and the certain. Well intentioned efforts to develop inclusive policy and legislation appear to always lead to the repetition of exclusion and add to the confusion, frustration, guilt and exhaustion experienced by teachers. This chapter considers policy and legislation relating to inclusion, and questions why exclusion is so impossible to resist. The fragmented policy arena within which inclusion is wedged is examined. An example of legislation, The Additional Support Needs Act in Scotland, which replaced the system of formally assessing disabled children, is considered alongside the Parliamentary Inquiry which recommended the change and to which I was Adviser. This example is discussed in some detail and whilst it is particular to Scotland, the insights through being unusually close to the policymaking process may be of interest. As Slee (2003) has demonstrated with his commentary on his own sortie into government in a more formal capacity as Deputy Director General within Education Queensland, an insider/outsider perspective can contribute significantly to policy analysis. The House of Commons Education and Skills Select Committee report on special educational needs (House of Commons Education and Skills Select Committee, 2006), which contains some damming accusations of the government's failings, but which produces some spectacularly exclusionary pronouncements of its own, is also examined. The absence of children and young people in the policy and legislative processes is also considered.

INCLUSION POLICY: DISSEMINATING DOUBT

Inclusion 'policy' is as much a mindset as a set of texts. It is recognised as an expectation, and even an imperative, as much as it exists in written form. It is an ideology for some, and a harmful one at that. It is presented as rational, coherent and explicit yet it is 'unscientific and irrational' (Ball, 1990a, p. 3) and is certainly opaque. Furthermore, its inherently political nature is downplayed, as is the way in which teachers, children and others are constructed *through* policy, becoming its effects, for example 'the included child' but no longer, according to HM Inspectors, the child with 'special educational needs'. The consensus which is assumed to characterise the policymaking process, however, is far from the reality:

> There is ad hocery, negotiation and serendipity within the state, within the policy formulation process . . . The point is that quibbling and dissensus still occur with the babble of 'legitimate voices' and sometimes the effect of quibbling and dissensus result in a blurring of meanings within texts, and in public confusion and a dissemination of doubt (Ball, 1994, p. 16).

Policies themselves are also transient, subject to shifting interpretations – indeed to 'interpretations of interpretations' (Rizvi and Kemmis, as cited in Ball 1994, p. 16) – and particular representations. As Ball (1994) notes, sometimes the policy texts are not read in the original but are mediated and delegitimized, for example by teachers unions. Even where they are read, however, this is done in a very particular way, with teachers' readings and reactions constructed for them by the very nature of the text and its positioning in relation to the teachers' professional contexts.

Ball helpfully distinguishes between policy as text and policy as discourse. As was seen above, the texts themselves are full of contradictions and contestations. As discourses, policies create effects through the way they speak of objects and of people. It is the discursive aspect of policy that is the most significant because it works on people in their local situations and masks its own effects:

> It changes the possibilities we have for thinking *otherwise;* thus it limits our responses to change, and leads us to misunderstand what policy is by misunderstanding what it does. Further, policy as discourse may have the effect of redistributing voice, so that it does not matter what some people say or think, and only certain voices can be heard as meaningful or authoritative (Ball, 1994, p. 23; original emphasis).

Inclusion policy is perhaps among the most problematic kind, since, as Ball (1994) notes:

> the more ideologically abstract any policy is, the less likely it is to be accommodated in unmediated form into the context of practice; it confronts *other realities*, other circumstances, like poverty, disrupted classrooms, lack of materials, multilingual classes (p. 19; original emphasis).

There is a plethora of policies on education, social welfare and even health in which inclusion is inscribed and since the emergence of New Labour's social inclusion agenda in the UK, it has reached into many areas of life and work. As Warnock (2005) bitterly notes, inclusion is a fundamental concept in government's thinking about schools, leisure, employment, higher education and the arts and performs, not as policy but as ideology.

Analyses of inclusion policy have shed little light on its contradictions and complexities. They either conflate policy and legislation into generalisations about *context* (eg Riddell and Brown, 1994; Peter, 1995), ignore what Ozga (1990) calls the bigger picture or take the meaning of policy for granted. As Ball (1994) points out, 'theoretical and epistemological dry rot is built into the analytical structures they construct' (p. 15). Analysis of educational policy has not been well done, as several commentators have noted (Ball, 1994, Scheurich, 1994). The problem, according to Scheurich (1994), is that they treat social problems like diseases and assume that a policy remedy will suffice. Even policy analysts who claim to be writing from a postpositive perspective, viewing the policy process as a struggle over symbols, retreat into commentaries of social deficiencies and of the relative merits of different prescriptions (Hawkesworth, 1988; Scheurich, 1994). One analysis of policy which has resisted such a deficit orientation is Fulcher's (1989) depiction of inclusion policy 'struggles' (p. 8) in which she demonstrates how discourse is deployed as both tactic and theory. Her analysis highlights how inclusion policy is located within a moral system of values which in turn is set in a political system which has a hierarchy of values. This creates normalised expectations, for example about what children can be expected to do, and permissions, for example to label and exclude, if they do not meet these expectations. Gillborn and Youdell's (2000) *Rationing Education* is another exceptionally good analysis of policy and illustrates how the Conservative Citizens' Charter and the subsequent New Labour social inclusion agenda led to a deepening of inequalities.

Ball's text and discourse distinction is useful for thinking about inclusion policy. It is difficult to point to particular texts which exist as 'inclusion policy', but there are key documents, an assortment of legislation, policy texts and 'guidance' which are accepted as the official inclusion rubric. Within the UK, the *Warnock Report* (DES, 1978) has been the vade mecum of inclusion. More recent texts include the DfES's *Excellence for all children: meeting special educational needs* (1997) and Ofsted's (2004) *Towards inclusive schools* for England and Wales; *Supporting children's learning: The Code of Practice* (Scottish Executive, 2005), the guidance accompanying the Additional Support Needs Legislation, would be recognised as current Scottish policy, together with *Count us in: achieving potential in Scottish schools* (HMIe, 2003) and the set of documents on inclusion and equity within the HMI's *How good is our school.* (HMI, 2004). In the US, Ware, 2005 and Danforth 2006 describe *The Individuals with Disabilities Education Act (IDEA)* as the principal authority and Slee (2003) identifies inclusion policy as being embedded within the major Queensland reform of *Queensland State Education – 2010.* The persistent refrain from commentators on these policies is that they offer little insight on how to *do* inclusion and are themselves messy, complex and confused (Riddell, 2002; Danforth, 2006). Dyson (2001) is less inclined to read UK policy as confused, suggesting that the elision of inclusion with social inclusion by New Labour is a more calculated form of slippage which ties it to the standards agenda. The inclusion policies certainly appear to do little to assuage the confusion, frustration, guilt and exhaustion experienced by teachers. The fragmentation of policy in relation to different arenas of inclusion/exclusion creates further confusion, chaos and considerable damage in the shape of inequality. Race/ethnicity, gender and disability are all addressed in different ways, by different government departments, with different *solutions,* and with varying degrees of success. Social class is generally not acknowledged in policy; there is some concession to social disadvantage in UK policy but even this has been a hard won battle in a context in which any suggestion that educational failure is linked to poverty was 'almost a taboo subject in public policy debate' (Smith and Noble, 1995, p. 133) and in which New Labour had asserted that poverty was no excuse for failure (Whitty, 2002). The obsession with examination results has led politicians and policymakers to claim great improvements by students overall, while inequalities on the basis of gender, ethnic origin social class worsened (Arnot et al, 1998; Connell, 1993; Gillborn and Youdell, 2000). The impact of policies on these inequalities has not been scrutinised and as a consequence:

> At every turn there is scope for a worsening of social inequality. As our data testify, despite the best intentions of some teachers and the struggles, effort and resistance of many pupils, the reforms seem relentlessly to embody an increasingly diverse and exclusionary notion of education (Gillborn and Youdell, 2000, p. 41).

Joined up working (Milne, 2005), applied to inclusion and other aspects of educational, social welfare and health practices, appears to be more of a cliché than a policy, ordered by government departments which are themselves disconnected and not accompanied by thinking about how such connected practice will lead to greater inclusiveness.

Inclusion policy as discourse appears to function in two ways. On the one hand, its quasi-philosophical intent and language of social justice and belonging gives it a status (at least an aspirational one) alongside other 'erudite knowledges' (Ball, 1990a, p. 24) such as neo-liberalism and management theory. On the other hand, it is placed within a heavily technicist context which reduces the practice of inclusion to a set of techniques and skills. These pull the teacher in different directions and create impossibilities. Dyson (2001) notes the fundamental contradiction in the UK educational system between 'an intention to treat all learners as essentially the same and an equal and the opposite intention to treat them as different' (p. 25). The teacher is caught somewhere in between these intentions and with an awful sense of foreboding that children are being let down and for which they are being held responsible.

The highly charged challenges to inclusion policy by teachers unions have already been witnessed. On a more mundane level, policy may be challenged through a series of what Riseborough (1992) calls 'secondary adjustments':

> Teachers can create, through a repertoire of individual and collective, "contained" (i.e. fitting in without introducing pressure for radical change") and "disruptive" (i.e. attempts to radically alter the structure or leave) strategies, an empirically rich underlife to policy intention (Riseborough, 1992, p. 172; original emphasis).

These enable teachers to cope with what is imposed upon them, but do not, he suggests, amount to significant resistance.

ADDITIONAL SUPPORT NEEDS: WHO DISAPPEARED 'SPECIAL?'

Long before Warnock delivered her devastating attack on inclusion (2005), she had been muttering about the problems associated with the process of statementing. This statutory form of assessment of children with special educational needs had been established by the 1981 legislation which her report in 1978 (DES, 1978) had generated but had created winners and losers among individual children and among schools. In her pamphlet, she vociferously denounced the statementing process, saying that it 'is wasteful and bureaucratic and causes bad blood between parents and local authorities and schools' (Warnock, 2005, p. 29). There is also, Warnock said, 'a crucial lack of clarity in the concept of a statement' (p. 12) and she rather sheepishly acknowledged her own contribution to this: 'I personally feel a degree of responsibility for what has turned out to be not a very bright idea' (p. 29).

The Scottish equivalent of statementing, recording, was also recognised as problematic and a Scottish Parliamentary Inquiry into special educational needs (Scottish Parliament, 2001a) documented its iniquity, inefficiency and failure to meet the needs of children and their parents. The Inquiry, undertaken by the Education, Culture and Sport Committee, set out to examine the diversity of provision across Scotland in special needs education; to investigate the effectiveness of current integration strategies at all levels of pre-school and school education; to investigate the effectiveness of transition arrangements for special needs pupils at each stage in the school education system; and to consider how effectively the requirements of special needs families are understood and fulfilled by education services. Among its many recommendations was a call to the National Advisory Forum on Special Needs to review the recording procedures to 'consider the options of either replacing the system or revising it substantially' (Scottish Parliament 2001a, p. 3). I acted as Adviser to the Inquiry and assured the Members of the Scottish Parliament (MSPs) that such a bold move would be regarded with interest and perhaps even respect from outside Scotland.

The creation of a Scottish Parliament, in 1999, had been heralded as a way of remoralising politics (Cohen 1996), reawakening civic engagement and restoring the jaded Scottish humanity. The Parliament was seen by commentators as the chance to revive Scotland's distinctive social capital and to assert some new values in the shape of greater accountability and openness (Paterson, 2000a & 2000b). Bryce and Humes (1999) saw great prospects for improving education and urged Scottish politicians to 'interrogate senior officials and hold the Executive to account in ways that have not been possible before'. Taking the step to remove the system of recording was, for me at least, an example of what the Scottish Parliament should be about.

The Scottish Executive responded swiftly and, following a series of consultations, drafted The Education (Additional Support for Learning) (Scotland) Bill which went onto the statute in 2005, replacing the existing system of recording with a new approach. The new legislation, however, will recreate exclusion on a number of counts, as key figures who have given evidence in Parliament have pointed out.

The first problematic area concerns the language used in the definitions in the legislation, the confusion and the potential exclusions that these create. When I first came across the new term to replace special educational needs, additional support needs, I was confused and, anxious about the prospect of sounding thus during a planned conversation with an education journalist, looked for clarification of the term within the Consultation on the draft bill (Scottish Executive, 2003). There was little comfort to be had:

> A child or young person has additional support needs for the purposes of this Act where, for whatever reason, the child or young person is, or is likely to be, unable without the provision of additional support to benefit from school education provided or to be provided for the child or young person (p. 1).

After struggling with this tautology for some time, I eventually gave up and confessed my confusion to the journalist, who, as an English graduate, revealed that he had also struggled to make sense of the definition. When I was invited back to give evidence in Parliament, I was still confused by the language and said so. Another source of confusion and potential exclusion related to Co-ordinated Support Plans (CSPs), the statutory document which, like its predecessor the Record of Needs, set out the education authorities' obligations and would be subject to regular monitoring and review. It appeared that only children who required support from an external agency would be entitled to a CSP. These documents would be in addition to Personal Learning Plans (PLPs) and Individualised Education Plans (IEPs) and children could potentially be multiply coded with CSPs, PLPs and IEPs. Donna Martin, of Parents Awareness Forum Fife, described the angst which the uncertainty over who will and will not receive particular plans, and the support that went with it, had caused parents:

> I agree that we need change, but I am very concerned about which children will get a co-ordinated support plan, which children will get a personal learning plan and where our children will fit into the system (Scottish Parliament, 2003a, Col. 443).

George Reilly, a representative of Dyslexia Scotland highlighted the space for slippage within the language of the legislation:

> I do not know how a sentence that uses words such as 'practicable' and 'reasonable' would be rephrased, but I can easily foresee local authorities using such a measure to make even less provision for dyslexic children than they do at present. In the vernacular, that could be a means of copping out (2003b, Col. 391).

Concerns were also raised in Parliament about the impact that the legislation would have on teachers and on their capacity to provide support. Speaking on behalf of the Convention of Scottish Local Authorities, Councillor the Rev Ewan Aitken voiced some fears:

> We are concerned about the demands that the bill will place on teachers and other school staff, especially in the context of the national teachers agreement. Who exactly will manage each of the plans? (Scottish Parliament, 2003c, Col. 254).

These concerns were echoed by George Haggarty of the Headteachers Association of Scotland, who feared that schools could be blamed for failing to make provision:

> We hope that the bill will not lead to a system that is more demanding of the school sector – we are thinking of the focus that could be put on the apparent failure of schools to deliver additional support needs (Scottish Parliament, 2003d, Col. 301).

The legislation was also criticised for making inadequate provision to secure children's rights. Their rights are acknowledged, but not guaranteed, within the legislation and Katy Macfarlane of the Scottish Child Law Centre argued that unless these rights were statutory, then adults would continue to have primacy over children:

> Unless children's rights are enshrined in the legislation, children will simply not have them because, let us face it, it is much easier to take decisions about children – especially children with additional support needs – without their input. It is much easier, more efficient and much less time consuming. That is what is happening now (Scottish Parliament, 2003a, Col. 428).

George McBride of the Educational Institute of Scotland pointed to a subjugation of children's voices over those of their parents:

> There are requirements for children's voices to be heard at some stages, but that is very much after the parent has exercised his or her rights (Scottish Parliament, 2003c, Col. 282).

As the Bill went through its subsequent parliamentary stages, the Scottish Executive (2003) responded to some of the criticisms made and to the advice given and introduced some amendments. These included the introduction of a duty on Education Authorities to provide additional support to certain children under the age of three and added protection in the short term for those with a Record of Needs. Whilst these were important accommodations, there were still reservations that the legislation would not adequately serve children and young people and their families. Once again, the 'monstrous world of difference and repetition' (Ansell Pearson, 1997, p. 5) had proved irresistible.

ONCE MORE FOR EXCLUSION?

When the MSPs presented their report, which included their recommendations to abolish the system of recording, to the Scottish Parliament, there was cross-party consensus and strong emotions. Members of each of the main parties expressed pride in realising their ambition to secure an 'inclusive education for all children' (Scottish Parliament, 2001b, Col. 770). The report was, as one MSP contended:

> another example of Scotland becoming a much better place to live in because of the existence of the Scottish Parliament, which is able to address subjects that would not have been given any kind of political airing under the old political system with which we are all too familiar (McAllion, Labour, Scottish Parliament 2001b, Col. 801).

The MSPs were pleased with their own departure from the 'We know best orthodoxy' (Peattie, Labour, Scottish Parliament 2001b, Col. 785) and contended that 'We are on our way to producing a more civilised society' (Gorrie, Labour, Scottish Parliament 2001b, Col. 801). During the debate on the report, even a Scottish Nationalist MSP, whose attention was normally devoted to issues that were more newsworthy than inclusion, was voluble on the focus of the debate:

> today's debate is not about statistics, money or . . . minutiae . . . Instead it is about supporting, helping, caring for and involving the children who are in the chamber today and many others. If we see the debate in such a way, the Parliament is not some dry and arid place, but part of the living development of the Scottish community . . . The debate is not about figures, politics or . . . dogma; it is about belief, faith caring and the creation of community . . . it is about human rights and human beings (Russell, SNP, 2001b, Col. 816).

During the process of the Inquiry I was impressed by the extent to which the MSPs understood the need to alter their terms of reference from an examination of integration to inclusion and recognised the significance of the distinction. They were also quick to remove phrases such as 'special needs families,' which both individuals submitting written evidence and I had suggested was patronising. The MSPs came to the realisation that inclusion was not just about children with special needs, but was about schools and professionals changing to ensure that no-one was left out (Barton, 1997). Although they were clear on this point, they also recognised the complexity associated with inclusion and accepted that many problems had been generated by simplistic policy solutions. In private sessions following the questioning of witnesses, and with the microphones switched off, the MSPs confessed to their mounting uncertainty about how inclusion for all pupils might be achieved. The experience of the Inquiry had affected some MSPs profoundly as they had been forced to confront their own ignorance and prejudice and they revealed this publicly:

> I will make something of a confession. When I began my part in the Committee's Inquiry process, back in November 1999, I was sceptical of mainstreaming, probably because of my own experiences as a child. I never encountered any children with special educational needs in my classroom – they went away in a

bus to a school somewhere else, because they were different, and could not be educated with me. Looking back on that, I realise that that is exactly the kind of impression that we must challenge among young people who are growing up now. Children with special educational needs, despite those needs, are not different from other children in Scotland and should not be treated differently. They should be able to expect the same high standard of education that every other child does (Gillon, Labour, Scottish Parliament 2001b, Col. 819–820).

I knew very little about this subject when the Inquiry started. I approached the subject and my first visit to some schools involved with trepidation, but I have scarcely seen more caring, loving and enjoyable places in which to spend time (Russell, SNP, 2001b, Col. 781).

The MSPs involvement in the 'special needs' inquiry had a profound experience upon them, amounting to what (Deleuze and Guattari, 1987) have called 'deterritorialization' (p. 9). This process is explored in more detail in the following chapter on Deleuze and Guattari's philosophy, but for the MSPs, it meant that their existing knowledge and assumptions were unravelled and recognised as part of the problem of exclusion. The new legislation, on the other hand, appeared to be an act of reterritorialization:

not . . . returning to the original territory, but . . . the way in which deterritorialized elements recombine and enter into new relations in the constitution of a new assemblage or the modification of the old (Patton, 2000, p. 101).

During the Inquiry, they fulfilled their duty to hold the Scottish Executive to account, often doggedly refusing to let officials off the hook with inadequate or obscure answers:

I did not think that the answer to [Jenkins', Lib Dem] question was clear. He asked whether having a special unit in a mainstream school would count as mainstreaming of youngsters with special needs. Could you give me a shorter answer to that question? (Monteith, Cons, Scottish Parliament, 2000a, Col. 1101).

The responsibilities of holding the Executive to account were met effectively within the official Parliamentary sessions, but the MSPs have been less successful in seeing the process through and ensuring that the civil servants carry out their recommendations. As a result, the officials have been able to reinstate fudge and blur within policy and to refuse anything that requires significant change. One example of this is their rejection of the definition of inclusive education contained in the MSPs' report as 'maximising the participation of all children in mainstream schools and removing environmental, structural and attitudinal barriers to particpation' (Scottish Parliament, 2001b, Col 770). This form of words has been accepted by many writers on inclusion (Allan, 1999, Barton, 1997; Slee, 2003) and was met with enthusiasm among the MSPs. The Executive, however, saw the definition as inappropriate and rejected it in their response to the report:

The Committee's definition makes a welcome contribution to the debate about inclusive education. However, there is a wide spectrum of views about approaches to inclusive education and a commonly agreed definition, which

> might also refer to the removal of educational barriers, would be difficult to
> secure (Scottish Executive, 2001a, p. 2).

When the MSP who was opening the debate in Parliament invited me to offer any suggestions for her address, I suggested that she challenge this refusal:

> I am disappointed that ministers felt unable to endorse our definition of
> inclusive education or to accept the need for a clear and agreed definition.
> I hope that the minister will inform us of the actions that he will pursue in
> the light of our recommendations (McGugan, SNP, Scottish Parliament,
> 2001b, Col. 772).

The Minister, in his response, claimed to have accepted the definition of inclusive education after all, but seemed to have missed the important second part of the formula, concerned with removing barriers:

> A key feature of that approach is to assist education authorities to include
> children with special educational needs in mainstream education wherever
> possible and wherever that is appropriate to the needs of the child. That fits
> with the committee's recommended definition of inclusive education . . . That
> does not mean that we take a dogmatic view on inclusion in the main stream
> regardless of the needs of the individual child. We want every child to receive
> a quality education that is appropriate to his or her needs (Nicol Stephen,
> Deputy Minister for Education, Europe and External Affairs, Scottish
> Parliament, 2001b, Cols. 773–774).

Inclusive education does not get a mention in the draft 'code of practice' issued to provide guidance on the implementation of legislation (Scottish Executive, 2005). However, within the series of reports on inclusion and equality in *How good is our School*, the 'self evaluation' armaments for schools (HMIe, 2002), one was devoted specifically to the education of children with additional support needs (HMIe, 2004). Here the Inspectors attempted to pin down a definition of inclusive education and did indeed make reference to barriers to participation. Although the HMIs acknowledged that these barriers may relate to external aspects of the structure, environment and attitudes within schools, they saw them as also residing within the child:

> The barrier or barriers may also relate to the pupils' physical, sensory or
> intellectual disabilities, to emotional and social needs, challenging behav-
> iour, autistic spectrum disorders and communication difficulties, and to
> chronic illness and absence from school. Barriers to learning may also arise
> from difficult circumstances such as parents who abuse drugs or alcohol.
> Children who are looked after may also face barriers to learning
> (HMIe, 2004).

So what happened? How did we get, so quickly, from this proud sense of achievement to a position where the new legislation was being pronounced 'a disaster in the making for every child, every family and every local authority in the country, and, ultimately, for the Government' (Eileen Prior, The Equity Group, Scottish Parliament, 2003c, Col. 442)? At one level, this can be explained as an effect created by the Scottish Executive personnel who responded to the requirement to produce new legislation. At another level, the repetition of exclusion may be part of what Derrida (1991a) calls a 'gramophony' (p. 596), in which we are forced to repeat exclusion endlessly because we are unable to function in any other way. In other words, we cannot avoid the valorization of the negative (Ansell Pearson, 1997) and any difference which manifests itself as intensity is necessarily cancelled out into 'extensity' (ibid, p. 14), evolving into something homogenous and identitical, and producing:

> An irreversible decline from the more to the less differentiated, from difference produced to difference reduced and ultimately to the annihilation of difference . . . *Reason* is installed as the power which identifies and equalises difference (Ansell Pearson, 1997, p. 11, original emphasis).

The repetition of exclusion appears to occur through what Deleuze and Guattari (1977) name as a territorial social machine, a socius, which regulates and codifies desire: 'to inscribe them, to record them, to see that no flow exists that is not properly dammed up, channelled, regulated' (p. 33). The socius exists on the basis of disequilibrium and the imbalance of debt and credit, creating a psychic economy (Nietzsche, 1994) of inequality. Baker (2002) portrays a more sinister dimension of the inevitability of the repetition of exclusion, arguing that we – as teachers and as researchers – are unable to resist hunting down disability and difference. Baker contends that we *need* to find the pathological in order to function ourselves. This negative ontology goes on relentlessly; even when we pursue alternatives, we simply reinvent the hierarchies that help sustain these negatives and social order, Baker suggests, is a euphemism for the colonisation of privilege.

The quest for certainty and the calculable within educational policy and practice may also effect reterritorialisation and the repetition of exclusion. This closes down possibilities for creating the kinds of policy and legislation which will generate inclusiveness and allows for the deferral of responsibility. Furthermore, the certainty with which recommendations – for example about what constitutes good practice – need to be made, enables responsibility to be evaded. The increasing emphasis on *what works* pushes us towards technical solutions and further away from understanding the features of inclusion which might be meaningful to children and young people and their families. The guarantees and assurances (of quality, value added, or enhancement), which are increasingly expected within education, set up an inertia from which it is impossible to break away:

> Any presumption of guarantee and of non-contradiction in so paroxystic a situation . . . is an optimistic gesticulation, an act of good conscience and irresponsibility, and therefore indecision and profound inactivity under the guise of activism or resolution (Derrida, 2001a, p. 71).

This kind of inertia, according to Derrida, created by the pressure to reach a decision, produces an instant of 'madness' (Derrida 1992a, p. 25) which cannot be tolerated and which forces a decision and consequently closure. This limits the possibilities for achieving inclusion which, by its nature, is 'infinite, incalculable, rebellious to rule and foreign to symmetry, heterogenous and heterotropic (Caputo, 1997, p. 140) and for achieving justice. The pursuit of justice, Derrida argues, must embrace the undecidable and the incalculable; if these are absent, then there is injustice and irresponsibility. It is this very moment of madness when one has to decide what to do, but yet a just decision is impossible (Edgoose, 2001), which opens the door to the possibility of justice. The prospects of creating a more just and responsible inclusion through the creation of policy and practice aporias (Derrida, 1993) are explored in Chapter 4.

The Education and Lifelong Learning Committee of the National Assembly for Wales began a review of its Special Needs Policy at the end of 2004. This included an examination of assessment procedures and they visited the Scottish Parliament and the Scottish Executive in order to learn from their experience of the legislative change. Once again, I was wheeled into Parliament and was able to outline the problematic areas which had been identified by those giving evidence in the Scottish Inquiry. I had neither the inclination nor the capacity to offer advice on how to avoid the repetition of exclusion; rather I highlighted some of the tensions and contradictions in the task of establishing a just system and issued some general enjoinders to involve children in the review process – properly, in a way that invites them to *make* policy – and to consider radical reform of teacher education. They left promising to avoid some of the Scottish blunders but created a discomfiting sense of déja vu.

HOUSE OF COMMONS: 'UP FRONT' ABOUT SPECIAL SCHOOLS

The Education and Skills Committee of the House of Commons conducted an inquiry into special educational needs within England, which it reported on in 2006. It took written evidence from over 230 individuals and organisations, took evidence in Parliament from 50 witnesses and visited schools. They also received a report from BBC's Radio Four which broadcast an edition of *You and Yours* on the topic. The Committee appointed three advisors, Professors Alan Dyson and Ann Lewis and a Director of Education and Children's Services, Mark Rogers. In its report, attention was drawn to some of the contradictions confusions, frustrations and exclusion caused by the Department for Education and Science's policy and legislation on special educational needs and inclusion. The Committee's perceptiveness and criticality was impressive, yet its own recommendations were hardly likely to resolve matters and indeed were more likely to encourage a greater degree of segregation.

The Members of Parliament serving on this Committee took the task of scrutinising the policy and legislation produced by the Governmental Department for Education and Science – and holding it to account – seriously and at one point in the proceedings, underlined the Government's responsibilities:

> Lord Adonis' [Minister for Education] evidence that the government does not have a policy of inclusion, but was 'the will of Parliament' is unhelpful. Parliament is governed by the majority party of the day and therefore the will of Parliament reflects the will of the incumbent government of which he is a Minister. Therefore, the Minister should take responsibility for his

government's policy (House of Commons Education and Skills Select Committee, 2006, p. 123).

The Committee, in its report, produced a robust set of accusations of how 'the SEN system is failing' (p. 9) and offered evidence from a range of sources to demonstrate the impact upon children and their parents:

> We have received a large number of memoranda from parents who have had terrible experiences of their children suffering in an unsuitable mainstream setting and having to fight to achieve a place for their child in a special school. Equally we have also received a large number of memoranda from parents whose children have been placed in a special school and they have had to fight to allow them to be included in a mainstream school (p. 44).

The Report described training for teachers as inadequate and reiterated the 'serious flaws in the SEN system' (p. 40), identified by the Audit Commission (2002) and Ofsted (2004) reports, relating to standards and consistency of provision, the statutory assessment process, fair access to schools and outcomes for children. The Committee declared that it found it 'both surprising and highly concerning' (p. 40) that these problems had still not been addressed.

In addition to the identification of these failures, the Committee offered a highly sophisticated analysis, drawing attention to a number of contradictions within the Government's policy and legislation which produced exclusion and inequality. The first of these was in relation to the Government's policy on inclusion, whether it in fact had one and if so, whether this meant the closure of special schools. When they called upon the Education Minister to clarify the Government's position, his response that there was 'no policy whatever ... of encouraging local authorities to close special schools' (p. 12) led the Committee to conclude that 'The Government's position on inclusion seems confused and there is a need for clarification' (p. 12). They highlighted a 'radical u-turn' (p. 25) by the Minister who told the Committee that the Government would be content if the numbers of children within special school remained static:

> This directly contradicts the stated aim in the 2004 SEN Strategy that 'the proportion of children educated in special schools should fall over time' *The Minister's words demonstrate a significant change in policy direction* (p. 26; original emphasis).

The Committee succeeded in teasing out the fact that, although there was considerable confusion on the part of the Government, there was a discernible shift towards 'a third way' (p. 26) which recognised the place of special schools in a 'flexible continuum of provision', but found the lack of clarity about its position unacceptable:

> Seeking change through evolution not revolution is one thing, but changing a key policy focus and hoping to tie it back in to a particular reading of the existing SEN Strategy is not acceptable. The Government should be up-front about its change of direction on SEN policy and the inclusion agenda, if this is indeed the case, and should reflect this in updated statutory and non-statutory guidance to the sector (p. 27).

The second contradiction which exercised the Committee concerned the standards agenda and special educational needs and it cited a number of witnesses' commentaries on how children with special educational needs were disadvantaged by an emphasis on the narrow outcome of academic attainment. Here, the Committee identified another source of slippage from the Government in relation to personalisation:

> The Minister described personalisation as the 'key' to the Government's strategy on SEN. This had not previously been stated anywhere. It had been said that SEN 'should play a central part in the personalisation agenda,' and the SEN strategy says that the Government will 'put children with SEN at the heart of personalised learning' but this is quite different to putting personalised learning at the heart of the SEN strategy. This is further indication that the Government is re-thinking its policy on SEN (p. 64).

With forensic detail, the Committee searched for the presence of SEN within the Schools White Paper (DfES, 2005) in which personalisation featured and found 'little more than a passing mention of SEN' (p. 64). It did however, find a claim that 'Children and young people with SEN already benefit from the personalisation inherent in the SEN framework, which provides an individualised assessment of need and tailored provision' (p. 64). The Committee did not share this view.

A contradiction concerning parental choice was highlighted and the Committee remarked on the limited rights which parents have in relation to their child's provision. They have the right to 'seek' a special school place if they so wish, but the local authority does not have to provide this. Furthermore, parents have a right to choose a school for their child, but only one which is outside the state sector. Thus, they can remove a child from the public education, but they cannot choose within it. This created a troubling situation over which parents had no control:

> There are many parents that believe either their children are educated in mainstream schools against their wishes or that their children are not being given access to mainstream schooling when they should be . . . For children with SEN, the qualification regarding the efficient education of other children puts the final decision making power in the hands of officials and professionals rather than the parents of children with SEN. Parents increasingly have their expectations raised with regard to parental choice and this is understandably causing conflict and frustration when their experience is so different (pp. 47–48).

Parents were further disadvantaged by two further contradictions relating to statementing, the statutory system of assessment and the cost of tribunals. The Committee identified a conflict of interests in the linking of assessment and resources which had led to some bad practices within Local Education Authorities, including refusing to assess children and adopting blanket policies of avoiding quantifying educational provision in statements. Tribunals, the means through which parents can appeal the Local Authority's decision with regard to statementing and/placements, involve, in principle, no direct costs. In practice, however, parents may incur considerable costs if they commission expert reports or engage a lawyer and some parents have spent up to £18,000 on a Tribunal. The ideal of equal access to appeals is, the Committee suggested, far from the reality and it cited a head-teacher's view that 'tribunals are a complicated process and it's often only the dogged, middle class parents that are prepared to take the process on' (p. 53).

The Committee's analysis of the current system of providing for children with special needs showed an impressive level of sophistication, drawing attention to the exclusion and inequalities, the contradictions in the Government's policy and legislation and the shifts and elisions in the Government's position. The Committee undertook some skilled detective work on documents and in its questioning of the witnesses. It presented the contradictions within the system as what Derrida (1993) calls aporias or double contradictory imperatives, and wondered about how, or if, these could be squared. It is somewhat disappointing that in its recommendations, the Committee called for measures which would inevitably create closure and rein-scribe the exclusion it sought to banish. The Committee called upon the Government to 'resolve apparent contradictions in its strategy' (p. 82) and clarify its 'position on inclusion' (p. 12); to 'give greater priority to SEN and take full account of its need to have a central position in education' (p. 12); and to ensure compulsory 'SEN training' (p. 70) for all teachers. Demanding that the Government makes its position clear is both unlikely to produce a result and misses the opportunity to offer guidance to the Government on what its position ought to be. The Committee's call to prioritise and make SEN a central part of the mainstream is curious and it is hard to fathom why it should be SEN, rather than inclusion or, better still, the children who have experienced exclusion who are to be brought in from the margins. Equally hard to understand is why the Committee insisted on a 'clearly articulated national framework, linked to quality standards' (p. 62). During the Committee's deliberations on the draft report, a plea was made to reject the national delivery model with minimum standards on the grounds that it would lead to the imposition of the 'one-size-fits-all' (p. 131) policies 'in much the same way that the policy of inclusion became the orthodoxy despite the opposition of parents' (p. 131). These pleas, however, were rejected and the recommendation of a national framework was allowed to stand. Most puzzling of all is the Committee's proclamation that 'for many children with SEN and disabilities, special schools are invaluable' (p. 45) and should be placed on an equal footing with mainstream schools:

> It should be acknowledged by the government that both mainstream and special schools play a very important role in meeting the needs of children with SEN; whilst this provision may be very different, they are of equal value and worthy of equal acceptance (p. 121).

The calls for greater recognition and valuing of special schools have been met with dismay in some quarters, viewing it as a further nail in the coffin of inclusion. The Centre for Studies on Inclusive Education urged the government to 'step up inclusion' (CSIE, 2005) in spite of the criticisms of the Select Committee, arguing that segregation was 'damaging to society and individuals and a violation of their rights' (ibid).

MISSING THE CHILDREN

Schools are highly striated and sedentary spaces (Patton, 2000), with clear hierarchies. Difference is continuously verified and valorised and the individuals upon whom inclusion is to be practised are marked out with a special status. The young people themselves have no say in what kind of provision might make a difference to their lives and remain, in Linton's (1998) words, 'the missing voices' (p. 142). We have legislation which enshrines children's rights but there are few opportunities to exercise these rights because schools are more concerned to ensure children are passive, under control and subject to discipline. Attempts to seek children's views through formal consultation exercises are symbolic gestures which rarely lead to changes in practice. Ballard (2004) goes further to express concern about the removal of children from policy discourses to be replaced by what he sees as a sinister neutralising descriptor of the 'learner' (p. 2), which, he contends, ensures that values are kept at bay:

> Our cat is a learner. Interesting as he is in his own whiskery way, I would not equate him with the invaluable complexity, wonder and joy that is a child. If people decided to refer to cats in a new way – 'companion animal' is one such terminology – I would probably regret the loss of an essential 'catness in the language, but not take it too seriously. But I think it is a very serious matter when we stop talking about children in our classrooms and schools (p. 2).

The Scottish Parliament Inquiry into special needs, unusually, heard from, and learned a great deal from, children and young people who had experienced exclusion, in both special and mainstream schools. One individual described herself as having 'escaped' from special school with her dignity just about intact; another young person used the same phrase, but was referring to his escape from the mainstream. For this student, mainstream schooling amounted to a refusal of his deaf identity and an attempt to assimilate him, which had led to his exclusion:

> At breaks and lunch time, all my hearing friends would go into groups. They would listen to music and talk about pop records, so I felt very isolated. I went through some depression. It was also extremely difficult to communicate with the teachers who could not sign. How was I supposed to ask questions? I had an interpreter, but I did not have the interpreter for all classes – only for English or maths. For classes such as physical education, there was no interpreter. Therefore, I would have to write things down. I felt embarrassed about that . . . During my time at mainstream school, my confidence had deteriorated and I decided that I could not go back. I stayed at home for six months (Scottish Parliament, 2000b, Cols.1141–1142).

This youngster had moved to a special school for the Deaf and had been astonished at the contrast:

> I was shocked; the college was so different from mainstream schooling. I had not realised how good it would be for me. I thought that it was just the equivalent of mainstream school, but in fact it was the opposite. At the mainstream school I was bullied, but that never happened to me at Donaldson's College. Now, looking back, I feel that I made the right decision in going to Donaldson's

> College . . . the communication is there and it is very easy. Everyone can sign –
> the teachers, children, cleaners and gardeners – communication is vital and it is
> very easy (200b, Cols. 1141–42).

For this young person, the effortless communication that was possible in his new
school, but had been denied in the mainstream, made the difference between inclusion
and exclusion. Further evidence from children and young people alerted the MSPs to
the need to move beyond considerations of the physical placement of children to recognise the potentially highly exclusionary nature of some mainstream settings:

> Inclusion is about more than being in the same building; it is about being with
> others, sharing experiences, building lasting friendships, being recognised for
> making a valued contribution and being missed when you are not there.
> Inclusion is not an issue of geography. Yes, we need buildings to be made
> accessible, but change can happen only if people have accessible minds. We
> need to realise that it is a fundamental right of all children to be educated
> together. We all need to realise that today's children are tomorrow's future.
> We need to work together in partnership to secure that future (Scottish
> Parliament, 2000b, Col. 1190).

The children and young people who gave evidence to the Scottish Parliament inquiry
demonstrated an acute understanding of inclusion and exclusion, which was striking
when compared with some of the confusion experienced by adults. They described
the most significant barrier to inclusion as being negative attitudes towards them and
low expectations of what they could achieve:

> Often kids get stuck in a cycle of diminished expectation because of social
> perceptions and beliefs. I wish there could be a shift in perception (2000b,
> Col. 1201).

One individual described barriers which were placed in his way by professionals and
which almost denied him a mainstream placement, but his parents fought on his behalf:

> Both my parents were adamant that I should have the same rights, opportuni-
> ties and life experiences as other kids . . . After many months of fighting with
> doctors, psychologists and local authorities, I was finally given the green light
> to begin my schooling in a mainstream class (2000b, Col. 1188).

Although this young person had finally been able to attend a mainstream school, he
had encountered further obstacles within school, for example by being denied the
opportunity to go on a foreign exchange trip with his peers or participate in after-
school activities.

The House of Commons Education and Skills Select Committee considered evidence
from children and young people, but only indirectly through a project on participation
in education and the *Powerful Voices* conferences and in written submissions from
organisations representing children and young people. It is curious that the MSPs did not
choose to hear what children and young people had to say. Had they done so, they might
have learned a great deal and produced a rather different set of recommendations.

3.   EXCLUDING RESEARCH

Research on inclusion appears to have made little contribution to understanding the concept and has produced limited insights into how it might be achieved in practice or even where to begin. Research on inclusion and disability has even, it has been suggested, contributed to the marginalisation and exclusion of disabled people (Oliver, 2002), while ethnic minority groups have argued that research done *upon* them has been damaging because of the labels with which it is constrained to work (Artiles, 2004). More generally, educational research has come under attack for failing to produce knowledge that is useful to the policy and practice community. This chapter considers some of the problems associated with research on inclusion and disability and the damaging effects on those upon whom it is practised and reflects on some of the wider criticisms of educational research. Researchers entering the field of inclusion either as students or as novices face a particular challenge. They are expected to manoeuvre their way through a highly contested area, but without signposts marking researchers' positions and the kind of assumptions they are working with. As a consequence, new researchers may end up undertaking research which is highly exclusionary, but which they do not recognise as such. The failure of research on inclusion and disability to make a difference to those most affected have led to frustration and pain for some and for others has reinforced a sense of futility about the whole inclusion enterprise.

DO NO HARM

Oliver's (1999) frustration, 'pain and disillusionment' (p. 185) with the disabling and exclusionary nature of research has been shared by others who have regarded the process as an intrusion into their life and even a form of rape or voyeurism' (Bury, 1997, p. 244). Disabled scholars such as Oliver (1999) have contended that able bodied researchers, because of their lack of attention to the material consequences of their research, have done little for disabled people. He argues that research involving disabled people has failed to expose the 'real oppression and discrimination that people experience in their everyday lives' (2002, p. 16) and has merely contributed to

43

'the classification and control of marginalised groups who seek nothing more than their full inclusion into the societies in which they live' (p. 16). At one level, as has been argued repeatedly (Slee and Allan, 2001; Slee, 1998), the problem with research on inclusion is that it has never been able to shed itself of the formidable special edu-cation – positivistic – paradigm and continues to be shaped and judged by it. At another level, research in this field lacks a number of key elements without which exclusion is perpetuated: the voices of the researched are absent from the process; there has been little or no debate about the purpose of inclusion and hence there is uncertainty about what would constitute evidence for its success. Educational research more generally has been roundly criticised, but judgements about it are based on criteria which are inappropriate and which ignore values and issues of power.

ABSENT VOICES

Children and young people, the people upon whom inclusion and exclusion is prac-tised, are the most troubling absent voices in research. They and their families are best placed to comment on the kind of inclusion outcomes which would be acceptable to them, yet there have been limited efforts to work systematically with children and young people to obtain their views on their experiences of inclusion and exclusion. Several researchers have contended that their 'hidden voices' (Ainscow et al, 1999, p. 139) are potentially hugely informative about inclusive practice, but their presence within research projects is often as an exotic other, with their viewpoints placed alongside, or more often subjugated beneath, those of the professionals. Notable exceptions are Davis and et al's study of the lives of disabled children (2001) and Benjamin's (2002) ethnography of the micropolitics of inclusive education. The researchers in both these studies recognised the importance of altering the power rela-tions within the research process and finding ways of enabling children and young people to collaborate in 'creating a shared understanding of aspects of their lives' (Ballard and McDonald, 1999, p. 97).

As Masson (2005) notes, legislation in relation to children is concerned with care and protection and this may extend to limiting their participation in research, but parents and teachers may be the most effective gatekeepers. The uncertainty surrounding childhood (James et al, 1998) leads to children being constructed as having an ambiguous status both in research and in educational policy and practice more generally.

The absence of the voices of minority groups has been a major problem in research in inclusion and Linton (1998) argues that the missing voices of disabled people has created serious gaps in knowledge:

> New scholars of all stripes must recognize their moral and intellectual oblig-ation to evaluate gaps and faults in the knowledge base they disseminate to students that result from the missing voices of disabled people (p. 142).

This exclusion has been both wilful and unintentional. It has been wilful where research has deliberately kept minority groups from speaking, by a preference for doing research *on*, rather than *with*, them, or has concentrated solely on the professionals speaking about them (Diniz, 2003). The effect has been to render minority groups invisible in research (Netto, et al, 2001). It has been unintentional where individuals have been consulted in a genuine attempt to hear their voices, but then these have been subjected to *interpretation*, reductive explanations based on professional frameworks of knowledge or on judgements about the competence of disabled people (Alderson, 1995). Research on inclusion which seeks to represent minority groups often perpetuates the marginalisation of these same groups, by marking students as 'passive carriers of categorical markers of difference (e.g., race, class, gender) together with their assumed nefarious consequences (e.g., low achievement, dropout, delinquent behaviour)' (Artiles, 2004, p. 552).

Alongside concerns about the absence of the voices of minority groups, attention has been drawn to the *presence* of ethnic minorities within special education (Artiles et al, 1997; Ferri, 2004). Whilst acknowledging that the empirical evidence of the problem of overrepresentation of particular groups of students is convincing, Artiles (2004) questions the appropriateness of the focus on 'representation' within research of any group, because of the assumptions and expectations associated with these markers. As Gillborn and Youdell (2000) remind us, categories of class, gender, 'race', ethnicity and sexuality are socially constructed and research which is based around these tends to treat these as neutral and biological determinants and ascribes certain properties to the individuals labelled in this way. Artiles and colleagues (1997) are hugely critical of the failure of research involving minority ethnic groups to address issues of language and culture and the varying contexts of practice. They are also critical of the interpretation of research findings and application to culturally and linguistically diverse students, particularly when these groups have not been included in the sample or demographic information, when other relevant information about them has been under-reported or when there has been no disaggregation of the data to show how particular interventions may have differentially affected students from diverse backgrounds. So whilst there is a caution against forcing students to carry the markers of diversity within research, these authors also urge for greater recognition within research of the particular cultural contexts and circumstances of minority ethnic groups.

The representation of disabled people within research has been problematic because researchers have appropriated and written about 'experiences that they have no access to save through their own research techniques' (Oliver, 1999, p. 187). These representations lack an appreciation of the complexity of disabled people's lives, possibly not because they have been investigated by non-disabled people, but because the researchers fail to comprehend the multiply layered meanings assigned to them and are unable to resist the 'dogmatism of a single tale' (Grumet, 1991, p. 72). Both experiential and participatory accounts of disability have been unsatisfactory, according to Oliver (1999). Experiential accounts are inadequate because they privilege individual experience above everything else and such 'faithful accounts' (Oliver, 1999, p. 4) are simply not enough. Their individual nature is also a problem and as Oliver notes 'after nearly 200 years of social research we still do not have the faintest idea of how to produce collective accounts of collective experience' (Oliver, 1999, p. 4). Oliver also suggests that those involved in experiential research get caught up in highly emotionally charged arguments about who has the right to obtain such accounts. Most significantly, experiential research fails disabled people because it fails to tie itself to emancipatory theory or praxis, offering no way out for the subjects of the research. Participatory research, in Oliver's view, also fails disabled people. Attempts at enhancing participation are usually tokenistic and restricted to involving a few disabled people in some of the research processes, whilst retaining control over the important aspects of resources and agendas. As Oliver points out, this ensures that disabled people continue to be positioned in oppressive ways:

> Whether we like it or not, failing to give disabled people through their own representative organisations complete control over research resources and agendas inevitably positions disabled people as inferior to those who are in control (Oliver, 1999, p. 5).

Oliver acknowledges that researchers are themselves 'trapped between the material and social relations of research production' (Oliver, 1999, p. 12) and by funding bodies which privilege methodological individualism. He also suggests that they are naïve and unable to make sense of their own position as researchers and of their role in producing exclusion and oppression in the work they do. The effects upon disabled people are, according to Oliver, devastating. Although Oliver himself has decided not to pursue disability scholarship further after offering his 'final accounts' (Oliver, 1999, p. 183), he offers an alternative framework of research as production, which shifts the control of the research process from the researchers to the researched (Oliver, 2002). This is explored in Chapter 9.

The continuing domination of research in inclusion by the special education paradigm appears impossible to shake off. An escape route from special education knowledge has been provided by disabled people (eg Barnes, 1996; Oliver, 1996) in the form of the social model of disability, which shifts the focus of attention onto the environmental, structural and attitudinal barriers within institutions and society. There has, however, been a reluctance to use the social model to guide research. In spite of the many calls to investigate inclusion and exclusion simultaneously (Ballard, 2003b; Booth and Ainscow, 1998), there are few pieces of research which contain detailed social model analyses of the barriers to participation, especially within schools. The apparent indifference to the social model by educational researchers has angered the disabled scholars who were responsible for its development (Oliver, 1999). Oliver (1999) has been particularly critical of the lack of regard for the social model of disability by researchers who have instead appropriated the experiences of disabled people and contends that in so doing they have been '*shitting* disabled people' (Oliver, 1999, p. 187; original emphasis). Oliver also dismissed an earlier debate by Tony Booth (1991) and Marten Söder (1990) as 'intellectual masturbation' (Oliver, 1992, p. 20). Oliver may have been misguided in accusing them of being intellectual, but he was raising a serious point concerning the right of non-disabled people to discuss the labelling of disabled people, without involving them, and their failure to be influenced by the thinking of disabled scholars. Shakespeare (2006) contends that there are significant problems with the social model and it has become an obstacle to the development of the disability movement and to disability studies:

> I have come to the conclusion that the British social model of disability studies has reached a dead end, having taken a wrong turn back in the 1970s when the Union of Physically Impaired Against Segregation (UPIAS) social model conception became the dominant UK understanding of disability . . . At one time I was a critical friend of the social model, defending it against external attack (Shakespeare and Watson, 1997): I am now among those who argue that it should be abandoned (pp. 3–5).

Shakespeare suggests that the problems of the social model are, paradoxically, also its successes. It was developed as a political intervention rather than a social theory; it was strongly tied into identity politics; and it was defended as *correct* by its initial proponents, but not subjected to revision over the thirty years of its life. The bracketing of impairment from disability was an important move to privilege the material causes of society and to force the removal of these, but this has led to a disavowal of impairment which many disabled people have found difficult to accept:

> As individuals, most of us simply cannot pretend with any conviction that our impairments are irrelevant because they influence every aspect of our lives. We must find a way to integrate them into our whole experience and to identify for the sake of our physical and emotional well-being and, subsequently, for our capacity to work against Disability (Crow, 1992, p. 7).

French (1993) is sympathetic to the need to present disability in a 'straightforward, uncomplicated manner in order to convince a very sceptical world' (p. 24) that it is society, rather than individuals, which has to be changed. Nevertheless, the dogmatic defence of the social model as orthodoxy is, according to Shakespeare (2006), problematic and has contributed to the exclusion of the disability movement:

> Alone amongst radical movements, the UK disability rights tradition has, like a fundamentalist religion, retained its allegiance to a narrow reading of its founding assumptions (Shakespeare, 2006, p. 34).

Shakespeare and other commentators (Paterson and Hughes, 1999) have contended that a social model needs to become more sophisticated if it is to be relevant to the lives of disabled people or at least used more reflexively (Corker, 1999).

Research on inclusion which focuses on one area of oppression, for example in relation to disability, effectively silences other aspects, such as gender, class or ethnicity. Davis (2002) suggests that this 'intersectionality' (p. 148) occurs because anti-discrimination legislation revolves around a 'single axis framework' (Crenshaw, 1994, p. 40), but it may also be the case that researchers are unable to manage the investigation of one aspect of exclusion at a time. Notions of double and triple oppression have been fiercely contested because of the ways in which these have been constructed (Wright et al, 2000) and the question of what should be identified as the greater determinants of an individual's success, academically, socially and economically remains a source of debate.

NO DEBATE ABOUT THE PURPOSES OF INCLUSION

Researchers have done little to initiate a debate on the purposes of inclusion or on the question of what precisely is one to be included in. There is either an assumption among researchers that there is a shared understanding of what is meant by inclusion or an acknowledgement that it is a contested and complex area, but with little explication of these contestations and complexities. Researchers have often merged unreflexively 'terms such as 'special educational needs', integration', 'normalisation', mainstream-ing', 'exceptional learners' and 'inclusion' into a loose vocabulary' (Slee, 1998, p. 131). The failure to position research on inclusion *phronetically*, by foregrounding values and power, ensures that it can never get at how individuals are implicated within inclusion or to ascertain the purpose which inclusion might have.

In place of any meaningful debate about the purpose of inclusion and what this might look like for those most directly involved, we have a series of bland exchanges about valuing diversity (Benjamin, 2002) and a somewhat clichéd use of inclusion (Thomas and Loxley, 2001). Research outcomes appear to consist of superficial state-ments about disabled students' location within mainstream schools and the proportions of time spent in ordinary classrooms. There is a reliance on the physical presences and essences of students and towards research that is fixed by medicalised constructions of disability (Barnes, 1997) and which are readily measured, but as Artiles (2004) points out, such an obsession generates 'myopic understandings of the role of culture and his-tory' (p. 552) and ensures that agency is denied. Alternatively, researchers have gone in search of the inclusive school (Dyson and Millward, 2000; Corbett, 2001; Rouse and Florian, 1995) and are surprised when they find little evidence of inclusivity or can only offer generalised accounts of effective strategies from 'lessons learned' (Rouse and Florian, 2001, p. 399). Skidmore (2004) is deeply critical of such approaches which, he argues, reveal the researchers' 'determination to use their findings to put for-ward yet another abstract blueprint of the ideal school' (p. 23). Dyson and colleagues (2004) subsequently took the line that looking for the inclusive school had been a mistake while others have acknowledged that exclusion and inclusion can occur simul-taneously (Ballard, 2003b; and Ainscow, et al, 1999). This level of insight has still, however, eluded some and they continue to pursue the effective inclusive school. Some recent research has attempted to identify the impact of inclusion on educational out-comes, either for the disabled children themselves or for mainstream students. Research producing outcomes of this kind are generally attractive to funders of research with a concern for the costs of inclusion and may be tempting to a novice researcher. The flood of texts in the form of guides on how to 'do' inclusion (Sebba and Sachdev, 1997; Farrell and Ainscow, 2002) are based on limited research evidence but affect an authority as they rehearse children's pathologies and entrench further the notion of inclusion as some idealised final state. Most importantly they sidestep the important question: inclusion into what?

There is an awareness by some that certain aspects of inclusion are 'contested ground' (Sheehy, 2005, p. 1) and 'open to confusion' (Lunt and Norwich, 1999, p. 32), but those exploring this contestation are few and far between and there is little dialogue between them. Those who have admitted to stumbling over the meanings associated with inclusion (Slee, 2005), have challenged the assumption that 'with proper analysis, inclusion can in some way be disambiguated' (Thomas and Glenny, 2005, p. 9). Those researchers who have produced work with more questions than answers (Allan, 2003b; Baston, 2003) have felt troublingly exposed or have been accused of inadequacy for failing to provide satisfactory definitions. The absence of a debate on the nature and purpose of inclusion is extremely problematic for researchers who can only guess at what it might be and hope that they will know it when they see it.

THE FAILINGS OF EDUCATIONAL RESEARCH

Educational research has been subjected to intensive criticism over recent years for its failure to make a significant impact on the policy and practice community. Within the UK, the critiques by James Tooley (1998) and David Hargreaves (1996), although themselves deeply flawed, still had a considerable impact and contributed to an obsession with educational research which is useful and relevant (Nixon and Sykes, 2003). This and the 'fetishism with methodology' (Oliver, 2002, p. 4) ensures a continuing privileging of positivistic research and 'physics envy' (Sennett, 1995). These obsessions also create further confusion through the imperative to simplify, define and measure and the expectation of 'science as usual' (Flyvbjerg, 2002, p. 166). Many researchers have been lured away from forms of inquiry which problematise phenomena (such as inclusion and exclusion) and towards research which is oriented towards *what works*. This is of little use because it assumes such complex phenomena are understood, when they are not, and seeks to find solutions which can be packaged and disseminated to teachers and others.

Perhaps the most sinister manifestation of 'physics envy' (Sennett, 1995) within educational research can be seen in the predominance of systematic reviews. The limitations of the systematic review process have been addressed comprehensively and persuasively by Hammersley (2001) who is critical of the vast areas of research that are excluded and by Hodkinson (2004) who argues that they ignore embodied judgement and impose a single model. Maclure (2005a) has been particularly forthright in her dismissal of the quality controlled nature of systematic reviews, which strip them of their rhetoric and lead to the pursuit of 'clarity bordering on stupidity' (Maclure, 2005a, p. 393). In spite of these criticisms, they remain a formidable part of the educational research canon and command respect in some quarters. The inappropriate use of systematic reviews is one thing, but their use in inclusion research appears to have been highly irresponsible, directing the researchers' gaze in inappropriate and unproductive directions, and which are ultimately unjust. Dyson and his team (2002) who undertook a systematic review of research on inclusion found that there were few 'golden solutions' in the existing research. Although this was not surprising, there were wails of protest that researchers' efforts had not revealed any useful insights about how to achieve inclusion. Subsequent systematic reviews on inclusion (Nind et al, 2004; Rix et al, 2005) followed the protocols equally slavishly and eliminated vast amounts of inclusion literature before concentrating on a tiny number which met their criteria. Their not very illuminating finding that the teacher is of central importance in engaging children and young people does raise some questions about the value of such reviews and the direction of public resources towards them.

The culture of accountability operating within higher education places controls and constraints on educational researchers which force them towards particular kinds of research. In the UK, the Research Assessment Exercise acts as a particularly negative driver for researchers, but research in higher education in Australia, New Zealand, Canada, the US and other countries have also been described as moving in the direction of accountability frameworks (Vidovitch and Slee, 2001; Ballard, 2003a). Vidovitch and Slee (2001) warn that if accountability frameworks within higher education are not problematised they could become the 'midwives of globalization . . . which deliver market ideologies uncritically around the globe' (Blackmore, as cited in Vidovitch and Slee, 2001, p. 451). Barnes (1997) bemoans the way in which it steers researchers away from undertaking work which has practical value and contends that new researchers are unable to do anything other than 'kow tow to convention' (1997, p. 240). Moore et al (1998) describe explicit efforts by their Local Education Authority research sponsor to push their research in particular directions and to dictate who and what was to be included. This led them to do what they saw as disabling research and they reveal their 'despondency' (p. 35) at their own powerlessness to resist these pressures, partly because their own careers and qualifications were tied into the research contract. More upsettingly for them, they felt they let down the teachers, for whom they could produce little in the way of findings, and the d/Deaf children in their study, who became 'fetishised into things' (Riseborough, 1993, p. 140) through the research practices.

INTO THE ACADEMY? THE SCHOOLING OF NEW RESEARCHERS

New researchers enter the field of inclusion, usually with a commitment to understanding – and perhaps doing something about – exclusion, inequality and injustice. They are also likely to come with some belief in the value of inclusion, but they may be given the message that values are problematic in so far as they interfere with the pursuit of the epistemic (predictive and explanatory) research. New researchers may find themselves forced to deny or bracket off their values and beliefs whilst they undertake their research and may, not surprisingly, find this impossible. There is a further difficulty in relation to the rubric of research on inclusion which they enter into. The rubric continues to be haunted by special education and novices may find themselves unwittingly enlisted into a series of unwritten special education *codes*. These codes force researchers, experienced as well as novices, to search out the pathological and to hunt down students with particular labels. Before they know it, researchers may find themselves constructing a sample of students within particular categories of need and formulating interview questions which are informed by a deficit model of disability and which assume certain characteristics among the students in accordance with the categories being deployed. Researchers may thus be forced to collude in the repetition of exclusion through their work because the special education codes are not always immediately apparent and they may not have required sufficient skills in reflexivity to spot this.

Those undertaking research on inclusion have little to go on beside conventional texts on educational research. These deal with each aspect of the research and will occasionally delve into issues around ethics and sensitivity in the research process. There is little, however, to guide the researcher on 'how to capture what is inevitably elusive and complex' (Corbett, 2001, p. 38) and to avoid creating exclusion in his or her own research. Researchers of inclusion have been unwilling, or perhaps unable, to be explicit about their positions in relation to ontology – the nature of reality – and epistemology – the nature of the knowledge – they produce. Perhaps worse than a failure to be explicit is the superficial deployment of a particular methodological 'lens', such as a 'postmodern lens' (Harklau et al, 2005), for which one might read 'gloss'. The failure by researchers to be explicit about the ontology and epistemology of their work is a feature of educational research more generally, but it seems particularly problematic within inclusion because of the closure it creates for novice researchers and the disincentive to scrutinise their own positions. Slee (2006), in calling to inclusion researchers to 'let's get metaphysical (with apologies to Olivia Newton John)' (p. 117), likens their work to that of a gymnast:

> Herein is the intersection of discourse and interest. This is the art of the balance beam. I have never been a gymnast and claim no knowledge of this apparatus, but I should imagine the execution of the cartwheels, handstands and pirouettes, not to mention the splits, defies the pull of gravity. So too for inclusive education; the gravity of interest and traditional special/regular educational domination of the field brings us crashing to the mat of compromise all too often (p. 117).

As someone who was, in fact, a gymnast, I found that a good knowledge of biomechanics and constant practice were the best weapons with which to manage gravity. The challenge for the researcher on inclusion, however, is more complex, however. The equipment is non-standard and the balance beam, for example, is glazed with butter or some other slippery substance while the horse to be vaulted is constantly being repositioned. The researcher, thus, has to try to orientate him or herself in relation to fixtures which are themselves uncertain and given to change and to try to avoid coming to grief.

Research students undertaking a higher degree qualification are in a particularly invidious position, with uneven power relations between them, their supervisors and the institution in which they are enrolled. In putting together their research proposal and designing their research, they may not be encouraged to dwell on the uncertainty of inclusion and may be constrained, in constructing their research, to define their terms in a way that creates closure. If they are lucky enough to be given encouragement to remain open to contested meanings, they may find this difficult to handle alongside the other epistemological and ontological uncertainties and insecurities about theoretical positions and paradigms. In the scary world of postgraduate research, the definable and measurable may prove more comfortable and reassuring.

GOING ON WITH INCLUSION?

The picture painted so far is a bleak one and suggests that inclusion is difficult, if not impossible, to achieve. There appear to be many negative commentaries on inclusion and a sense that the cost to some is simply too great. The repetition of unjust and exclusionary effects in legislation and policy appear to be inevitable and we seem unable to stop ourselves hunting down the different and the pathological. Research on inclusion has done little to help understand what the purpose of inclusion is supposed to be and how this might be achieved. Worse still, some of the research on inclusion seems to have had an opposite – exclusionary – effect for some upon whom it has been undertaken. In spite of this bleak prognosis, there are, I am arguing, possibilities for engineering shifts in thinking and in practices – our own and others'. It involves, in Deleuze and Guattari's (1986) terms, 'diabolical powers to come or revolutionary forces to be constructed (p. 18). The remainder of the book is thus dedicated to putting the philosophers of difference to work on inclusion, in an attempt to rescue it from it from its own impasse and to reframe it as something that we can *go on* with.

PART TWO: PUTTING THE PHILOSOPHERS TO WORK ON INCLUSION

4.   DELEUZE AND GUATTARI'S SMOOTH SPACES

> We constantly lose our ideas. That is why we want to hang on to fixed opinions so much (Deleuze and Guattari, 1994, p. 202).

I have attempted to illustrate how the spaces of schooling, teacher education and education policy and legislation, which are rigid, striated and hierarchical, with clear lines of demarcation, produce exclusion. This chapter considers how the key ideas of Deleuze and Guattari might enable a reworking of educational spaces as smooth. The smoothing out of educational spaces is effectively about shifting power and altering the way in which people can engage within these spaces. In the final part of the book I will suggest some subtle and not so subtle ways of engineering this in schools, in teacher education and within the wider policy arena. This chapter attempts to set out some of the key ideas from Deleuze and Guattari which appear likely to assist in this process. They do not offer solutions to the 'problem' of inclusion, but they offer new ways of understanding it and 'new lines of flight' (Deleuze and Guattari, 1987 p. 161) for considering how it might be faced. Before considering what Deleuze and Guattari have to offer, and as a prelude to this and to the next two chapters dealing with Derrida and Foucault, I offer some thoughts on why philosophical ideas, rather than more practical guidance or solutions, are needed to revive the inclusion project.

ALL IN THE ABSTRACT? PHILOSOPHY AS ACTIVE EXPERIMENTATION

As Arcilla (2002) has noted, philosophers and educators have tended not to speak to one another, yet if we are to keep asking ourselves how should we educate (Bredo, 2002), then such an alliance is necessary. St Pierre (2004), lamenting the 'science as usual' (Flyvbjerg, 2002, p. 166) mentality which dominates education, declares that:

> We are in desperate need of new concepts, Deleuzian or otherwise, in this new educational environment that privileges a single positivist research model with its transcendent rationality and objectivity and accompanying concepts such as randomization, replicability, generalizability, bias, and so forth – one

that has marginalized, subjugated knowledges and done material harm at all
levels of education, and one that many educators have resisted with some
success for the last fifty years (p. 286).

Deleuze (1995) sees philosophy as an essential for education which, he notes, has
become a business, yet philosophy's chief role in relation to pedagogy has been as a
repressor, representing:

> A formidable school of intimidation which manufactures specialists in
> thought . . . an image of thought called philosophy has been formed histori-
> cally and it effectively stops people from thinking (Deleuze and Parnett, 1987,
> p. 13).

Deleuze (2000) contends that the big mistake of philosophy is to 'presuppose within
us a benevolence of thought, a natural love of truth' (p. 16) and, following Nietzsche
(1968), contends that there needs to be mistrust of concepts created by others.
Philosophy, thus, is profoundly political 'and takes the criticism of its own time to
its highest point' (Deleuze and Guattari, 1994, p. 99). The artist Paul Klee (1961)
points to the mobilising effects of analysing others' work, suggesting that it allows
us to 'set ourselves in motion' (p. 91), while Ansell Pearson (1997) points out that
philosophy is always forward thinking, speaking of values that are to come: 'philosophy is often sad, though never nostalgic' (p. 3) and it is this imaginative function of
philosophy which is of most value in relation to inclusion, to take us from the
impasse in which we find ourselves to new beginnings:

> [Philosphy] is imagination which crosses domains, orders and levels, knock-
> ing down partitions, co-extensive with the world, guiding our bodies and
> inspiring our souls, grasping the unity of mine and nature; a larval conscious-
> ness which moves endlessly from science to dream and back again (Deleuze,
> 1994, p. 22).

Gregoriou (2004) suggests philosophers of education have been 'unbecoming
philosophers' (p. 236), moving away from philosophy and into, for example feminist anthropology or liberal political-science. This has not, she argues, served education well in practical terms and has discouraged consideration of the central
normative question of how we should educate. She calls upon educationists to establish a 'minor philosophy of education' (Gregoriou, 2004, p. 234) 'which isn't
haunted by the big figures of philosophy's fathers, picks up these ideas from social
science without anxiety about risking its identity and connects these ideas in new
encounters' (p. 234). These next three chapters operate in this vein, identifying those
ideas of Deleuze and Guattari, Derrida and Foucault which can be put to work on
inclusion in, perhaps, new and surprising ways. Whilst every attempt is made to
understand the essential meanings of these constructs and to use them with integrity,
there may be aspects which purists of these scholars may balk at. It is to be hoped
that any offence is short lived and that misunderstandings or collisions prove to be
productive. It is also hoped that the suggested forms of engagement with the ideas
may provide platforms from which others can launch themselves into their own
creative and analytical trajectories.

Deleuze and Guattari, Derrida and Foucault, along with Irigary, Kristeva, Lyotard and others, have been recognised as philosophers of difference because of their concern with achieving the recognition of minority social groups and their attempt to formulate a politics of difference which is based on an acceptance of multiplicity (Patton, 2000). Each of these writers have in common an orientation to philosophy as a political act and a will to make use of philosophical concepts as a form, not of global revolutionary change, but of 'active experimentation, since we do not know in advance which way a line is going to turn' (Deleuze and Parnet, 1987, p. 137). Their work is a philosophy of affirmation which is a 'belief of the future, in the future' (Deleuze, as cited Rajchman, 2001, p. 76) and is intended to lighten and provide release:

> *To affirm is not to take responsibility for, to take on the burden of what is, but to release, to set free what lives.* To affirm is to unburden: not to load life with the weight of higher values, but to create new values which are those of life, which make life light and active (Deleuze, 1983, p. 185; original emphasis).

Nietzsche's notion of the creation of 'untimely' concepts (1983, p. 60) is taken up by Deleuze and Guattari as depicting the kind of political work they see as important: 'acting counter to our time and thereby acting on our time and, let us hope, for the benefit of a time to come' (Nietzsche, 1983, p. 60).

A key role for philosophy, if it is to be put to work on inclusion, is in relation to language and the challenge here is complex. It requires overcoming the complacency and lack of reflexivity through which inclusion has come to be understood as a catch all for everything and everyone and is now regarded as a vacuous concept or a 'prettifying euphemism' (Shapiro, 1993, p. 33); it also involves disrupting *the special needs empire* in a way that has lasting effects. In short, following Deleuze (1998), we need to make the language of inclusion stutter, creating 'an affective and intensive language, and no longer an affectation of the one who speaks' (ibid, p. 107). This is no easy task, as it involves taking language out of its natural equilibrium where there is security with definitions and meanings, but Deleuze suggests this is essential in order to move forward:

> Can we make progress if we do not enter into regions far from equilibrium? Physics attests to this. Keynes made advances in political economy because he related it to the situation of a "boom", and no longer one of equilibrium. This is the only way to introduce desire into the corresponding field. Must language then be put into a state of boom, close to a crash? (Deleuze, 1998, p. 109; original emphasis).

Derrida (1976) contends that language itself has lost some of its meaning and significance:

> The devaluation of the word 'language' itself, and how, in the very hold it has upon us, it betrays a loose vocabulary, the temptation of a cheap seduction, the passive yielding to fashion, the consciousness of the avant-garde, in other words – ignorance – are evidences of this effect (p. 5).

Disruptive work on language has the potential to create inclusiveness and a high degree of reflexivity because disjunctions that are created 'follow a rolling gait that concerns the process of language and no longer the flow of speech' (Deleuze, 1998, p. 110). The process of causing language to stutter also creates a silence:

> *When a language is so strained* that it starts to stutter, or to murmur or stammer . . . *then language in its entirety reaches the limit* that marks its outside and makes it confront silence . . . To make one's language stutter, face to face, or face to back, and at the same time to push language as a whole to its limit, to its outside, to its silence – this would be like the *boom* and the *crash* (Deleuze, 1998, p. 113 original emphasis).

Whilst there is no prospect of coming close to the exemplary writers cited by Deleuze, such as Kafka and Becket, whose 'affirmative disjunctions' (Deleuze, 1998, p. 111) create 'fragments, allusions, strivings, investigations (ibid), the philosophical concepts in this, and the subsequent chapters, will, it is hoped, offer the means of disrupting some of the current understandings and practices which get in the way of inclusion.

DELEUZE, DELEUZE AND GUATTARI AND . . .

> The two of us wrote *Anti-Oedipus* together. Since each of us was several, there was already quite a crowd (Deleuze and Guattari, 1987, p. 3).

The work of Deleuze and Guattari (1987) can be best described using their own concept of an assemblage, in the sense that it is non-linear and connects multiple systems of thought formation, and as a 'line of flight' (ibid, p. 9), in the way in which the work diverges and refuses to be reduced to a set of themes or elements of theory. Deleuze has also been described as a 'stutterer, thinker of the outside' (Boundas and Olkowsky, 1994, p. 3). Deleuze's way of working with others is somewhat abberant: 'we don't work, we negotiate. We were never in the same rhythm, we were always out of step' (Deleuze and Parnet, 1987, p. 17). Deleuze and Guattari's (1987) book, *A Thousand Plateaus,* was described by them as a 'rhizome . . . composed of plateaus: 'We have given it a circular form, but only for laughs' (p. 22). Guattari, a nonphilosopher, had a major impact on the philosopher Deleuze, taking his work onto new planes, some of them apparently inconsistent, but this seemed to be something which did not concern Deleuze. Indeed, Deleuze and Guattari (1994) contended that nonphilosophy was necessary to think new thoughts: 'Philosophy needs nonphilosophy that comprehends it; it needs a nonphilosophical comprehension just as art needs nonart and science needs nonscience.' (p. 218). Rajchman (2001) describes Deleuze's philosophy as consisting of:

> different conceptual 'bits', each initially introduced in relation to a particular problem, then re-introduced into new contexts, seen from new perspectives. The coherence among the various bits shifts from one work to the next as new concepts are added, fresh problems addressed; it is not given by 'logical consistency' among by the 'series' or 'plateaus' into which the conceptual pieces enter or settle along the web of their interrelations' (p. 21; original emphasis).

This is all rather unsettling for anyone attempting to get a grip on Deleuzian constructs, but as Deleuze (1995) himself said, 'there's nothing to understand, nothing to interpret' (p. 9). He has also spoken playfully of how when his students interacted with his work, 'nobody took in everything, but everyone took what they needed or wanted, what they could use' (Deleuze, 1995, p. 139). His work offers an opportunity to respond ontologically, with a series of questions:

> Does it work? What new thoughts does it make possible to think? What new emotions does it make possible to feel? What new sensations and perceptions does it open in the body? (Massumi, 1992, p. 8).

Problems for Deleuze 'do not exist only in our heads but occur here and there in the production of the actual historical world' (Deleuze, 1994, p. 190) and the significance of this is that they can be worked upon through thought. The act of thought, for Deleuze, is a throw of the dice, a form of experimentation. His philosophy, thus, consists of the concept, which has a multiplicity, a history and a 'becoming' (p. 18), the 'plane of immanence' (ibid, p. 35) on which the concept can emerge; the conceptual personae who can activate the concept, such as the nomadic teacher or the rhizomic learner; and the existing concepts which are the materials for the creation of new thought. Deleuze's work is profoundly ethical and his aspiration has been to create an ethics which is grounded in immanent modes of existence that have no externality, rather than in an appeal to a transcendental subject (Smith, 1998). Modes of existence, the elaboration of which has been influenced by both Nietzsche and Spinoza, are determined by and through the body. The advantage of this is that the body can be expressed in terms of its functions and capacities, for example for movement and expression. Modes of existence are created through the 'transvaluation of negation into affirmation, reactive into active' (Smith, 1998, p. 263) and the effect is a shift of orientation away from the universal and toward the singular and from the historical to the actual. Modes of existence are evaluated in terms of their power, but it is not the amount of power they create for individuals that is important; rather it is the extent to which the power can be deployed to push the limits that is significant.

Four of Deleuze and Guattari's conceptual 'bits' are selected on the basis that they appear to offer prospects for doing the kind of work on inclusion which will carry us 'across our thresholds towards a destination which is unkown, not foreseeable, not preexistant' (Deleuze and Parnett, 1987, p. 125). These are the rhizome, deterritorializations, difference and becoming.

THE RHIZOME

> Never interpret; experience, experiment (Deleuze, 1995, p. 87).

Deleuze and Guattari (1987) offer the rhizome as a model of thought, which challenges conventional knowledge and the means of acquiring this knowledge. According to Deleuze and Guattari, conventional knowledge is rigid, striated and hierarchical and with an 'arborescent' or tree like structure. This kind of structure relies on the logic of binarism, for example normal/abnormal; or able/disabled, and places these hierarchically within the system, identifying those on the negative side of the binary as targets for remediation and control. Learning within these spaces is concerned with the transfer of knowledge through a process of representation 'which articulates and hierarchizes tracings' (Deleuze and Guattari, 1987, p. 12), emphasises facts and asserts the binary distinctions between teacher and taught. Students are required to display their learning merely through repetition of these facts, with little opportunity for variation:

> The tree and root inspire a sad image of thought that is forever imitating the multiple on the basis of a centered or segmented higher unity (ibid, p. 16).

This kind of learning is inadequate because it is partial, with meaning being lost through continual fracturing, for example in the translation of texts or in forms of assessment. Inclusion in these learning processes is also partial, contingent, and tied to individuals' pathologies which in turn fragment and locate them within the striations of the school system. Inclusion, within these arborescent structures, is understood as a final destination.

In place of the arborescent tree structure of knowledge, Deleuze and Guattari propose the notion of a rhizome, which grows or moves in messy and unpredictable ways. The examples of rhizomes which they give include bulbs or tubers, but also rats and burrows: 'the best and the worst' (ibid, p. 7). Rhizomes have multiple connections, lines and points of rupture, but no foundation or essence, and the connectivity of these lines make a rejection of binarism inevitable:

> That is why one can never posit a dualism or a dichotomy, even in the rudimentary form of the good and the bad. You may make a rupture, draw a line of flight, yet there is still a danger that you will reencounter organizations that restratify everything, formations that restore power to a signifier, attributions that reconstitute a subject – anything you like, from Oedipal resurgences to fascist concretions (Deleuze and Guattari, 1987, p. 9).

The rhizome as a model of learning 'releases us from the false bondage of linear relationships' (Roy, 2003, p. 90) and allows for endless proliferation, new lines of flight and new forms of knowledge:

> Expression must break forms, encourage ruptures and new sproutings. When a form is broken, one must reconstruct the content that will necessarily be part of a rupture in the order of things (Deleuze and Guattari, 1987, p. 28).

Each rhizome contains:

> lines of segmentation according to which it is stratified, territorialized, organized, signified, attributed, etc.; but also lines of deterritorialization along which it endlessly flees (ibid, p. 18).

These 'ruptures and new sproutings' present new challenges and new ways of experiencing learning and inclusion. They are not, Deleuze and Guattari (1987) caution, secure spaces where individuals can be passive but a series of lines in which they must participate.

Deleuze and Guattari identify key characteristics of the rhizome which enable it to function effectively and do its disruptive work. The first of these concerns connectivity and heterogeneity: 'any point of a rhizome can be connected to anything other and must be' (ibid, p. 7), distinguishing it from the fixed – and rooted – nature of a tree. Secondly rhizomes privilege multiplicities, which take the form of lines and connections, rather than points or positions, and which disrupt unity and 'expose arborescent pseudomultiplicities for what they are' (ibid, p. 8). Thirdly, the rhizome has the potential to be ruptured or shattered and yet to start up again on one of its old lines or on a new line: 'you can never get rid of ants because they form an animal rhizome that can rebound time and again after most of it has been destroyed' (ibid, p. 9). A fourth aspect of the rhizome is the absence of any genetic axis, on which successive stages can be based, and of a deep structure, which can be broken down into constituent parts. These absences make it impossible to trace the rhizome, as one might the leaves of a tree. A final feature of the rhizome is 'that it has no beginning or end; it is always in the middle, between things, interbeing, *intermezzo*' (Ibid, p. 25; original emphasis) Rhizomic learning, thus, is always *in process,* having to be constantly worked at by all concerned and never complete. This in-betweenness is an inclusive space in which everyone belongs and where movement occurs:

> The middle is by no means an average; on the contrary, it is where things pick up speed. *Between* things does not designate a localizable relation going from one thing to the other and back again, but a perpendicular direction, a transversal movement that sweeps one *and* the other away, a stream without beginning or end that undermines its banks and picks up speed in the middle (Deleuze and Guattari, 1987, p. 25; original emphasis).

Whilst the rhizome has obvious metaphorical appeal, establishing it as the model for thinking about learning and inclusion is much more complex:

> It is not a matter of exposing the Root and announcing the Rhizome. There are knots of arborescence in rhizomes and rhizomatic offshoots in roots. The rhizome is perpetually in construction or collapsing, a process that is perpetually prolonging itself, breaking off and starting up again (Gregoriou, 2004, p. 244).

The market economy and the standards agenda have laid down their own roots and defined learning along linear and hierarchical lines which differentiate learners and exclude some of them. These structures may be impermeable to attempts to introduce rhizomic processes or may reassert themselves against them. It may be, however, that the rhizome has to be deployed creatively – to subvert, subtract and invent - and I offer some tentative suggestions in this regard in part three of the book.

DETERRITORIALIZATION

The striation of space is, according to Deleuze and Guattari (1987), one of the main tasks of the state and this functions to include some people and exclude others.

Smooth spaces within striated spaces are used as a means of communication in the service of space and in order to control flows of people and activities:

> The *relative global:* it is limited in its parts, which are assigned constant directions, are oriented in relation to one another, divisible by boundaries, and can interlink; what is limiting (*lines* or wall, and no longer boundary) is this aggregate in relation to the smooth spaces it "contains," whose growth it slows or prevents, and which it restricts or places outside (Deleuze and Guattari, 1987, p. 382; original emphasis).

The certainties which are pursued within state apparatuses or, as Deleuze and Guattari describe them, assemblages, seek to control individuals within their locales. As De Landa (1991) notes, these assemblages are ineffective since 'instead of leading to the achievement of total certainty, centralized schemes lead to 'information explosions' which increase the overall amount of uncertainty' (p. 66; original emphasis). De Landa contends that the most effective command systems are the ones that manage to 'dissipate uncertainty throughout the hierarchy' (1991, p. 60).

Schools are highly striated spaces in which the flow of students – through the building itself, through the curriculum and in relation to teachers, other adults and other students – is intensively regulated:

> The gates of the city, its levies and duties, are barriers, filters against the fluidity of the masses, against the penetration power of migratory packs' (Virilio, 1986, pp. 12–13).

School rules bind students to certain flows of activity, deviation from which brings a pathologising regime down upon them. Relationships between teachers in these rigid spaces are defined by authority and control and expressed through 'order words' (Deleuze and Parnett, 1987, p. 22), which are simply to be obeyed:

> When the schoolteacher explains an operation to the children, or when she teaches them grammar, she does not, strictly speaking, give them information, she communicates orders to them, she transmits 'order words' to them, necessarily conforming to dominant meanings (p. 22).

The communication of these 'order words' extend beyond the information that children are supposed to absorb to children's place and demeanour in the school, for example 'sit down', 'be quiet' or 'take your jacket off'. The ordering of children to remove their jackets has sometimes provoked a confrontation between the student and the teacher which is only resolved when the student obeys; recently, however, attempts by individual schools to prohibit certain forms of dress by ethnic minorities has met with a more strenuous challenge from communities and the occasional litigation, drawing its warrant from Human Rights legislation.

Deterritorialization seeks to knock existing understandings and ways of acting into a different orbit or trajectory (Roy, 2004). Its purpose is to undo the 'processes of continuous control and instantaneous communication' (Smith, 1998, p. 264). It is a performative breaking of existing codes which is also a 'making' (Howard, 1998, p. 115). That is, it is an escape, but in a positive sense, so that new intensities open up:

> The result is a return to a field of forces, transversing the gaps, puncturing the holes, and opening up the new world order to a quite different and new world of the multiple (Howard, 1998, pp. 123–124).

Deterritorialization creates 'chaosmos' (Deleuze and Guattari, 1994), a term coined by James Joyce and which Deleuze and Guattari considered an apt account of the effects of deterritorialization: 'composed chaos, neither forseen nor preconceived' (p. 204) and precipitating new ways of thinking and acting: 'once one ventures outside what's familiar and reassuring, once one has to invent new concepts for unknown lands, then methods and moral systems break down' (Deleuze, 1995, p. 322). The potential areas for deterritorialization cannot be specified; rather it is a case of being alert to opportunities to interrupt:

> This is how it should be done: Lodge yourself on a stratum; experiment with the opportunities it offers, find an advantageous place on it, find potential movements of deterritorialization, possible lines of flight, experience them, produce flow conjunctions here and there, try out continuums of intensitities segment by segment, have a small plot of new land at all times (Deleuze and Guattari, 1987, p. 161).

Deterritorialization has the potential to attack the rigid, striated – or territorialized – spaces of schooling, teacher education and policy, replacing these with ones which are smooth and full of creative possibilities. Within these newly created spaces 'life reconstitutes its stakes, confronts new obstacles, invents new paces, switches adversaries' (Deleuze and Guattari, 1987, p. 500). These smooth spaces are depicted by Deleuze and Guattari (ibid) as 'holey space' (p. 413), like Swiss cheese. Crucially, deterritorialization takes us from communication – through 'order-words' (Deleuze and Parnett, 1987, p. 22), imperatives for others to act – to expression. Smooth spaces are not, as was the case with the rhizome, safe spaces and deterritorialization is just part of an assemblage of territorialization and reterritorialization, each precipating the other. The Members of the Scottish Parliament, experienced the 'special needs' inquiry as an act of deterritorializion as it unravelled much of their pre-existing knowledge and assumptions and made them think anew about inclusion as a different kind of problem. Their own bewilderment at some of the contradictions had created a smooth path for them to imagine things differently, but their imaginings were very quickly reterritorialized and enveloped within the rigid striations of the new legislation, which created very clear boundaries and territories. Whilst this was disappointing, having even a glimpse of the possibilities offered through deterritorializion provides grounds for optimism and suggests that it is worth further efforts to secure smooth spaces for inclusion.

For deterritorialization to be achieved in relation to inclusion, there appear to be four elements which need to be considered. The first of these is a requirement that we become foreigners in our own tongue, experiencing the world around us as new, a 'becoming-intense' of language (Roy, 2004, p. 310). This allows us to question taken for granted notions, such as inclusion, and to develop atypical expressions. For Deleuze and Guattari (ibid), such stammering as if in a foreign tongue 'consitutes a cutting edge of deterritorialization of language' (p. 99). It has the effect of bringing language to a standstill, whereby 'suddenly things are not perceived or propositions not articulated in the same way' (Deleuze, 1988, p. 85). It also creates a kind of limbo, 'an *intermediate state* between content and expression' (Deleuze and Guattari, 1987, p. 44 original emphasis). This effect is desirable because it forces us to confront existing certainties by inserting a doubt 'blow by blow' (Deleuze and Guattari, 1994, p. 76). The recognition that these certainties are flawed will enable a process of starting again, with regard, perhaps, for more acceptable values.

The second element of deterritorialization is a refusal of essences or of signifieds, effecting instead, what Roy (1994) calls a 'de-*monstration* which replaces the Idea' (p. 310; original emphasis).

> Every time we will be asked about signifieds such as 'what is beauty, Justice, Man? we will respond by designating a body, by indicating an object . . . Diogenes the Cynic answers Plato's definition of a man as a biped and feath-erless animal by bringing forth a plucked fowl (Deleuze, 1990, pp. 134–135).

The point of this refusal is to stop language in its tracks, in an effort to find some sense:

> By the same movement with which language falls from the heights and then plunges below, we must be led back to the surface where there is no longer any-thing to denote or even to signify, but where pure sense is produced (p. 136).

This pure sense is produced through 'a reorientation of thought following its initial disorientation' (Bogue, 2004, p. 341), forcing the learner to encounter the new.

Creative subtraction represents a third element of deterritorialization and this is particularly significant in the context of inclusion specifically and education more generally, in which more and more is being expected of teachers and who, under-standably, are finding this overwhelming. Creative subtraction involves a calculated loss, rather than an acquisition:

> It is an ascetic practice, an awareness of the movement of sense and nonsense as well as the paradoxicalities of language, and that substracts in a creative manner in order to make openings for new becomings (Roy, 2004, p. 311).

Samuel Beckett saw his work in a similar way and as in contrast to that of his contemporary, James Joyce, who sought to embellish and add to his writing:

> I realised that my own way was an impoverishment, in lack of knowledge and in taking away, in subtracting rather than adding (Knowleson, 1996, p. 147).

Another element of deterritorialization is an acceptance that there is no-one behind expression. Individuals may be part of expression, but not the authors of it: 'there is no individual enunciation. There is not even a subject of enunciation' (Deleuze and Guattari, 1987, p. 79). Instead, individuals may be 'interpellated' (Haraway, as cited in Roy, 2004, p. 309) into 'the currents and cross-currents of this infinitely dispersed discourse'(ibid, p. 309) and any identity that is revealed is 'essentially fortuitous' (Deleuze, 1990, p. 178). This frees them up to contribute to new combinations of expression, without worrying about their own implication in these forms. The removal of agency from expression is part of a wider ambition by Deleuze and Guattari to think outside of identity in their theorising on difference, and this is discussed below.

Achieving deterritorialization within schools and within teacher education is, as I have suggested, no easy task, but in Chapter 6, I will explore the role of children and young people in working on their own school spaces and in Chapter 7, I will consider how teacher education might be deterritorialized in a way that offers new maps, rather than tracings, for becoming teachers.

DIFFERENCE

Inclusion has been plagued by platitudes with regard to difference, in which teachers are urged to 'celebrate' diversity and difference. Apart from the absence of any indication of how such celebration might be done, the language itself is patronising and amounts to the kind of tolerance which provoked such rage in Slee's (2003) disabled colleague. The emergence of these empty, vacuous platitudes was associated, as was seen in Chapter 2, with an inability to avoid the repetition of exclusion and the use of a complex system of pathologies to define, divide and treat difference. The inevitable and irresistible repetition of exclusion arises from a fear of difference and a need to control it or make sense of it and the teachers unions have made it clear that some difference is more frightening for their members than others. Deleuze understands this fear fully: 'That which is new is not orthodox but paradoxical, and hence its sense seems nonsense, not good sense' (Bogue, 2004, p. 333). Howard (1998) goes further to suggest that the New World Order 'levels all differences; alliance politics becomes identity politics and all members treat otherness as enemy' (p. 113). Difference, according to Deleuze (2004), is therefore 'mediated' (p. 38) by being subjected to identity, opposition, analogy and resemblance. The purpose of this is to try to equalise difference or reduce it to make it 'livable and thinkable' (ibid). The unspoken question implied by such a treatment of difference is 'wouldn't you rather not be [different]' (Ware, 2003b, p. 121).

Deleuze seeks to privilege difference over identity and to establish a concept of difference which involves 'no necessary connection with the negative or with negation' (Patton, 2000, p. 31). He rejects the Hegelian link between difference and contradiction:

> It is not difference which presupposes opposition but opposition which presupposes difference and which far from resolving difference by tracing it back to a foundation, opposition betrays and distorts it (Deleuze, 2004, p. 62).

Such a struggle, he argues, is characterised by 'cruelty, even monstrosity' (ibid, p. 36), in which 'the distinguished opposes something which cannot distinguish itself from it but continues to espouse that which divorces it' (Deleuze, 2004, p. 62). Difference in itself, in contrast, implies 'a swarm of differences, a pluralism of free, wild or untamed differences' (p. 61). Deleuze makes an important distinction between difference and diversity:

> Difference is not diversity. Diversity is given, but difference is that by which the given is given . . . Difference is not phenomenon but the noumenon closest to phenomenon . . . Every phenomenon refers to an inequality by which it is conditioned . . . Everything which happens and everything which appears is correlated with orders of differences: differences of level, temperature, pressure, tension, potential, difference of intensity (Deleuze, 2004, p. 280).

Deleuze's politics of difference is affirmative, attempting to 'rescue difference from its maledictory state' (p. 37) and refusing to treat it as 'secondary, derivative or deficient' (Patton, 2000, p. 46) in relation to identity, but it also provides a basis for the recognition, and responsiveness to, individual differences. Deleuze's version of difference is immanent, that is, difference *in itself*, rather than in relation to identity. It is set only in relation to other differences and as such, is 'material and forceful' (Patton and Protevi, 2003, p. 5), requiring difference to be shown 'differing' (Deleuze, 2004, p. 68). It is also, according to Deleuze (2004), 'light, ariel and affirmative' (p. 65), allowing individuals to perform their own difference. The shift towards a more affirmative conceptualisation of difference could be useful for inclusion, possibly reducing the fear of difference or reverence for those who present differently.

Deleuze and Guattari's notion of affirmative difference has implications for minority groups and the way in which they are seen. A minority, they contend, is identified by the gap which separates it from the standard, or the mainstream:

> The opposition between minority and majority is not simply quantitative. Majority implies a constant, of expression or content, serving as a standard measure by which to evaluate it. Let us suppose that the constant or standard is the average adult-white-heterosexual-European-male-speaking a standard language . . . It is obvious that 'man' holds the majority, even if he is less numerous than mosquitoes, children, women, blacks, peasants, homosexuals etc. That is because he appears twice, once in the constant and again in the variable from which the constant is extracted. Majority assumes a state of power and domination, not the other way around (Deleuze and Guattari, 1987, p. 105).

Deleuze and Guattari criticise the goal of promoting membership of the mainstream by minority groups; instead, they introduce a concept of majority-minority, which is intended to evoke becoming-minor or minoritarian. This, they suggest, involves an explicit articulation of difference and divergence of minorities from the majority, forcing the majority to examine their own standard:

> The power of the minorities is not measured by their capacity to enter and make themselves felt with the majority system, nor even to reverse the necessarily tautological criterion of the majority, but to bring to bear the force of the non-denumerable sets, however they may be, against the denumerable sets (Deleuze and Guattari, 1987, p. 471).

Deleuze and Guattari caution us against a form of differentiation through which segregation could be justified as a means of protecting difference. The establishment of faith schools, regular calls for black boys to be educated separately and, of course, special schooling are examples of this kind of erroneous differentiation. Each of these further negates, rather than affirms, difference and has little impact on the mainstream. Deleuze and Guattari's proposition enables difference among minorities to function as 'transformational multiplicities that threaten the status of the majority' (Patton, 2000, p. 48). Everyone, not just minority groups, are intended to be minoritarian or 'becoming revolutionary' (ibid, p. 48), working against the normalising power of the majority.

Howard (1998) reminds us that is not enough to proclaim 'long live the multiple' as we are trapped in our Hegelian roots of the enlightenment and this will force us to hunt down the different as negative. And, as Deleuze himself says 'a slave does not cease to be a slave by taking power' (2004, p. 66). This affirmative version of difference must be constantly repeated and there must be an anticipation of the dangers – and of the likelihood – of negation. In Chapter 7, the possibilities for enabling student teachers to explore both difference and desire within their teacher education programme are considered and Chapter 8 considers some examples of the disabled artists who produce difference as a work of art.

BECOMING

The final concept of Deleuze and Guattari that is being suggested for appropriation to the inclusion project is that of becoming, 'the action by which something or someone continues to become other (while continuing to be what it is)' (Patton, 2000, p. 78). This kind of becoming is 'revolutionary' (Deleuze and Parnett, 1987, p. 147) and extends beyond mere resistance to territorialization, involving the invention of new forms of subjectivity and new connections (Patton, 2000). It is also regarded as being open to everyone, including, or perhaps especially, those whose identities are considered fixed and immutable. Old habits can be transformed into new modes of existence: 'new percepts and new affects' (Deleuze, 1995, p. 164). Percepts, according to Deleuze (2004), differ from perceptions in that they are independent of the person who experiences them; affects, following Spinoza (1985), differ from affections and feelings by going beyond the strength of those who undergo them, but also denote transformations in bodily capacities. So percepts and affects are separate '*beings* whose validity lies in themselves and exceeds any lived' (Deleuze, 2004, p. 164 original emphasis). The notion of becoming has already been invoked in relation to all of us as becoming minor or minoritarian to enable the majority or the mainstream to be worked upon.

Desire is a key element of becoming for Deleuze and Guattari: 'there is only desire and the social and nothing else' (Deleuze and Guattari, 1977, p. 29). Desire is seen as a primary reactive force, rather than a reactive response to unfulfilled need (Patton, 2000), which connects with power to produce intensities in the relations between bodies. Deleuze and Parnet (1987) describe desire as revolutionary because

it 'always wants more connentions and assemblages' (p. 79). The becomings
produced by desire are not transcendent; rather, they enable individuals or things to
become other whilst also retaining their original state. To become something else, for
example becoming-animal or becoming-woman, and to which we could add becoming-teacher and becoming-student, is empowering because of the impact of desire;
one can form an 'inter-individual body with the real or imagined powers of the
animal in question' (Patton, 2000, p. 79). Thus, individuals appropriate these additional characteristics and wear these as part of their own 'affects', an enhanced
bodily capacity. Crucially, Deleuze and Guattari (1987), see only minorities as
capable of becoming:

> There is an entire politics of becomings-animal, as well as a politics of sorcery, which is elaborated in assemblages that are neither those of the family
> nor of religion nor of the State. Instead they express minoritarian groups that
> are oppressed, prohibited, in revolt, or always on the fringe of recognized
> institutions, groups all the more secret for being extrinsic, in other words
> anomic (p. 247).

Minorities can create becomings for themselves only insofar as they cease to be
'a definable aggregate in relation to the majority' (Deleuze and Guattari, 1987, p.
291). However, Patton (2000) has also suggested that we are all capable of becoming-minoritarian, by creating divergence from the norm: 'becoming revolutionary is
a process open to all at any time' (p. 83).

Becomings, for Deleuze and Guattari, are events rather than essences, experiences from which 'ever new, differently distributed 'heres' and 'nows'' emerge
(Deleuze, 2004, p. xix). Becomings are also infinite and, like the rhizome, move in
unpredictable directions 'of the zigzagging line' (Deleuze, 1995, p. 45). They are
created, not by 'looking for origins, even lost or deleted ones, but by setting out to
catch things where they were at work, in the middle: breaking things open, breaking
words open' (Deleuze, ibid, p. 86). Crises and predicaments are material for becoming and indeed the vicious circle may become virtuous, because the individual's
capacity to invent new concepts and articulate new values is contingent on the
dynamics of experience (Semetsky, 2004). This is perhaps the most exciting prospect
for inclusion so far: the crisis, characterised by frustration, guilt and exhaustion,
could represent an important moment which preciptitates new becomings. In other
words the troubles and failures with inclusion which have been experienced so far
could be the transformative material for becoming-inclusive for those who, according to Ballard (2003b), have lost their souls. For new teachers, a becoming identity
is far more constructive than their existing one as not yet competent and is one which
they can map out, at least partially, for themselves.

The relevance of Deleuze's ideas to education has increasingly been recognised
(Bogue, 2004; Gregoriou, 2004; St Pierre, 2001; 2004) and their value in transforming education into a problem which could then disrupt it and open it up to new possibilities, experimentations and challenges has been discerned (Costa, 2005). There
have, however, been few successful attempts to apply these to educational practice.

Roy's (2003) *Teachers in nomadic spaces* is an imaginative attempt to explore the ways in which curriculum and pedagogy might be rethought, but his analysis remains at the structural level and fails ultimately to show how practice might be changed by Deleuzian concepts. Honan's (2004) impressive rhizo-textual analysis of policy texts reveals both how the teacher is positioned within policy and teachers' readings of the texts. Honan calls for others to engage with Deleuze in a similar way and hopes that groups of educational researchers might come together to construct an 'apparatus of social critique' (2004, p. 280).

The concepts of Deleuze and Guattari which have been explored here have been selected because of their disruptive and creative potential for inclusion. Whilst writing this chapter, immersed in the writings of Deleuze and Guattari, the relevance of other concepts, such as the nomad and Bodies without Organs, became apparent. These were not developed in this chapter in the interests of containment and in order to avoid creating a rhizomic text, which, unlike Deleuze and Guattari, I would struggle to manage and remain coherent within. The concepts which are elaborated here do, however, represent prospective lines of flight for others to take up and to evaluate their potential contribution to the inclusion project.

5. DERRIDA AND THE (IM)POSSIBILITIES
OF JUSTICE

What is this strange desire for words?

(Van Manen, 2002, p. 240)

Derrida, like Deleuze, can be characterised as a philosopher of difference and whilst much of his work has been denounced as highly complex and often unnecessarily obscure (Rorty, 1989), there is general acceptance that his method of deconstruction has been a key legacy for philosophy. Deconstruction can potentially help with the reframing of the inclusion problem because of its role in disrupting the 'decidability' (Patrick, 1996, p. 141) within texts and in undermining or subverting the 'ideology of expertism' (Troyna and Vincent, 1996, p. 142) that plagues inclusion practice. This chapter will try to unpack, not so much what deconstruction is – since Derrida cautioned against such essentialist attempts at definition – but will try to show what it does *in practice*. The possibility of a political – and ethical – version of deconstruction, drawing on Derrida's Levinisian orientation to ethics, will be considered. In the absence of any practical guidance from Derrida himself, which he refused because this would be inappropriate and would take us back to essentialism, the question of how deconstruction might be accomplished will be addressed. The notion of the aporia or double contradictory imperative will be explored as a means of writing and presenting the outcomes of deconstruction to policy and practice communities.

DECONSTRUCTION: WHAT?

Derrida was frequently called upon to explain what he meant by deconstruction; he was always evasive about the essence of deconstruction, contending that all ontological statements about *what is* missed the point:

> What deconstruction is not? everything of course! What is deconstruction? nothing of course! (Derrida, 1991b, p. 275).

A significant problem with deconstruction is that it has become omnipresent, and is claimed as being done by many people. It is used synonymously with criticism or critique, and is not seen as confined to the reading of texts. Shortly before his death

71

in 2005, Derrida railed against the fact that deconstruction was everywhere and indeed there is a European Punk Rock festival tour called *Deconstruction,* a *Deconstruction Institute,* devoted to the taking down of buildings, an *Electronic Deconstruction Broadcast,* and even a film, *Deconstructing Harry.* On the event of his death, critics saw the ubiquitousness of deconstruction as a sign of Derrida's impact. His own concern, however, was that the prevalence of deconstruction had diluted the effect of what he saw as something special. His unwillingness to say what his version of deconstruction was and how it was distinguishable from critique may have contributed to its comprehensive adoption as an 'approach', but as Caputo (1997) observes, the prevalence of deconstruction has provoked 'a certain "axiomatics" of indignation' (p. 37) and 'high dudgeon' (ibid, p. 38) in some quarters:

> Critics of deconstruction feel obliged to rush to their closets, dust off and don their academic suits of armor, and then collectively charge this enemy of the common good, their lances pointed at his heart (ibid).

Derrida's resistance to defining deconstruction was tied to a fear of it becoming amenable to a set of rules and procedures, which, he argued, would destroy it. More importantly, however, he contended that its value lay in its elusiveness and its impossibility:

> I would say that deconstruction loses nothing from admitting that it is impossible; also that those who would rush to delight in that admission lose nothing from having to wait. For a deconstructive operation *possibility* would rather be a danger, the danger of becoming an available set of rule-governed procedures, methods, accessible practices. The interest of deconstruction, of such force and desire as it may have, is a certain experience of the impossible (Derrida, 1991c, p. 209; original emphasis).

For Derrida (2001b), the experience of the impossible is not just the opposite of the possible or something that is inaccessible; rather it is a responsibility towards thinking where it is most inconceivable.

Deconstruction is seen by Derrida as inventive and creative, giving the commonplace and taken-for-granted a 'new bent or twist, on twisting free of the containing effects of both essentialism and conventionalism' (Caputo, 1997, p. 103) and forming its own rules of engagement through its own process:

> Deconstruction is inventive or it is nothing at all; it does not settle for methodological procedures, it opens up a passageway, it marches ahead and marks a trail; its writing is not only performative, it produces rules – other conventions – for new performativities and never installs itself in the theoretical assurance of a simple opposition between performative and constative. Its *process* involves an affirmation, this latter being linked to the coming [venir] in event, advent, invention (Derrida, 1991c, p. 218).

This kind of invention necessitates calling into question the conventional understanding of invention itself, which, Derrida argues, would neutralise with the stamp of reason. In trying to 'reinvent the future' (Derrida, 1991c, p. 218), Derrida seeks a greater openness to what is to come, to the other and to the incalculable. Caputo

(1997) describes Derrida as an 'in-ventionalist' (p. 109) because of a kind of hyper-vigilence in which:

> his eye or ear is always turned to what is to come and because he keeps a constant watch for all these forces that would contain what is coming, that would forestall or prevent the invention of the other (p. 109).

Claiming that his intention was not to be deliberately unhelpful, in his *Letter to a Japanese friend* (1991b), Derrida suggested that it was easier to say what deconstruction was not. It was not negative, not a process of demolition, not analysis, not a methodology (in the sense that it can be taught), not an act, and not an operation. Having clarified what deconstruction is not, then, perhaps we can ask what deconstruction is concerned with and Derrida is at least specific on this point: deconstruction is about justice. Or rather, for him, deconstruction *is* justice because it always 'has to do with the other' (Derrida, 1997a, p. 17). Deconstruction, which Critchley (1999) describes as a 'philosophy of hesitation' (p. 41), is directed at decidability and closure, for it is these which create injustices. Derrida regards the instant of the decision as profoundly irresponsible:

> When the path is clear and given, when a certain knowledge opens up the way in advance, the decision is already made, it might as well be said that there is none to make; irresponsibly, and in good conscience, one simply applies or implements a program . . . It makes of action the applied consequence, the simple application of a knowledge or know how. It makes of ethics and politics a technology. No longer of the order of practical reason or decision, it begins to be irresponsible (1992b, pp. 41–45).

Injustice arises, according to Derrida, through a kind of forgetfulness of the other, effected through the rush to reach a decision and this can be seen both in practice and in the logocentrism of texts:

> Injustice – not to mention racism, nationalism and imperialism – begins when one loses sight of the transcendence of the Other and forgets that the State, with its institutions, is informed by the proximity of my relation to the Other (Critchley, 1999, p. 233).

The function of deconstruction is to interrupt closure and certainty within texts and to create undecidability about their meaning and intent. Existing concepts such as justice, democracy, decision and responsibility are reinvented with a double meaning, relating to their absolute and unconditioned form and their contingent version into which the other is allowed to come (Caputo, 1997; Patton, 2003). Texts are read with an eye to the way in which they 'get into trouble, come unstuck, offer to contradict themselves' (Eagleton, 1993, p. 134). The creation of undecidability is seen by Derrida as an act of responsibility which 'keeps an inventionalist eye open for the other to which the law as law is *blind*' (Caputo, 1997, p. 131; original emphasis). It is only when undecidability is acknowledged that ethics and politics can begin (Derrida,1992a).

Deconstruction attempts to give expression to the 'unheard of thoughts' (Derrida, 1973, p. 102) and to open up 'that-which-cannot-be-thought' (Critchley, 1999, p. 29).

It invites us 'think again and afresh' (Biesta, 2001, p. 34) about the things that matter, but which may have lost meaning or significance. The unthought relates, for Derrida, mostly to the other and this makes deconstruction an act of affirmation of the alterity of the other: 'Yes to the stranger' (Critchley, 1999, p. 189). It is an affirmation which for Derrida (1988) is unconditional.

Some writers on inclusion and special education have represented their work as deconstruction. Skrtic (1995), for example, claims that his deconstruction delegitimises modern (special) education theory and practice, arguing that his bracketing of special is a 'political tactic' (p. xiv). Thomas and Loxley (2001) present their deconstruction as a way of '*thinking* behind special education' (p. ix; original emphasis). Whilst both these texts are laudable attempts to go beyond the atheoretical and 'epistemic jumble' (ibid, p. 17) that special education has been and inclusion has become, they are troubling in a number of respects. First, it is hard to see how their work constitutes anything more than critique. There is a risk of sounding either precious or essentialist in suggesting that what they have done is not recognisable as deconstruction, but it seems odd to claim it as such when what they appear to have offered is a detailed critique, each of which is very powerful as such. A second, more worrying, problem concerns the way in which the so-called deconstruction serves as a prelude to a reconstruction: Skrtic reconstructs (special) education for postmodernity while Thomas and Loxley follow their deconstruction with a construction of inclusion. Such a move seems precipitate and in danger of the kind of repetition of exclusion which we have witnessed. It may be more helpful to dwell in the undecidability offered by deconstruction, exploring the role of our own misunderstanding in creating exclusion before rushing to such closure by pinning down and fixing meaning. Nevertheless, there are important questions about deconstruction's political function which need to be addressed and it is to these which I now turn.

AN ETHICAL DECONSTRUCTION?

Undecidability, recognised as a key 'product' of deconstruction, is also at the heart of its failure for those critics who denounce its inability to 'navigate the treacherous passage from ethics to politics ... from responsibility to questioning'. (Critchley, 1999, p. 189). The impasse created by deconstruction's undecidability fails to account for the activity of political judgement, political critique and political decision. Rorty suggests that in deconstruction and in Derrida's work more generally there is a quest for 'ironical private perfection that is politically useless and perhaps even pernicious' (as cited in Critchley, 1999, p. 200) whilst others have dismissed deconstruction as "wild nonsense and irresponsible play' (Caputo, 1997, p. 36). These accusations have been refuted by Derridean scholars, sometimes obstinately, as Midgely's (1997) suggestion that the 'devilry' (p. 26) in deconstruction did not need to be apologised for 'and is its delight' (ibid) illustrates. As Critchley (1999) contends, ethics is the goal or horizon towards which Derrida's work tends and he is deeply concerned with making the future better (Patton, 2003). Attridge (1995) points out that the 'ethics and the political are not avoided by deconstruction but are implicated at every step' (p. 110). Derrida himself has attempted to answer the charges of irresponsibility and to set out the ethics of deconstruction more coherently. For Derrida (1988), 'there can be no moral or political responsibility without this trial and without this passage by way of the undecidable' (p. 116). In other words, he does not think the political moment can be reached without the kind of dissonance created by the undecidable. Deconstruction can show how a regime is based on a set of undecidable propositions and can force institutions to open up a passage toward the other (Derrida, 1992a). Nevertheless the criticisms that he does not make this leap from undecidability are well made and, as Critchley (1999) notes, Derrida is evasive about the shift to questions concerning the political:

> But how is one to account for the move from undecidability to the political *decision* to combat that domination? Yet decisions have to be taken. But how? And in virtue of what? How does one make a decision in any undecidable terrain? (Critchley, 1999, p. 199).

An important question here concerns the nature of the political within our state and our institutions. Invariably, when decisions are taken, the political is masked and decisions are presented as rational and ordered: 'in this way, politics can claim to restore the fullness of society and bring society into harmony with itself' (Critchley, 2002, p. 2). The foregrounding of justice within the political creates obligations based on the surplus of duties over rights and this is precisely what Derrida implies by his version of the political. Derrida makes a distinction between the law and justice. The law comprises the judgements that are made in favour of, or against, individuals, drawing on the statutes and precedence. The law is 'stabilizable and statutory, calculable, a system of regulated and coded prescriptions' (Derrida, 1992a, p. 22). Justice, on the other hand, is: 'infinite, incalculable, rebellious to rule and foreign to symmetry, heterogeneous and heterotropic' (p. 22). Decisions that did not encounter undecidability might be legal, but not necessarily just:

> A decision that didn't go through the ordeal of the undecidable would not be a free decision, it would only be the programmable application or unfolding of a calculable process. It might be legal; it would not be caring [juste] . . . And once the ordeal of the undecidable is past (if that is possible), the decision has again followed a rule or given itself a rule, invented it or reinvented, reaffirmed it, it is no longer *presently* fully caring [juste] (1992a, p. 24).

Derrida describes a decision without the risk of the undecidable as a non-decision or a calculation, as well as being unjust. He sees justice as characterised by caring and by an openness to the other, a form of hospitality in which one is inviting and welcoming to the stranger. He distinguishes between the law, which is amenable to deconstruction, and justice, which is not, but this tension is what gives the moment of deconstruction both its weight and its anxiety:

> This moment of suspense, this period of *épochè*, without which, in fact, deconstruction is not possible, is always full of anxiety, but who will claim to be just by economizing on anxiety? (ibid, p. 20).

Critchley (1999) recognises in Derrida's deconstruction a Levinisian stance in relation to ethics and, through this understanding, views deconstruction as ultimately responsible and providing new resources for thinking about ethical responsibility. Deconstruction helps this process by providing a disruption of totalising politics such as anti-semitism or anti-humanism. The subsequent approach to the political, following Levinas (1969), is governed by the 'double movement of withdrawal: a withdrawal and a retrait' (Critchley, 1999, p. 206) and this withdrawal has to be total for it to be effective. A vital consideration here is in relation to democracy and the recognition that while we might hear that we live in a democracy, there is no democracy and we must, therefore, invent it. Derrida (1997b) contends that we need to think of democracy as futural, an infinite task and an infinite responsibility directed towards the other:

> If I knew that tomorrow democracy would be present, that democracy was a
> necessity of History, that it is a law of History, that it is programmed, as some
> people think today, then in *that* case I would be a fatalist. It is because we
> know that this is not the case that we should struggle for democracy. But
> I agree this is a concept of democracy that is not very common among democ-
> rats, among politicians or political philosophers (p. 30).

Deconstruction can help us with that futuring and Derrida (2002) helpfully distinguishes between several registers of debt with regard to others:

> Between a finite debt and an infinite debt, between debt and duty, between a
> certain erasure and a certain reaffirmation of debt – and sometimes a certain
> erasure in the name of reaffirmation (pp. 16–17).

Derrida also specifies ethical responsibility, always excessive or not responsibility at all, as a surplus of one's duties to the other over one's rights, and democracy as a promise, the desire or the movement toward the other to come (Dronsfield and Midgely, 1997). Politics *towards* democracy is constructed as a space of questioning which is mediated ethically. Deconstruction takes us to the politics of the multiple which goes beyond mere respect for difference; rather, it 'thematizes difference and reduces the thematized to difference' (Critchley, 1999, p. 238).

The moment from undecidability to the political, to the *decision,* is found in the relationship with the other and this is both an unequal and assymetrical relationship and one which opens up onto a relation to a third other and to humanity as a whole: 'that is to a symmetrical community of equals' (Critchley, 1999, p. 226). For Levinas, ethical obligations to the other open up onto wider considerations of justice for others, or to a third party, and that leap to the political is a leap with the other (Edgoose, 1997). It is in the interaction with the other, where speech 'cuts across the vision of forms' (Levinas, 1969, p. 193), that closure is eluded and one becomes the hostage of the other, infinitely responsible. Here Levinas distinguishes between the Said and the Saying. In exchanges with the other, the - ambiguity of language is such that the shared meaning sought by speaker and listener is denied. The Said of speech strives for clarity and universality, but in so doing becomes the Saying, which is ethical, but is also full of ambiguity:

> Ethical Saying is precisely nothing that can be said; it is rather the perpetual undoing of the Said that occurs in running against its limits. One does not comprehend the ethical Saying within the Said; the Saying can only be comprehended in its incomprehensibility, in its disruption or interruption of the Said (Critchley, 1999, p. 43).

As Edgoose (1997) points out, schools and other institutions pay attention only to the Said, which contains the formal knowledge students are expected to gain, and the Saying is rendered silent. It is the Saying which reveals one's relationship with the other and the very fact that one cannot limit one's responsibility to that other. These Sayings constitute moments of hesitation which highlight ethical sensitivity, but they are often quickly closed down and overruled by the Said. Edgoose (2001) suggests that teachers may assert the Saying in order to interrupt the Said and refuse its power, but this is to place teachers in an uncertain, and therefore vulnerable, position:

> To converse is to become vulnerable to the uncertainty of the other's reaction and thus to take the risk of responsibility for him or her. When one does not know how one's students will react, the inescapable uncertainty of one's reception highlights one's vulnerability and responsibility (p. 123).

Derrida has troubled the position of the other within the community and indeed has expressed some reservations about the notion of community itself (Derrida, 2001a). He was particularly disturbed by the connotations of fusion and identification inherent in depictions of the relationship between individuals and community, and has argued that the notion of a universal community which excluded no-one was an oxymoron because a community always had an inside and an outside. Like Young (1990) he saw the privileging of consensus which took place around community as problematic:

> If by community one implies, as is often the case, a harmonious group, consensus, and fundamental agreement beneath the phenomena of discord or war, then I don't believe in it too much and I sense in it as many threats as promises (Derrida, 2001a, p. 66).

In deconstructing community, Derrida showed how what was understood as a warm and welcoming term was full of hostility and that its need to retain its identity as a community led it to be unwelcoming and to impose limits on who belongs. This is an example what Derrida terms an 'aporia' (1992a, p. 22) a necessary ordeal of impossibility which one has to go through in order to make a decision and take responsibility:

> The paralysis that it connotes, the aporia for me, is not paralysis, it is a chance; it is a chance; not so-called 'luck', but something which conditions affirmation, decision and responsibility (p. 63).

Where communities are concerned, the political – and aporetic – question is how they can remain a place for commonality whilst also being an open, uninterrupted community that respects difference and resists closure from totalitarianism and immanentism (Critchley, 1999). At the level of justice, 'I and the other are co-citizens of a common polis' (ibid, p. 232). Derrida's 'vision' of community was one in which these limits were also openings and rather than individuals identifying with and belonging to a community homogenously, they would have a 'porous and heterogenous identity that differs with itself' (Caputo, 1997, p. 114). Such a community, in Derrida's imagination, would pursue a refusal of immanence or the restriction to the sphere of the subject and would root itself instead in that which lies outside the subject, a transcendence or incompletion (Critchley, 2002).

Derrida's troubling of difference further underlines the ethical 'take' of deconstruction. The problem with difference, as he saw it, is its ontological imperative that requires the use of arbitrary and differential signs to separate individuals and phenomena and which set up binary oppositions. As he points out, 'a difference generally implies positive terms between which the difference is set up; but in language there are only differences *without positive terms*' (Derrida, 1991d, p. 63) His invention of différance, which he has playfully pointed out sounds the same as difference, so has to be seen to be distinguished from it, is an attempt to get beyond ontology and is concerned with being, to account for the 'open-ended, uncontainable, generalizable play of traces' (Caputo, 1997, p. 105). Différance, he describes, is a double word, combining to differ and to defer. It is not intended to be a word or a concept which can be defined or described; rather it is a condition of possibility that produces words and concepts: 'It is because of *différance* that the movement of signification is possible' (Derrida, 1982 p.13). Différance introduces temporization and spacing, a kind of third space which encompasses movement and which replaces the binaries with options for other differences. So, for example, he is not denying that we have 'truth and principles', but is merely 'reinscribing these within the un-arche of *différance* ' (Caputo, 1997, p. 102). Deconstruction, because it allows for the play of these differences, is différance.

HOW MIGHT WE 'DO' DECONSTRUCTION?

The process of deconstruction, for Derrida, is always a reading of texts, for there is nothing outside the text (Derrida, 1976). It involves a double reading, a reading with at least two layers, usually by first repeating the 'dominant interpretation' (Derrida, 1988, p. 143) of a text, which takes the form of a commentary; and then opening up the text to its own blind spots, which lie behind and are protected by commentary. But these have to be managed simultaneously, forcing the deconstructor to operate with 'two texts, two hands, two visions, two ways of listening. Together at once and separately' (Derrida, 1982, pp. 65) or reading both from the inside and the outside. Derrida (1976) depicts the deconstructor as a tight-rope walker who risks 'ceaselessly falling back inside that which he deconstructs' (p. 14). It is a double reading that traverses the text and achieves 'the destabilization of the stability of the dominant interpretation' (Derrida, 1988, p. 147). Deconstruction seeks to locate a point of otherness and opens up a discourse on the other which has been appropriated through logocentrism (Critchley, 1999). How one reads the text depends on the text itself and the less a text deconstructs itself, the more it can be deconstructed, opened up to itself, showing the flows of thought and assumptions which direct it and what it excludes. The deconstructive process has to enter into the text's own trajectories and engage with them to find their moments of undecidability.

There have been a few bold attempts to prescribe a method for deconstruction. Suggesting that one could use deconstruction to 'astonish friends and confound enemies'. Swirl (n.d.) offers 'two easy steps'. The first step involves the identification of a binary opposition, achieved by noticing what a text takes to be natural, normal or self evident, such as that women are inherently nurturing and how a distinction is made between this and something else, for example men. The second step involves deconstructing the opposition, by showing how it is derived from or an effect of something else, even though its existence is determined by being defined against that something else. This could then lead to a demonstration that what is presented as *normal* is really a special case. These steps are distinguished from reversal, which merely reorders the relationship between two things; deconstruction is presented as having a higher order than reversal because it subverts the hierarchy of the relationship and demonstrates its instability. The provision of practical examples may be of use in illustrating what one might look for in a text, but the degree of prescription could be said to cut across the ethos of undecidability which is so central to deconstruction.

Maclure (2005b) offers some extremely useful guidance on reading texts which amount to what she calls a deconstructive ethos. First of all, she recommends that the researcher sees the world, their data and themselves as text and thinks of such things as 'the classroom', 'the child', 'the researcher' with invisible quotation marks round them. These constructs, she contends, are not natural, not self evident and never innocent. Second, she suggests looking for binary oppositions in texts, eg normal/abnormal, including the researcher's own biases and assumptions. Finally, she encourages the researcher to challenge the taken-for-granted – not in a destructive spirit, nor in an effort to find the truth, but in order to open up textual spaces that seem closed and to confound things which seem simple.

The search for binary opposites is a fruitful form of deconstructive activity and the field of inclusion is full of these: special/ordinary; disabled/able bodied; normal/abnormal. Deconstruction of these oppositions both takes us to the space *in-between* and undermines the polarities themselves. However, Balkin (1994) urges us to view these oppositions as necessarily 'nested' (p. 5), that is seeing the two terms as simultaneously having relationships of similarity and difference. This enables us to avoid the essentialism between the two oppositions and forces our attention on the shifting similarities and differences in the contexts in which they arise and are given meaning.

If what has been said so far about how to 'do' deconstruction appear difficult to put into practice, this is precisely because of the impossibility at the heart of deconstruction which Derrida regards as an ordeal, and that we have to come through: our own aporia in effect. Perhaps the first thing which has to be done is to effect a positive reorientation towards language and communication as problematic:

> Don't you believe that all language and all interpretation are problematic?
> More than problematic even, which is to say, perhaps an order other than
> problematicity? Isn't this also a stroke of luck? Otherwise, why speak, why
> discuss? How else would what we call "misunderstanding" be possible?
> (Derrida, 1988, p. 120).

Derrida regards this problematisation of language as part of an affirmative ethos. One can at least begin the process of deconstruction by combining a direct reading of a text with an eye on *what else* and with an eye on the other.

Deconstruction has been seen as having a potential value within education by several scholars. Biesta and Egéa-Kuehne's (2001) impressive collection, *Derrida & Education* contains some excellent papers of the significance of Derrida's work for the educational project and these have particular regard for the ethical dimension of deconstruction. (Edgoose, 2001; Biesta, 2001). These papers, whilst helpful in explicating deconstruction, do not, however, offer illustrations of this in practice. Some examples can be found in the work of Lather (2004; 2005; 2006) and Maclure (2005c). Lather deconstructs the scientificity (2006) inherent in educational research, while in Maclure's deconstruction, frivolity is used as a way of 'discomposing the language of policy and thereby of unsettling its totalising ambitions' (p. 1), effectively using frivolity as resistance. Maclure argues that attention to the frivolity forces researchers to attend to the 'marginal, the embarrassing and the recalcitrant' (p. 10) and offers a powerful illustration of the power of deconstruction. Beyond education, there are some impressive examples of deconstruction, by Brannigan (1996) and Wolfreys (1996), which problematise the notion of applying Derrida and underline the ethical responsibility of deconstruction.

WRITING DECONSTRUCTION: INCLUSIVE APORIAS

The notion of an aporia was developed by Derrida in the context of identity and concerns about nationalism and racism. It is a Greek word, meaning a non-way along which one can walk no further. What is at stake in the word aporia is 'not knowing where to go' (Derrida, 1993, p. 12). As Wills (2001) points out, there is a certain inevitability of aporias if we accept that language is always necessarily double or necessarily both communication and dissemination: 'one will necessarily say something double, one will necessarily walk into an aporia the moment one opens one's mouth' (p. 72).

As an Algerian living in France, describing himself as an 'over-acculturated, over-colonized European hybrid' (Derrida, 1992b, p. 7), this issue was both personal and political for Derrida. He was absorbed by the dilemma of how we might respect and respond to, on the one hand, differences and minorities and, on the other hand, the 'universality of formal law, the desire for translation, agreement and univocity, the law of the majority, opposition to racism, nationalism and xenophobia' (Derrida, 1992b, p. 78). He concluded that any responsible notion of European identity had to incorporate both the universal and the individual, in effect the aporia or double contradictory imperative. These aporias highlight dual responsibilities which need to be faced without privileging one or the other:

> That is not easy. It is even impossible to conceive of a responsibility that consists in being responsible *for* two laws, or that consists in responding *to* two contradictory injunctions. No doubt. But there is no responsiblility that is not the experience and experiment of the impossible (ibid, pp. 44–45; original emphasis).

These double duties are not in opposition to one another; rather, there is 'the haunting of the one in the other' (Derrida, 1995, p. 20).

Schools are full of aporias. There is a requirement, for example to raise pupils' attainment *and* promote inclusion; or to keep children with behavioural problems within school *and* ensure the safety of staff and other students. Furthermore, the policy and legislation relating to inclusion, as I have illustrated, are full of certainties, closures and pronouncements on how to do things more effectively, yet often merely recreate exclusion. These double duties are generally experienced as absolute contradictions which compromise those in the middle, the teachers. Teachers unions have closed down the aporia of behavioural problems and safety in their explicit refusal of the uncertainty and by underlining the unacceptability of the threat posed to them and other children by inclusion. Aporias are also rife within teacher education. Staff involved in this enterprise are expected to provide teaching and support to ensure student teachers achieve the 'standard' for full registration *and* continue to see themselves as in a process of development. They are supposed to exhort student teachers to operate autonomously *and* to collaborate with other professionals. They operate within University contexts which demand high standards of excellence *and* compliance with legal requirements to avoid discrimination.

Fairclough (2000) has analysed the multitude of aporias created by New Labour in its policies, through the language of 'not only . . . but also' (p. 49), with both elements given equal weighting and assumed to be compatible: 'education is not just the great liberator, it is critical to economic development' (p. 49). When Fairclough turns these rhetorics on the New Labour discourse, he shows how effectively the discourse is deployed to control public perception. He also demonstrates how effectively it is used to deny the irreconcilability between the political discourses of the right, with such elements as responsibilities and enterprise, and those of the left, for example rights and tackling poverty.

A deconstructive reading of the General Teaching Council's (GTC Scotland, 1995) *Fitness to Teach* and the *Code of practice for students with disabilities*, issued by the Quality Assurance Agency for Higher Education (QAA, 1999), revealed some of the exclusionary pressures they created for the disabled students they claimed to be encouraging into higher education (Allan, 2003a). Inclusion, in these documents, had a spectral quality, being introduced and ghosted out, but always appearing to be there, like an unread text which legitimised the displacement of authority: 'not read, not yet read, awaiting reading' (Wolfreys 1999, p. 280). The GTC document, for example, acknowledges the desire of disabled people to distance themselves from the medical model, whilst also conjuring up an image of the unfit teacher as a dangerous subject, who threatens the wellbeing of children. The image, the would-be teacher and inclusion, therefore, all have to be disavowed. In the QAA document, the under-representation of disabled people is reflected upon and attributed, in part, to problems of access, teaching methods and attitudes and in this move, inclusion is conjured as a wish to be more 'welcoming' to disabled students. But inclusion is also banished by the very notion that disabled students need to be welcomed, like some guest who would otherwise not be there. Both documents claim to be inclusive, yet manage to avoid this in ways which appeared, on the surface, to be rational and well intentioned. Inclusion, in both documents, has been 'there without being there. It was not yet there. It will never be there' (Derrida 1998, p. 144). A deconstruction of this kind might be seen as negative and critical, but it at least alerts us to the ways in which exclusion can become inscribed in documents.

GO ON, SAY SOMETHING DOUBLE

The 'findings' of deconstruction could be presented, not as a destruction of the well intentioned products of the writers, but as an illustration of some of the impossible choices we face in trying to be inclusive and in trying to educate more generally. 'Recommendations' could be presented as a series of aporias, double contradictory imperatives, which cannot – and must not – be reduced to singular choices.

> The condition of possibility of this thing called responsibility is a certain *experience and experiment of the possibility of the impossible: the testing of the aporia* from which one may invent the only *possible invention, the impossible invention* (Derrida, 1992b, p. 41; original emphasis).

Writing of this kind refuses the closure of the solution or the choice but creates openings for debate about how we should educate and how we might include. It forces all of us to examine our responsibilities towards the other and to recognise our own implication in exclusion. Because this recognition is not brought about by accusation, finger pointing which makes those being pointed at deflect elsewhere, but is part of a broader demonstration of the irresistibility of our own exclusionary practices, we can accept our culpability and find a way to go on. Deconstruction, thus, operates as a form of 'hyper-political radicalization' (Derrida, 2001a, p. 73), allowing us 'the possibility of permeating and displacing borders' (Gregoriou, 2001, p. 146). Because it is the performance of justice and is always about the other, it is a way of avoiding assimilation: 'we have to cross the border, but not destroy the border . . . We should not erase the border by assimilating' (Derrida, 1997, p. 33).

Deconstruction offers us a practical tool for playing with some of the certainties and closures which dog inclusion and education more generally and which continually recreate exclusion. It is the practical experience and performance of philosophy at its best, providing new ways of seeing, thinking and being. It is a promising kind of philosophy which invokes justice and inclusion as yet to come. Deconstruction offers possibilities, not for reconstruction, because therein lies the inevitability of the repetition of exclusion, but a redescription of existing concepts. This involves two kinds of invention: an ordinary invention of the possible and 'an extraordinary or pure invention which would involve the appearance of something truly or radically other' (Patton, 2003, p, 18).

For those expecting to have found a template or a method for deconstruction, this chapter is likely to have disappointed, but I have attempted to show why providing such a thing would be wrong headed and unhelpful. Perhaps the only piece of useful advice, beyond the earlier enjoinder to view the 'problematic' of language and communication as positive, might be to purloin a sporting motif: Just do it.

6.   FOUCAULT AND THE ART OF TRANSGRESSION

> Maybe the target nowadays is not to discover what we are, but to refuse what we are. We have
> to imagine and to build up what we could be to get rid of this kind of political 'double bind',
> which is the simultaneous individualization and totalization of modern power structures
>
> (Foucault, 1982, p. 216; original emphasis).

This chapter considers some of Foucault's conceptual tools (Foucault, 1977a; Allan, 1996) for understanding how power is exercised upon individuals and how they are subsequently constrained to behave in particular ways. However the aspect of Foucault's work which has the most exciting potential for inclusion is his somewhat neglected writings on ethics and these are dealt with in greatest detail here. Foucault's ethics allows us to envisage individuals as capable of transgression, enabling them to challenge disabling barriers and find new selves, new ways of being in the world. This is important, because, as has been suggested so far, whilst we can attempt, following Deleuze and Guattari and Derrida, to work on the mainstream, and on society in an attempt to make them more inclusive, this is an awesome task and it may take some time before evidence of change is seen. In the meantime, there may be some value in helping individuals to find forms of tactical defiance and resistance and new ways of existing in a disabling and exclusionary world. Foucault's ethics also enables those of us involved in providing or promoting inclusion, whether as teacher, other professional, researcher or teacher educator, to identify the work we might do on ourselves to ensure the success of the inclusion project. It also enables us to consider how we might support disabled students' transgressions.

FINDING FOUCAULT, POWER AND KNOWLEDGE

> I think I have in fact been situated in most of the squares on the political
> checkerboard, one after another and sometimes simultaneously: as anarchist,
> leftist, ostentatious or disguised Marxist, nihilist, explicit or secret anti-
> Marxist, technocrat in the service of Gaullism, new liberal and so on. An
> American professor complained that a crypto-Marxist like me was invited in
> the USA, and I was denounced by the press in Eastern European countries for

> being an accomplice of the dissidents. None of these descriptions is important
> by itself; taken together, on the other hand, they mean something. And I must
> admit that I rather like what they mean (Foucault, 1997a, p. 113).

Foucault, like Derrida and Deleuze and Guattari, sought to defy categorization of himself as one kind of scholar or another. He is indeed something of a contradiction, issuing enjoinders to study power and knowledge at its roots, for example in schools and hospitals, whilst remaining largely at a structural level in his own analysis. He died of complications arising from Aids and, it is suggested, as a result of practising his own 'limit experiences' (Miller, 1993, p. 29) but his writings constitute an important legacy. Foucault's initial interest was in structures and discourses and in his archaeologies of knowledge (Foucault, 1972), of medicine (1973) and of madness (1967), he demonstrated deftly how discourses produced the '*restitution* of truth' (Foucault, 1967, p. 197; original emphasis). In the *Birth of the clinic* (ibid, 1973), for example, Foucault traced the development of medicine, illustrating how the gaze opened up a 'domain of clear visibility' (p, 105) and the hospital provided a regulated space in which medical knowledge was acquired, recorded and passed on through the rituals of teaching.

In Foucault's shift from archaeology to genealogy, the focus of his work moved from discourses to institutions such as prisons, schools (1977a), and to sexuality (1978; 1985; 1986), where, in his genealogies, he uncovered how knowledge and power were interlinked and constructed individuals as objects of knowledge and as subjects who were controlled, even - and perhaps especially - by themselves. His analyses overturned understandings of modern phenomena, driving home the realization that where we might think we have greater freedom, we are, in reality, more tightly constrained than ever before. In *Discipline and punish* (Foucault, 1977a), for example, a detailed and morbid account of a regicide being hung, drawn and quartered in the eighteenth century is followed by a portrayal of an equally detailed, but apparently more benign regime of imprisonment almost a century later. Foucault invites us to consider that the removal of the physical punishment as a spectacle has, in fact, led to a more insidious form of control over individuals' bodies and their souls. His analysis is extended to education and the 'disciplinary regimes' which turn young people into 'docile bodies' (Foucault, 1977a, p. 138).

Foucault developed a series of constructs about power and knowledge which he offered as a useful 'box of tools' (Foucault, 1977a, p. 208) for understanding how individuals were controlled and constrained. The most important of these is 'the rather shameful art of surveillance' (ibid, p. 172), a disciplinary technique for ensuring individuals were sorted, regulated, normalised and made to behave in particular ways. Foucault identified three ways in which surveillance was undertaken. First of all, hierarchical observation was a means of making it possible 'for a single gaze to see everything perfectly' (ibid, p. 173). Physical structures were created, based on Jeremy Bentham's panoptican design, to ensure maximum scrutiny of people:

> to render visible those who are inside it . . . to act on those it shelters, to pro-
> vide a hold on their conduct, to carry the effects of power right to them, to
> make it possible to know them, to alter them (ibid, p. 172).

Hierarchical observation, thus, encompassed a form of supervision of supervisors, with everyone accountable to authority from above. The effectiveness of the supervision was guaranteed by the fact that it was 'absolutely *discreet,* for it functions permanently and largely in silence' (ibid, p. 177) and since it was impossible to know when one was being watched, it was necessary to behave as if this was the case.

Normalising judgements are also used, according to Foucault, to justify correction and coercion in teaching and promote standardization and homogeneity. Individuals can be measured in terms of their distance from their norm and once the extent of their deviance from the norm is established, disciplinary techniques can be used to homogenize, normalise and, of course, exclusion can be justified as a means to these ends. Foucault regards normalisation as one of the great instruments of power at the end of the classical age, but alerts us to its continued use:

> It is easy to understand how the power of the norm functions within a system of formal equality, since within a homogeneity that is the rule, the norm introduces, as a useful imperative and as a result of measurement, all the shading of individual differences (1977a, p. 184).

Foucault's third dimension of surveillance, the examination, combines hierarchical observation and normalising judgements in a ritualized form which transforms the 'economy of visibility into the exercise of power' (Ibid, p. 187). The examination also introduces individuality in order to fix and capture and makes each individual a 'case', capable of being 'described, judged, measured, compared with others, in his very individuality' (ibid, p. 191). These mechanisms of surveillance create subjects who are known and marked in particular kinds of ways and who are constrained to carry the knowledge and marks. The kind of power exercised here, Foucault tells us, is not the negative kind which represses, masks or conceals; rather, he argues, it is the kind which produces 'reality; it produces domains of objects and rituals of truth' (Foucault, 1977a, p. 194) in the shape of individuals and what is known about each of them.

The child with *special needs*, the *disaffected*, and even the *included child* can easily be understood as having been constructed through a whole hierarchy of power and knowledge, with needs identified through a complex process of assessment which is aimed at distinguishing the abnormal from the normal; and perpetually kept under surveillance through a whole network of supervision (Allan, 1999). It is not just the child him or herself who is subject to this intense scrutiny; parents and all the professionals providing support are all caught in this web of surveillance. The formal process of statementing (in England and Wales) or recording (in Scotland) is a ritualised version of surveillance which requires documents to be kept of individuals and their pathologies. I reported that, following some public acknowledgement that the Records of Needs procedures in Scotland were unsatisfactory, these were replaced with a new system for assessing children's 'Additional Support Needs'. I argued, however, that the new procedures appear likely to replicate the problems of the previous system and have certainly recreated mechanisms of surveillance and the means of exerting authority where there is a dispute:

> The co-ordinated support plan is a statutory document which will be subject to regular monitoring and review for those children and young people who meet the criteria . . . Education authorities are still able to draw up co-ordinated support plans even where parents disagree that one should be prepared or where they refuse to co-operate (Scottish Executive, 2005, pp. 43–50).

Furthermore, the new procedures seem to have inserted greater uncertainty into the system, particularly at local authority level, leaving professionals with unclear criteria about where to draw the normalising line which will release resources and support.

Foucault's analyses of subjectification, in which he demonstrated so effectively how individuals were incapable of resistance, have proved seductive to many who have undertaken their own genealogies of educational contexts (Ball, 1990b; Blacker, 1998; Marshall, 1989; Fendler, 1998). Baker's (1998) 'history of the present' (p. 118) demonstrates how childhood was produced within the public school movement in the United States, without any debate about what it meant to be a 'child'. Special needs and disability have also been seen as ripe for Foucauldian analysis. Tremain's (2005) collection of papers on *Foucault and the government of disability* contain a wealth of analyses of epistemologies, ontologies, histories, governmentalities, ethics and politics which reveal 'some of the fascism which still runs round in our heads and still plays itself out in our everyday behavior' (McWhorter, 2005; p. xvii). These studies situate individuals as impotent, heavily constrained and with dismal prospects. Medical, juridical and administrative practices construct and demarcate the disabled subject and the discourses of inclusion are underpinned by a homogenising imperative. In spite of this, however, we are urged to 'think beyond accepted dogmas' (Tremain, 2005, p. 22) and to do what we can:

> The point here, I think, is not to feel bad about the injustice or the suffering in the world . . . The point is to pull up short before the possibility that what you thought was true might not be, that what you thought was normal or natural might be the product of political struggle, and to start – from just that place – to *think*, which means to question, to critique, to experiment, to wonder, to imagine, to try (McWhorter, 2005, p. xvii).

Just as Foucault (1982) encouraged us to read the 'modern state' (p. 214) of penal institutions, education and even sexuality as creating less, rather than more, freedom, we might question whether shifts from integration to inclusion and, before that, the 'Warnock watershed' which is said to have foreshadowed integration, were positive moves and indeed whether they were even moves at all. This is certainly the stance taken by critics such as Booth (1998) and Slee (2001b), who have questioned whether the inclusion movement has simply been a rebadging of special education which has enabled teacher education to carry on their old practices – of turning student teachers into 'card carrying designators of disability' (p. 171) – under a more publicly acceptable label. A number of critics have used Foucauldian constructs to read the lack of progress towards inclusion as effects of power and as part of a wider system of control. Simons and Masschelein (2005), for example, suggest that inclusion is offered only to 'exclusive pupils' (p. 208) as part of a double move of individualization and totalisation which characterises the modern state. Foucault (1982) describes this as the establishment of governmentality, a means of ensuring that each person is both an individual and part of a totality:

> I don't think that we should consider the "modern state" as an entity which was developed above individuals, ignoring what they are and even their very existence, but on the contrary as a very sophisticated structure, in which individuals can be integrated, under one condition: that this individuality would be shaped in a new form, and submitted to a set of very specific patterns (p. 214).

Drinkwater (2005) questions whether the move from institutionalized living to care in the community necessarily represents an emancipation or humanitarian reform and suggests that it might be a 'new dispersal of power relations, entirely in keeping with the modern drive to greater efficiency.' (p. 229). The othering of these institutions as dark bad places, he argues, encourages us to see the intensification of control over the subject as benign.

The moral panic, in the UK, over 'hoodies', youngsters wearing tops with hoods so that their faces and identities are obscured, can be read, in Foucauldian terms, as a a 'perverse implantation' (Foucault, 1978, p. 36), a means of naming deviance (and its distinguishing – hooded – characteristics) in order to then cure or remove them. Foucault developed the notion of a perverse implantation in relation to sexuality, describing the emergence of an elaborate set of codes for speaking about so called normal sexuality – between a married couple – and identifying what deviated from this norm. In this 'discursive explosion' (p. 38) in the eighteenth and nineteenth century, scrutiny was exercised over:

> the sexuality of children, mad men and women and criminals; the sensuality of those who did not like the opposite sex; reveries, obsessions, petty manias, or great transports of rage. It was time for all these figures, scarcely noticed in the past, to step forward and speak, to make the difficult confession of what they were (p. 38).

The depiction of hoodies as perverse enables them to be denounced as outside the social order and justifies the use of practical measures to control them. Desperate measures, in the form of Anti-Social Behaviour Orders (ASBOs), have been administered to these individuals, restricting their movements, in some cases banning them from wearing their hoods and ensuring they are closely monitored and controlled. The ASBOs also provide 'hoodies' with an elevated status and endorsement of their deviant identity, but commentators have questioned whether the anxiety about these individuals is really warranted (McLean, 2005). This implantation of perversion has been extended to children in schools who misbehave. Their presence, as was seen in the comments from the union officials, has become a threat to the education of pupils and the security of pupils and staff in schools. Their perverse identities provide a means for the refusal of inclusion on the grounds of risk and danger.

Whilst Foucault's critique of the way subjects are disciplined have appealed to so many scholars, it has also earned him criticisms that his work is overly pessimistic

(Rorty, 1990) and did little to encourage individuals to take action (Shumway, 1989). Others have argued that Foucault's depiction of 'docile bodies' (1977a, p. 138) denies agency and creates a 'fleshless passive body' (Hughes, 2005, p. 84) which is 'dissolved as causal phenomenon' (Schilling, 1993, p. 80) and with powers which are limited to those invested in them by discourse. Hughes argues that because of this underestimate of the body's agency, a Foucauldian analysis contributes little to disability studies and, consequently, to the emancipation of disabled people. Foucault's later work, ethics, contains a much more sanguine view of agency and depicts individuals as capable of working on themselves to achieve new kinds of existence. It is to this that I now turn.

FOUCAULT'S ETHICS

Foucault's framework of ethics focuses on:

> the forms of relations with the self, on the methods and techniques by which he works them out, on the exercises by which he makes of himself an object to be known, and on the practices that enable him to transform his own mode of being (1985, p. 30).

Foucault gave little advice on how one should undertake transformation of this kind in practice (Smart, 1998). He mentions the role of the counsellor, friend, guide or master who will tell you the truth about yourself, but does not discuss the nature of the relationships involved. Bernauer suggests that Foucault provides an invitation to others 'not to renounce the soul . . . but to transgress its borders, to reinvent one's relationship to it' (Bernauer 1999, p. xiv). This invitation enables individuals to see themselves as the main source of transformation, rather than waiting for a more substantial structural or material change. As Veyne (1997) observes, 'the self is the new strategic possibility' (p. 231), capable of responding to the dangers which are encountered:

> The ethico-political choice we have to make every day is to determine which is the main danger . . . My point is not that everything bad but that everything is dangerous . . . If everything is dangerous, then we always have something to do. So my position leads not to apathy but to a hyper- and pessimistic activism (Foucault, 1984, p. 343).

Foucault (1985) regards ethical practice as having four dimensions, which he elaborates upon in relation to Christianity and sexuality. He points out that the four dimensions of ethics will inevitably overlap and cannot be dissociated from one another or from the actions that support them. The four dimensions are:

1. *Determination of the ethical substance.* This dimension involves the identification of 'this or that part of oneself as prime material of his moral conduct' (Foucault, 1985, p. 26) Individuals decide which aspect of the self is to be worked on or changed and in Foucault's example of Chrisianity, one's beliefs, intentions or desires might be specified as objects for transformation in order to become a better Christian.

2. *The mode of subjection.* The second of the ethical dimensions concerns the way in which the individual recognizes how he or she operates in relation to certain rules and to find other ways of observing these rules. Foucault uses the example of fidelity and contends that there are many ways to practise austerity and 'be faithful' (Foucault, 1985, p. 26). An example of the mode of subjection, provided by Blacker (1998), is the Greek aristocrat who fashions his diet according to certain aesthetic criteria.

3. *Self-practice or ethical work.* This aspect involves what one does 'not only in order to bring one's conduct into compliance with a given rule, but to effect transformation of oneself into the ethical subject of one's behaviour' (Foucault, 1985, p. 26.). Thus, sexual austerity in Foucault's example can be practised silently through thought or by a much more explicit and 'relentless combat' (p. 26). It is a form of 'asceticism' (Blacker, 1998, p. 362) through which individuals transform themselves.

4. *The Telos.* The final dimension concerns the ultimate goal which an individual is trying to achieve through ethical work. In Foucault's example, fidelity is identified as part of a journey towards complete self mastery and he highlights the moral aspect of the transformation of self which is involved. Blacker describes this process as a kind of 'controlled and self-regulated dissemination of the subject into the world, a positive dissolution . . . not self-absorption, but being absorbed into the world: a losing-finding of the self' (1998, pp. 362–363; original emphasis).

These practices of the self are not acquired easily but have to be learned through disciplined training and through reading and writing and Foucault (1997b) underlines the importance of writing for oneself and for others:

> No technique, no professional skill can be acquired without exercise; nor can one learn the art of living, the *techne tou biou,* without an *askesis* that must be understood as a training of the self by the self . . . writing is regularly associated with "meditation" and with that exercise of thought on itself that reactivates what it knows, that makes present a principle, a rule, or an example, reflects on them, assimilates them, and thus prepares itself to confront the real (Foucault, 1997b, pp. 235–236 original emphasis).

Foucault's notion of writing as a form of meditation draws on Seneca and Epictetus and he sees this as proceeding in two different ways. The first is linear, taking the writer from meditation through to the activity of writing and onto *gumnazein,* 'training in a real and taxing situation: work of thought, work through writing, work through reality' (Foucault, 1977b, p. 236). The second is circular, going from meditation through to a rereading of notes which provoke further meditation. The reflexive function of writing, particularly in correspondence with others, is emphasised by Foucault: to write is thus to 'show oneself, make oneself seen, make one's face appear before the other' (ibid, p. 243). It is a way of 'summoning the gaze of the other' (ibid, p. 247). Reading is also seen as implied by the practice of the self because 'one cannot draw everything from one's own funds . . . As a guide or example, the help of others is necessary' (ibid, p. 236).

Foucault argues that one should become so accomplished in ethical practice that one engages in it unconsciously:

> You must have learned principles so firmly that when your desires, your appetites or your fears awaken like barking dogs, the logos will speak with the voice of a master who silences the dogs by a single command (1987a, p. 117).

While Foucault's ethical practice is directed towards a kind of sexual austerity, it can be viewed as a means of promoting inclusion, in a way which recognizes disabled students' desires as well as their needs.This work is not only ethical; it is also a political, social and philosophical endeavour which is put into practice through a kind of curiosity (Foucault 1988, p. 321), a practice, which he explains:

> evokes the care of what exists and might exist; a sharpened sense of reality, but one that is never immobilized before it; a readiness to find what surrounds us strange and odd; a certain determination to throw off familiar ways of thought and to look at the same things in a different way . . . a lack of respect for the traditional hierarchies of what is important and fundamental (p. 321).

Foucault highlights the necessity of establishing conduct which seeks the rules of acceptable behaviour in relations with others, but foregrounds the self as the principle object of care, and as the means through which care for others can occur. Smart (1998) claims that the contemporary version of caring for oneself, which is characterised by self-determination, self-expression and hedonism, has led to indifference towards the other, but this need not to be the case.

The contention that inclusion starts with ourselves has been voiced by several scholars (Ballard, 2003b; Slee, 2001b) and by this it is meant that everyone who is involved in inclusive practices – teachers, other professionals, researchers, teacher educators, parents and disabled people – has to turn the gaze on themselves to examine how 'what looks right and moral and beyond reproach, what seems natural and inevitable can be seen and experienced quite otherwise' (McWhorter, 2005, p. xvii). The framing of inclusion as an ethical project (Allan, 2005a) enables the work we each have to do on ourselves to be set out in terms of the determination of the ethical substance, mode of subjection, self practice or ethical work and a telos.

SIDESTEPPING EXCLUSION: THE PRACTICE OF TRANSGRESSION

Transgression emerged in Foucault's writings on ethics as a subversive tactic which could enable individuals to transform themselves. Transgression is a form of resistance involving the crossing of limits or boundaries. It is not antagonistic or aggressive, nor does it involve a contest in which there is a victor; rather, transgression is playful and creative. Among disabled people, transgression has been a significant means of challenging limits and disabling barriers. It is possible to recognise both collective transgression and more subtle and indirect transgression by individuals.

The development of the concept of transgression was sparked by Foucault's interest in Kant's critique of limits, but represents a more practical (and political) form of engagement. Foucault saw transgression as distinctively different from transcendence or transformation: he did not envisage individuals as gaining absolute freedom from limits, but instead suggested that individuals, in crossing limits or boundaries, might find moments of freedom or of otherness. Foucault's account of where transgression takes place is somewhat complex. In his *Preface to Transgression* (1977b), written as an introduction to the work of Bataille, he argues that 'It is likely that transgression has its entire space in the line it crosses' (p. 73). This implies a boundary that can only be there by crossing it. The limit and transgression depend on each other, but the relationship is not a simple one; rather, the relationship, according to Foucault, is like a spiral, with moments of crossing of the limit appearing as a flash of lightning in the night which give a darkening intensity to the night it obscures. Foucault also describes the interplay of limits and transgression as being regulated by a simple obstinacy. The act of crossing the limit does not violate it, but simultaneously affirms and weakens it. Foucault regards this as a form of non-positive affirmation, which has to be constantly repeated, and likens it to Blanchôt's notion of contestation, which does not imply a generalised negation, but an affirmation that affirms nothing.

Foucault uses sexuality to illustrate transgression, arguing that since the writings of Sade and, more recently Bataille, sexuality has been a fissure which marks the limit within us and designates us as a limit. Foucault has been criticised extensively for failing to provide empirical examples of his concepts and indeed his discussion of sexuality provides little guidance on the practical pursuit of transgression. His own sexual transgression can hardly be seen as a model for others to follow, given its contribution to his own untimely death (Miller, 1993). Transgression has, nevertheless, been viewed as an attractive construct in relation to marginalised and oppressed groups, not least of all because and forces a recognition of exclusion. For those who transgress, according to Boyne (1990), 'otherness lies ahead' (p. 82) and this allows individuals to shape their own identities by subverting the norms which compel them to repeatedly perform as subjects with a particular marginal identity, such as disabled or ethnic minorities. They are not required to – and indeed could not – reject these identities entirely, but can vary the way in which they have to repeat these performances. There have been few studies of transgression, but researchers studying resistance have uncovered strategies which could be read in this way. In Cooper's (1997) study of religious education, for example, resistance served the function of halting change and involved schools selectively incorporating the religious provisions of the 1988 *Education Reform Act*, while ignoring others. In Bloor and McIntosh's (1990) study of surveillance and concealment, new mothers avoided both breast feeding and the wrath of the health visitors checking up on them and their resistance was regarded as effective because it enbled 'a way of avoiding control without confrontation' (p. 176). Sullivan's (2005) study of paraplegics in a spinal unit revealed individuals' 'struggle for control of the body' (p. 39). Sullivan found their resistance harrowing, but as successful in rejecting the authoritarianism and totalising aspects of control.

Foucault (1977b) acknowledges a difficulty with words which hampers philosophy and sees the absence of a language with which to talk about transgression as inhibiting its practice. Nevertheless, he expresses his hope that one day transgression will be as much a part of our culture as contradiction was for dialectical thought.

Bataille also looks forward to the normalisation of transgression whereby silent contemplation would be substituted with language (Foucault, 1984). It could be said that transgression is indeed part of everyday culture, although it does seem to be concerned with marginal activities. Transgression has become synonymous with forms of eroticism and 'deviant' sex and I made this disconcerting discovery when searching the web for material in relation to an encyclopedia entry I was asked to write on transgression (here I can offer the reference, Allan, 2005b, rather than the plaintive 'your honour'). Transgression is also prevalent in the arts: Anton Chekov's short story, Kate Jordan's play and a film, written and directed by Michael DiPaulo all have the title of *Transgression* and Joyce Carol Oates' collection of short stories is entitled *Faithless: tales of transgression.* The kind of transgression which has become popularised is rather naughty and is some way from the kind of challenges to normalisation Foucault appeared to advocate.

Evidence of transgression by disabled students emerged in my own work (Allan, 1996; 1999) and came as something of a surprise. The work was conceptualised as a study of the experiences of students with special needs, and their mainstream peers, in mainstream schools and, having been immersed in Foucault's genealogical analysis, I expected to find students who were constrained and controlled by the discourses and practices of special education. This indeed was the case and the hierarchies of surveillance through the assessment procedures and teaching practices had disciplinary effects on the young people and their families. The transgression of the students through which they resisted these effects was particularly subtle and effective and moved the students both in and out of disability. Raschida, an Asian visually impaired student, first alerted me to the extent and scope of transgression, beaming as she described how the long cane which she hated, because it was so 'visible,' had been 'dropped [in the lake]'. The loss of the long cane, she reported gleefully, had annoyed her teachers, but had enabled her to escape the imperative to perform her visual impairment in public. She had acquired a smaller folding cane which was much less obvious and with which she was more comfortable. Raschida also described an episode of transgression in which she pretended to be 'blind drunk,' rather than blind, when she was with her boyfriend:

> I usually met him at nights and that and he was [drunk] . . .I used to always pretend that I was drunk as well. I [wasn't] really, but I was just saying that he'd think, if I couldn't see anything, he'd realize [laughs] . . . I decided to tell him. Because we used to meet up at my friend's house and I knew her house quite well as well, so I never used to bang into things or anything, I'd just act normal, casual (Allan, 1999, p. 106).

Other students revealed transgressive strategies which moved them away from a disabled identity. These included a hearing impaired student pretending to be able to hear and a physically disabled youngster avoiding going to the bathroom during school hours (in order to escape the indignity of being hoisted and undressed by his female assistant). A visually impaired student even spoke of demanding a punishment exercise which had been given to students for talking but from which she had been excused on account of her impairment. There were instances also of students transgressing in ways which made them more disabled. One pupil with behavioural difficulties, for example, regularly referred to himself as 'a spastic' (Allan, 1999, p. 54) and therefore unable to do certain things, while a wheelchair user encouraged her peers to run errands for her and proudly described how easily she manipulated people to help her: 'People will always do things for me because they know I can't walk' (Allan, 1999, p. 53). These acts of transgression enabled individuals to challenge the limits placed upon them and exercise control over themselves and others. They were, however, temporary and partial acts which had to be constantly repeated and reactions to them had to be monitored. Transgression also had certain costs for the individuals, the most obvious and troubling one being the health problems which the young wheelchair user who was avoiding the bathroom spectacle may have been storing up for himself.

Teachers were generally unsympathetic to, and critical of, the students's transgressive practices, reading these as evidence of their failure to accept the *fact* that they were disabled and of their refusal to accept help for their *needs*. Raschida's teachers were highly critical both of her attempts to mask the true extent of her visual impairment and her failure to accept what they saw as an inevitable decline. Her maths teacher was even negative about her ability to do complex operations in her head and whilst he rightly insisted that she had to demonstrate her calculations in order to gain some credit if the final answer was incorrect, it was nevertheless striking that this awesome capacity was constructed as a problem. Raschida's ethnicity was also pathologised:

> Blind Muslim women are unmarriageable (sic). If anyone did agree to marry her (it would be an arranged marriage from Pakistan) it would only last the minimum time and then the bloke would divorece her *but* would have gained British citizenship. She would then be cast aside; when Muslim women marry, they go to live with the husband's family. If the couple is divorced, the wife is cast out! (Allan, 1999, p. 82; original emphasis).

The notes on Raschida's 'file' also pathologised her puberty and denounced her efforts to enjoy a teenage existence because this amounted to a refusal to accept the teachers' help. The ignorance revealed in these notes is one shocking dimension; another is the depths which the professionals' gaze penetrated.

The teachers of the child with behavioural problems interpreted his transgression as mere attention seeking and as a pathological tendency to claim an inappropriate label, and accused his parents of encouraging this. The headteacher of the student who was refusing to go to the bathroom bemoaned the large amount of money which had been spent on a hoist that was not being used. There appeared to be a clash of discourses within schools, between, on the one hand, the students' discourse of desire, within which they practised transgression, and on the other hand, the teachers' discourse of special educational needs, within which they provided support. The only exception to this concerned a student with a degenerative condition which was causing a loss of mobility. The headteacher had recognised the discourse of desire and had worked closely with the student and his family to ensure that his desires were respected and responded to and that he had support when it was necessary. This involved an element of collusion with the student peers, to ensure they were always on hand and able to pick him up without a fuss if he fell over.

Recognition of, and support for, the transgression of disabled students from their mainstream peers was another surprising discovery. Mainstream students spoke admiringly of the disabled students' attempts to 'be treated normally' (Allan, 1999, p. 63) and were scathing about how teachers often looked past these and gave the students 'special treatment' (ibid). One visually impaired student described how inappropriate such conduct was:

> I think they sometimes go out of their way to help [disabled student], but she doesn't like that, she likes to be treated normally . . . If anybody makes a fuss of her she gets really embarrassed and she just doesn't like it. She's always complaining if people make a fuss of her. She'll say, 'Oh God, I wish they hadn't done that'. She just likes to be treated like everyone else (Allan, 1999, p. 63).

The mainstream students' highly sophisticated understanding of the significance of transgression included a recognition that their own uncertainty and discomfort about how to engage with their disabled peers was inevitable if they were to take account of their desires rather than their needs. The mainstream students also supported their disabled peers' inclusion, through a micro-regime of governmentality. This included legitimizing the transgressions of disabled students, even when these were somewhat troubling, for example, by breaching the 'normal' rules of engagement between students. The governmental regime also had pastoral and pedagogic elements, whereby the mainstream students offered assistance, for example by reinforcing certain behaviours or correcting mistakes. The mainstream students' governmentality could, however, at times be punitive, enabling them to justify and condone their own bullying and other exclusionary tactics. The mainstream students' governmentality had, like the governmentality of the state, both individualizing and totalizing effects, but these were, on the whole, positive and assisted and supported their disabled peers in their transgression and in their efforts to be included. The mainstream students saw their role in supporting transgression as significant and saw themselves as gaining from the process by being better informed about disabled students and more skilled at interacting with them. Although there was considerable othering of disabled students by their mainstream peers, there was very little evidence of the hostility which professionals see as characterising relationships between disabled and non-disabled students and seek to minimise.

Transgression appears to provide an important way for disabled people to engage playfully with limits imposed upon them by a disabling society. It seems to provide scope for challenging the very existence of some of these limits and finding new ways of being in a disabling world. As Foucault reminds us transgression does not lead to transcendence, but rather 'affirms the limitlessness into which it leaps as it opens this zone to existence for the first time' (1994, p. 74). At the same time, however, this affirmation is ambivalent since it 'contains nothing positive' (p. 74). Transgression operates within a discourse of desire and this discourse has to be extremely powerful to speak against the needs based discourses which dominate both education and services for disabled people. The governmentality of the state, with its double contradictory imperative of individualizing and totalizing, may limit the opportunities for transgression; alternatively, the micro-regime of governmentality within the school and among young people could have a positive and productive role in encouraging and supporting transgression.

THE PHILOSOPHERS OF DIFFERENCE: UNLOCKING POSSIBILITY

Fielding (2001) calls for an engagement with philosophy in order to rescue education from the 'tyranny of the technical' (p. 10) which has locked everyone – perhaps especially teachers – into impossibility and exclusion. Smyth (2001) acknowledges the exclusion experienced by teachers as well as children and contends that if we are prepared 'to think radically outside the frame' (p. 239) then we need to find ways of bringing people *into* the frame. The following chapters set out some practical ways of engaging the philosophers of difference in the hope of achieving this.

PART THREE: RETHINKING INCLUSION?

7.   TEACHERS AND STUDENTS: SUBVERTING, SUBTRACTING, INVENTING

How to begin? How to satisfy? How to ensure those who have picked up this book and have possibly waded through the earlier chapters are 'rewarded with a bit of sense' (Lyotard, as cited in Gregoriou, 2004, p. 234). The task of putting the philosophers to work on inclusion began in the earlier chapters on Deleuze and Guattari, Derrida and Foucault, where I attempted to illustrate the ideas which had particular relevance to inclusion. These were the parts of the philosophers' work which could, I was suggesting, help to understand and explore some of the complexities of inclusion and allow the inclusion 'project' to be reframed. The task of setting out how, in concrete terms, these ideas might be *used* – in practice – is a daunting one, presenting itself as an aporia or double contradictory imperative. How might I offer some guidance on what the key players (teachers, other professionals, teacher educators, researchers, children and their parents) might actually do with these ideas whilst avoiding reducing what is suggested to a set of practical tips or to the kinds of enjoinders which ensure special education continues to reign (Slee, 1993; Brantlinger, 2006a). Amidst this uncertainty, it is clear that what is offered needs to be both substantial and radical. Following Foucault, we know that power is so omnipresent and insidious that that we need to find cunning ways to *subvert* it; Deleuze and Guattari have helped us to recognise school spaces as highly striated and some creative *subtraction* is needed in order to smooth these out; and we know that the logocentrism in policy documents and official texts consistently achieves closure and denies the other, so we have to find ways to *invent* to secure the presence of the other and to produce undecidability. In the next three chapters, what is offered is not a recipe for inclusion, but is a series of propositions on how inclusion might be reframed as a struggle for everyone to participate in – to be included in – and on the strategic shifts which might produce new possibilities for inclusion. These amount to *subverting, subtracting* and *inventing*.

If inclusion was recognised, not as fixed entity, practised upon a discrete population, but as a continuous struggle, which, like the rhizome, was never complete, there would be less frustration and guilt among teachers about their apparent failures – children still waiting to be included. If the struggle for inclusion was understood, not as the responsibility of teachers, but as one in which everyone (adults and children) was included, there might be a greater likelihood of success through the collective investment. If the participants in the inclusion struggle were able to do so as practical philosophers, experimenting with and experiencing inclusion, difference could possibly become a source of interest and intrigue – a puzzle – rather than a problem to be defined and managed.

Perhaps a place to begin work on the struggle for inclusion is with Foucault's telos, the overall goal, for inclusion. This is something which has been omitted from policy discourses; attempts have been made to define what inclusion *is,* but these have led to bland platitudes, with little regard for what it is supposed to do and for whom. There is a need to refuse this kind of defining and pinning down; instead the purpose and function of inclusion needs to be addressed, not just by policy makers and professionals, but also by children and their parents, who have to be able to identify the kinds of consequences that are acceptable to them. Consideration of what inclusion ought to do should not be confined to those who are the usual targets for inclusion by virtue of their labels, but should be undertaken in respect of everyone. Having started at the fourth and final strand of Foucault's framework of ethics, it might be useful for teachers and children – both disabled and non-disabled – to return to the beginning and to elaborate on the practical work that they think they might do on themselves in order to achieve inclusion in their own setting.

The proposition that teachers and students talk together about inclusion and what it might look like may appear odd. Students are generally kept out of discussions about matters directly affecting them in schools, and where they do get to express views, for example through school councils, this is usually confined to matters such as uniforms and the playground. The topic of inclusion is avoided because it has been concerned with the placement of individuals and teachers have sought to avoid further stigma by drawing attention to their difference. If all children are involved in discussion of what it means to be included in their schools, classes, lessons and social groups and of what gets in the way of this, it becomes less about any individual and more about the processes of inclusion and exclusion. The disabled and non-disabled youngsters with whom I have talked and worked have astounded me with the sophistication of their understanding of inclusion and of learning more generally. The Scottish politicians involved in the Parliamentary inquiry on 'special needs' were also impressed by the insights offered by those who had direct experience of inclusion and exclusion. Furthermore, the youngsters I have engaged with have articulated a strong commitment to inclusion and have felt incensed when their teachers' practices get in the way of this. As Coffield (2002) has argued, children work well in the role as citizens and as 'bullshit detectors' and are able to spot injustices which affect them and others. There is little doubt that disabled and non-disabled children are capable of engaging in discussions about inclusion with their teachers. These discussions might also prove to be instructive for teachers and others.

INCLUSIVE MANOEUVRES (IN THE DARK?)

There are potentially four shifts that might be productive and could create openings for inclusion. These are in relation to teacher/student relationships, school spaces, learning and behaviour and each involves elements of subversion, subtraction and invention. Fundamentally, they involve addressing the power imbalances that exist within schools and shifting these in favour of students to enable them to participate more fully and effectively. The shifts are also about redirecting the huge amount of energy that already exists in schools in more useful and productive ways. As Connell (1993) reminds us, schools are 'busy institutions' (p. 27) which produce social hierarchies, select and exclude and this level activity could profitably be refocused towards social justice (Gillborn and Youdell, 2000).

TEACHER/STUDENT RELATIONSHIPS

The rigidly hierachical and bounded relationships between teachers and children and young people, with the latter subjugated by the former's authority, knowledge and power, could be interrupted by the teacher him or herself. The framework of Children's rights within the United Nations Convention of the Rights of the Child, and now enshrined in legislation in many countries (although not the United States), could provide the basis for shifting responsibility for some decision-making towards students. The Convention safeguards certain rights and provides a mandate for greater participation by children generally and in discussions about matters directly affecting them. As Lee (1999) has remarked, however, Article 12, which refers explicitly to children's participation, is a mixture of potential toothlessness and bold intent. This particular article is also more controversial than those concerned with protection and provision because it raises the issue of citizenship (Prout, 2003). More generally childhood is understood by adults as a highly ambiguous state and children are largely invisible in policy and professional practice. They only become visible when they are defined as 'troubled' or 'troublesome' (Foley et al, 2003, p. 107).

The interpretation and implementation of children's rights legislation within schools has so far been minimalist and indeed Freeman (2000) has identified a 'chasm between Convention and practice' (p. 279). School councils have been the most common way in which children's rights have been operationalised in schools. These forms of organisation operate within existing hierarchical school structures and constrain the young people to replicate adult processes of decision-making. The scope for decision-making is usually confined to matters of uniform, school lunches and the building, with little opportunity for incursions into teaching and learning (Allan et al, 2006; Ruddock et al, 1996).

The experience of one headteacher in Scotland in seeing how far she could take the children's rights agenda has been salutary (Allan and I'Anson, 2004; Allan et al, 2006; I'Anson and Allan, 2006). This headteacher had introduced children's rights in a previous school with considerable success and sought to repeat and extend the process in her new school. Over a period of 18 months, a group of researchers from the University of Stirling and Save the Children tracked activities and progress within the school. The journey on which the various participants travelled was a complex one which involved discovering what did not work as well as what did. The headteacher came to the realisation that attempting to bring children's rights into what we termed the 'bureacratic spaces' (Allan and I'Anson, 2004, p. 126), pupil councils and school assemblies, had little effect, largely because the power relations in the school were unchallenged. Incorporating rights within the curriculum was more successful as it enabled children to explore their own conceptions of power and their place within school and to make connections with subject content. This raised uncertainties for the class teachers, however, where, for example, issues emerged which highlighted an infringement of children's rights. Most successful was where children were able to experience and experiment with rights within ethical spaces. The Special Needs Observation Group (SNOG) was an example of success within ethical spaces and is described later in this chapter.

Children in the school were taught about the significance of their rights and how these related to responsibilities, and this took a considerable amount of time within lessons and in school assemblies. More importantly, staff had to be encouraged, continuously, to let go of their safe hierarchies of authority, knowledge and power. Everyone in the school, including the janitor, dinner ladies, administrative staff and playground supervisors, and others who were connected with the school, for example the community policeman and the home-school link worker, were 'recruited' and encouraged to alter the way they engaged with children. A key change for some was to no longer shout at children. The children took some time before they became confident enough to exercise their rights, but gradually became more assertive and more inclined to knock on the headteacher's door with issues and potential solutions. Towards the end of the research period, the headteacher was becoming more ambitious about extending children's rights still further to include them on interview panels for staff appointments and, at a future date, allowing children to chair their own care or special needs case reviews. These ideas were likely to cause splutterings (as opposed to stutterings) within the local authority hierarchies, and indeed the notion of children interviewing staff had already been vetoed at a higher level, but the headteacher was intent on persevering. The experience in this school highlights the time and effort it takes to shift teacher/student relationships and the challenge it presents to adults to relinquish familiar and habitual ways of working.

The appointment of Children's Commissioners in England and in Scotland is an important shift towards ensuring children's rights are upheld and these individuals, who have considerable powers, have already made their presence felt. The establishment of other 'Children's champions,' to protect and defend children's rights may also be advantageous, although the children's choices of champions – Ant and Dec – as the most popular, followed by David Beckham, then Prince William (CBBC, 2001) do not inspire confidence.

The shift in teacher/student relationships could be characterised as a move, in Deleuzian terms, from communication to expression or from the sender-receiver mode, in which information flows along 'established power grids . . . with the voltage a determination of unequal social relations' (Roy, 2004, p. 298) that exists between teachers and their students, to more messy forms of exchange which are events in themselves. This is likely to be unsettling since, as Foucault notes, there is a profound fear of the 'mass of spoken things, of everything in it that could possibly be violent, discontinuous, querulous, disordered even and perilous in it' (Foucault, 1972, p. 229). As Roy (ibid) suggests, there is a need to understand and try to overcome the phobias about disorder and the obsessive desire for certainty which leads to oversimplification. The challenge for teachers is to try to think from within confusion (Britzman, 2002) without seeking closure through a demand for a clear distinction between the teacher and taught and to be open to 'the ethically rich drama that runs through education' (Edgoose, 1997, p. 1). Pratt's (1992) suggestion that the teacher/student relationship be conceptualised as a 'contact zone' (p. 4), a space of confrontation which is positive, playful and productive, is useful:

> Social spaces where disparate cultures meet, clash and grapple with each
> other, often in highly asymmetrical relations of domination and subordination
> the spatial and temporal copresence of subjects (pp. 4–7).

Teachers may have to do some creative subtraction on themselves, removing, for example, the order words that they use, such as 'sit down'; 'be quiet'; or 'take your jacket off'. They might also practise paying attention to the Sayings, moments of hesitations and stammerings by students and rather than close these down with familiar content, teachers might keep them open and respond to them. Whilst this may be unsettling to teachers because of its departure from the intended content and may produce anxieties about achieving learning outcomes, such 'failure of fluency' (Edgoose, 1997, p. 6) makes a caring justice possible.

An example of an accidental stammering was relayed to me by a parent of a five year old child with Down's syndrome. This child had just started school in his local primary and the preparations for his start had been an model of effective partnership working: the various professionals had consulted and had prepared the class teacher for the start of term; good support was in place; the parents had been fully involved in advising the school of the child's particular interests and the class teacher felt very confident about supporting this child. But she happened to notice one of the child's classmates sitting looking very concerned and worried. Eventually she tried to find out what was troubling this other pupil and was told, 'you're not taking care of [the child's] legs. The teacher immediately became alarmed; nobody had told her about the child having any trouble with his legs. She racked her brains, went back through the notes, then talked to the child again only to learn the truth: 'we were told that [child] has special knees and you haven't been taking care of his knees'. An event like this could provide an opening in which to be playful, and to then move to new ground.

A second episode of stuttering came, again by accident, but this time with an adult who, in attempting to describe his wife's postgraduate research could not find the word inclusion and referred to it instead as being about enclosure. At the time I provided the missing word, but then suggested that his word was more apt and this apparent misnaming could provide the necessary jolt to thought and the basis for asking 'what do we want people to be included in?'

A third example of stuttering was a gift from a first year student responding to an examination question of mine on inclusive education but who wrote instead about 'inconclusive education'. This left me initially doing the stuttering and wondering if leg pulling was taking place, but as I reflected later, it seemed that this student had been insightful and that we should be thinking of the process as never being concluded. I began this chapter in this vein and would dearly love to acknowledge the student's contribution, but the anonymity of marking makes this impossible. I am, nevertheless, extremely grateful for the insight afforded by this stuttering.

Baroness Warnock found herself the hapless victim of stuttering on a recent visit to Scotland, where she was dining out on her pamphlet in praise of special schools (Warnock, 2005). The General Teaching Council, her hosts, misprinted the publicity materials and billed her as speaking on *From integration to exclusion*. The Council was uncharacteristically sheepish in pointing out its error, but one member of the audience exploited the pause offered by this stuttering to argue that the title was in fact correct and that what was going on in schools was exclusion rather than inclusion. Although this particular comment created closure, the gaffe provided an interruption which produced 'vacuoles of noncommunication, circuit breakers, so that we can elude control' (Deleuze, 1995, p. 175) and which might have enabled alternative possibilities to be considered.

Teachers might create opportunities for students to stutter together over constructs. So rather than dealing with fixed meanings, students could be invited to produce 'creative *murmurs* within language, plateaus of intensity that align in multiple ways constructing different worlds' (Roy, 2004, p. 311). This is an invitation to play with words and to invent new forms of expression. It is only through these new inventions that we can undo the orthodox.

Transgression, the practical and playful resistance to limits developed by Foucault, is an important way for disabled people to challenge the disabling barriers they encounter. Whilst it is necessary to continue to work to remove these barriers to inclusion which exist within schools and elsewhere, there is possibly a place for helping disabled and young people to recognise barriers, for example in the form of negative or patronising attitudes, and to find ways to challenge them. Teachers or other adults could work with children and young adults, individually or in groups, to agree tactics, either proactively or reactively. This could even be a project for disabled children and adults to work on with their non-disabled peers. More generally, students might be helped to become *readers of power*, learning to recognise how it is used to construct their identities and relationships with adults, control their movements, their learning and their behaviour. Developing literacy in relation to power would perhaps enable students to understand how adults are also implicated in this way and perhaps make them feel less antagonistic towards them. The students could then direct their resistance towards more productive and positive ends.

The suggestions so far relate to what teachers might do to shift their relationships with the students in their classes. It involves some bold subversion on their part, potentially undermining their own expertism and authority; subtraction, in the sense giving fewer 'order words' and inventing new language and new ways to go on with students. Teachers' fears of losing control may make them reluctant to undertake these actions, but more positively, they might look to students as having valuable insights and expertise, that they can learn from, particularly in relation to difference. Propositions for a more formal role for children, young people and parents, in relation to teacher education and staff development are offered in Chapter 7.

SCHOOL SPACES

The highly rigid and striated – territorialized – space of the school could be worked upon and smoothed out – deterritorialized – by students. This involves inventing new ways for students to experiment with and experience inclusion and participation. Where this has been made possible, students have achieved significant success as the following two examples illustrate.

In the school where the headteacher implemented a children's rights framework (Allan et al, 2006), a small group of children was formed to look at inclusion in the school. The Group, called the Special Needs Observation Group (SNOG) was initially formed by a parent of two disabled children in the school, but the children gradually assumed responsibility for their own activities. One boy in particular, Alistair, became a strong leader of the group, particularly in relation to shaping the others' understanding about inclusion. The group excelled in identifying the barriers to participation and encouraging the whole school community to think and act more inclusively. Interestingly, the members of the group very quickly and comprehensively identified the need to examine inclusion by looking simultaneously at exclusion, a point which inclusion scholars have grasped only relatively recently in spite of enjoinders from Booth and Ainscow (1998), Ballard (2003b) and others and which continues to elude some. They operationalized the social model of disability intuitively, without naming it as such, but identified the biggest barrier to participation as being the attitudes of teachers and students. The naming of the group was an accident of inventiveness and deterritorialization. My colleague, John I'Anson and I were sitting with the group as it explored possible names for itself and the acronyms which different letters would produce. I jokingly suggested the acronym SNOG and they responded to this with delight, while the parent offered to have tee shirts with 'SNOG' emblazoned across the front made up. This she duly did, but some time later the headteacher reported some complaints from some of the parents who were concerned about the impact of such a risqué name on their child's moral safety. The fuss eventually died down when the children demonstrated that having such an 'in your face' name got them noticed in the school, gave them a new level of authority and enabled them to get their message across to other children and to teachers. Their impact on the school space was significant and they made numerous suggestions for alterations which would remove barriers to participation. The headteacher remarked ruefully that the group's request that a particular door be altered to improve access was more likely to be heeded because it had come from students rather than from staff.

A second example of smoothing out space relates to the arts centre within the University of Stirling (the macrobert). When this was being refurbished, a group of Young Consultants, aged between 7 and 16, was established to provide guidance and support at all stages of the process, from the design through to the building (Mannion and I'Anson, 2004). The Young Consultants shaped the building into what it is today, interpreting accessibility in a deeper way than just ensuring people could get through doors. Their recommendations extended to the kind of information that was available to entice people to participate in the arts and they were extremely successful according to all of those involved, from the architect and the director of the centre through to the young people themselves. The adults quickly became aware of the importance of the distinction between listening to children and young people and hearing, and responding to, what they said and the Director of the Centre emphasised the responsibility this placed upon them:

> ... young people are very demanding, especially if you're going to involve them and you say 'Right we're going to listen to you'. You have a real responsibility to deliver and if you don't deliver you have to really be able to give very detailed answers about why ... Once you open yourself up to the flood gates of demands and expectations ... you know, there's no stopping it (Mannion and I'Anson, 2004, p. 307).

The sense that the Young Consultants were 'making [their] own environment' (Mannion and I'Anson, 2004, p. 310) was powerful for both them and the adults they worked with and had a profound effect on the architect, both as an architect and as an adult. His experience left him wondering why he had not taken account of young people's views in the past: 'Why did we miss out on an obvious group of people?' (Mannion and I'Anson, 2004, p. 313). The Young Consultants' commitment to the Centre has continued and they have been involved as reviewers in an annual international film festival for children.

The curriculum is a space that has been described as overcrowded with too many additional obligations being squeezed in (LTS, 1999; Scottish Science Advisory Committee, 2003) and it is in desperate need of some creative subtraction. In Scotland, following the publication of *A Curriculum for Excellence* (Scottish Executive, 2004), the Government promised to remove things to make room in the curriculum, inventing the term 'decluttering' (Scottish Executive, 2004) but it is hard to see how there will be agreement on what should go. Furthermore, at the same time there are calls to place greater emphasis on such things as citizenship and creativity. There seems to be some difficulty in avoiding seeing these as 'add ons', complete with their own content, forms of delivery and outcomes, rather than as vehicles for participation, learning and forms of expression. However, this is precisely where their value lies and they have the potential to make room and to free up space.

RHIZOMIC LEARNING

The quest for certainty, closure and *outcomes* in learning, could be replaced by a search for the undecidable, the incalculable, in which learning cannot be predicted. This does, however, involve a considerable subversion of the expectations contained within policy documents that particular behaviours will lead to particular outcomes. It also requires some inventive thinking about the alternative kind of learning that is to take place. The metaphor for the shift in learning used by Deleuze and Guattari (1987), involving the replacement of the arborescent tree structure with the rhizome, is particularly useful. Deleuze (2004) also helpfully talks about the shift from the actual – the acquisition of knowledge and content – to the virtual – the engagement with problems and ideas. He describes learning as the subjective acts carried out when one is confronted with the objectivity of a problem or an idea. Learners require to undergo the 'disorienting jolt of something new, different truly other' (Bogue, 2004, p. 341) and the process of learning is the explication of these new encounters, an 'undoing of orthodox conventions' (ibid). The film director Anthony Minghella (2004), speaking at a conference on film and education, underlined the need for teachers to 'confound' young people and to challenge them to think laterally. He exemplified this by talking about his own confounding by a teacher of English who played him a Leonard Cohen record – *Suzanne*. This episode set him on a love of poetry which has lasted a lifetime and which is sustained by reading poems every day. Teachers needed, he suggested, to acquire the confidence to be able to move young people in this way.

Deleuze (2000) also suggests that the only effective way to learn is actively and bodily and, using the analogy of learning to swim, compares this with other approaches:

> The movements of the swimming instructor which we reproduce on the sand bear no relation to the movements of the wave, which we learn to deal with only by grasping the former in practice in signs . . . We learn nothing from those who say: "Do as I do" . . . Our only teachers are those who tell us to "Do with me", and are able to emit signs to be developed in heterogeneity rather than propose gestures for us to reproduce (p. 23).

The effective teacher, according to Deleuze, emits signs for the learners to read, interpret and experience. Deleuze's swimming analogy helps us to understand the way in which 'learning always takes place in and through the unconscious, thereby establishing the bond of a profound complicity between nature and mind'. The children who participated in creative activities through *Art Lab,* which will be reported in Chapter 8, were clear that the best kind of learning was that in which they were required to 'do stuff'. This they contrasted with the passive and dull nature of much of their learning in school.

The shift away from knowledge and solutions, and from notions of learning which are about having these communicated by the teacher to the student, towards problems and ideas which are expressed through learning *events* is a profound one, particularly given the outcomes driven nature of education and the expectation that children and young people have acquired levels of knowledge and skills by particular ages and stages. Hannah Arendt (1968) says, education is where 'we decide whether we love our children enough . . . not to strike from their hands the chance of undertaking something new, something unforseen by us' (p. 198). Yet the prospect of children and young people learning things that have not been laid out by teachers seems to be unsettling and it may be necessary to examine why this is the case. The climate of accountability seems to have swamped education, taken away teachers sense of control over themselves, never mind their students, and made them into machines of performativity, delivering students to the specified outcomes and deeply unsatisfied with their 'profession'. It is not proposed that knowledge and solutions are abandoned, since these will always continue to matter within our education system; rather, it is being suggested teachers might place a greater emphasis on learning as expression. There might, however, be scope for teachers collectively to find ways of subverting the regimes of accountability and to explore more political forms of engagement.

There has been some recognition, at government level, of the need to ensure that learning is concerned with more than the communication of subject content. Education Queensland, for example, commissioned a longtitudinal study of teaching, learning, assessment and leadership (Luke et al, 1999) and recommended a move towards productive pedagogies, involving heightened intellectual demand on students, connectedness to the students' lives outside the school, a supportive classroom environment and recognition of difference. One of the key features of the productive pedagogies was that issues of social justice, equity and inclusion were central, not supplementary, to good pedagogy and were vital to ensuring high levels of academic achievement. This is a significant rejoinder to the argument that raising achievement and inclusion are mutually exclusive. It is clear that they are aporetic, pulling in different directions, but it may be that they are less of an either/or and more of an also/and.

The metaphor of the rhizome may be used to open up opportunities to acquire knowledge and solutions but in different ways. There is increasing interest in approaches which take account of different learning styles and this could be a valuable way of introducing more openness into the learning process, without leaving teachers feeling vulnerable and concerned about their students' success in achieving learning outcomes. There is a danger, however, that learning styles could be used to effect further closure, for example by differentiating students as particular types of learners and requiring them to retain particular labels. A key challenge for teachers will be to initiate dialogue with students about learning, enabling them to learn about how they learn. This will take time but my experience of researching children's learning (Allan et al, 1998; Allan, 2005c) suggests that they can become extremely articulate and welcome this kind of engagement, even if they initially find it difficult to talk about their own learning. The children we spoke to reported that the questions we asked them were easy but good answers were difficult, because they didn't usually talk about these things (Allan et al, 1998).

The invitation to students to narrate their own learner identities and experiences could be undertaken as an exercise in the practices of the self, allowing individuals to map their own learning. This would enable them to identify the work on themselves in order to become better learners, but they will need help in managing the uncertainty associated with rhizomic learning. Experiencing uncertainty as positive, rather than as evidence of a lack of knowledge or understanding of the rules and expectations, could free students up to pursue their own 'new lines of flight' (Deleuze and Guattari, 1987, p. 161) and avenues of thought and could be enormously liberating without posing a threat to the social order of the school.

Children's ideas about good learning are surprising for their ordinariness. In research on children's learning (Allan et al, 1998), children identified the following prerequisites:

- Being made to do class work and homework
- Being made to write down an example, not just watch it
- The teacher goes over work done, marks work, checks jotters
- New material is explained
- Questions about understanding are taken seriously and answered clearly
- The teacher grasps which point is not understood
- There are opportunities to experience 'real' activities
- Practical activities are balanced with writing
- Enough time is given together with a deadline for finishing.

Good explanations of subject content, rather than the same ones repeated *louder,* together with the need to be engaged actively, rather than being passive recipients of knowledge, are clearly important to children and young people and should not be too much to ask. Yet irritation and impatience was a more common experience for the children and young people we spoke to in this research:

> The teacher just rushes on, and people who get [grade] ones were putting their hand up. If you went out to ask for help he would give you a row . . . We didn't understand it, we asked and he never even heard you – you keep putting your hand up – that's when we get punishments . . . Ask the teacher and they'll help you . . . [but] some teachers crack up on you and say you've not been listening (Duffield et al, 2000, p. 270).

The youngsters we spoke to were keen to take responsibility for their learning but had been given little opportunity to do so. Their willingness to become more engaged is a good starting point for teachers.

The experience of the Special Needs Observation Group (SNOG), in the school in which the headteacher had implemented a children's rights framework (Allan et al, 2006), was a form of rhizomic learning in which they experimented with and experienced inclusion. They took rights – literally – on a walk through the school in order to discover the points at which exclusion arose. Simulation exercises of this kind, in which non-disabled individuals pretend to be disabled, can be superficial and essentialist, but these young people forced their gaze on the disabling barriers and found themselves constantly surprised, and capable of imagining more of the exclusion experienced by their disabled peers. This kind of learning about rights seemed to be particularly effective because it took them off in new and unanticipated directions. Having 'dealt with' disability, the group decided to move onto ethnicity, and identified some concerns about the level of participation of some individuals. They then decided to tackle size issues when they became aware of some of their peers' discomfort when changing for gym. Their experience and experimentation with rights had alerted them to new forms of exclusion which they wished to do something about.

Summerhill school, founded by AS Neil, is a somewhat unusual, but nevertheless interesting, example of rhizomic learning. It provides a unique insight into how children respond when given the 'freedom to learn.' The school came under the spotlight in 2000 when, following a negative Ofsted inspection, a number of complaints were served on it and it was threatened with closure. Summerhill lodged an appeal against the Secretary of State's complaints and a Tribunal was held in the High Court to determine the school's fate. I became part of a research team acting on behalf of Summerhill; my remit was to consider evidence in relation to the complaint by Ofsted that there was inadequate support for students with special educational needs and insufficient expertise in this area. The Tribunal folded within a week, with an agreement reached by both sides and accepted by the students of Summerhill, but at times the court case resembled high farce and the three judges, at one point, declared themselves astonished at what they were hearing. In considering an early complaint that the school, which functions as a home, in the familial sense, had no separate toilets for boys and girls and for children and adults, the judges' impatience was palpable and they quickly moved to an annulment of this. Later on, it became evident that the school had been placed on a 'to be watched list'. The list was in no way official and Summerhill had not been informed of this, a revelation to which the judges reacted with utter astonishment and anger. The renowned human rights lawyer, Geoffrey Robinson QC, milked the judges' incredulity and made mincemeat of one of the minions of the Secretary of State. This poor individual suffered a particularly gruelling encounter which at times smacked of Dickens: 'come come Mr Phipps', was sent home with homework which involved reading AS Neil's books and failed to reappear the next day on account of a migraine.

Forensic examination of the Ofsted Inspection process, which produced the 'evidence' on which the complaint was based, has been undertaken by Stronach (2005) who has highlighted gross ineptitudes and inappropriate and unjust practices. What is of interest here, however, is the young people's response to the invitation to choose whether to attend lessons or not. As part of the research team, I spent time with the students. The pattern, as the students described it, was one in which they initially did not go to lessons, but later did so when they were ready (and bored). When they took up their classes, their learning, as Robinson described to the Tribunal, was 'fast and furious' and this was certainly what was observed. The students were demanding learners, keen to make up time on their learning and I witnessed a science teacher being told by the students to bypass a particular experiment because they understood what would happen and wanted to move on. This he happily did and appeared quite unfazed by being directed by the students in this way.

The proposal put to the school by the DfEE amounted to a climb down. Carmen Cordwell, the 15 year old who chaired the meeting to decide whether this was acceptable, spoke to the press about what they saw as a triumph:

> This is our charter for freedom. It gives us the space we need to live and breathe and learn into the future. After 79 years, this is the first official recognition that A S Neill's philosophy of education provides an acceptable alternative to the tyranny of compulsory exams. With this one bound, we are free at last (Summerhill Press Statement, 23 March, 2000).

In spite of this 'victory', Summerhill continues to be placed under surveillance by Ofsted because of an unwillingness to tolerate difference of this kind within the education system. This is, as I have suggested, an unusual school which is not part of the state sector and there are few, if any, schools elsewhere in which students would get such freedom to choose when and what they learn. It is, however, an important example and a 'powerfully interesting experiment' (Purves, 2000, p. 96) because it illustrates that even when young people are given such extreme degrees of freedom, they do not descend into disorder.

BEHAVIOUR

At a recent meeting with an assistant headteacher of a local secondary school, we were interrupted by a senior teacher who was apoplectic with rage. She had just had an unpleasant encounter with a student who was attempting to use the lift, but who was not entitled to do so as he was not disabled. The teacher reported that she had ordered the student to get out of the lift, to which the reply was 'No'. She repeated her order, only to be met with the same answer: 'No'. On hearing this, the assistant headteacher responded with a smile and said 'oh that's good; before he would have said "No, f*** off."' The teacher had come looking for support and the promise of reprisal for the student and found the response disconcerting, but as an observer, I found the refusal to leap into opposition and confrontation impressive and inspirational. This episode is not intended to suggest that all misbehaviour be regarded positively, but to illustrate that negative confrontation is not an inevitable consequence when students challenge authority.

For one young person, Alistair, the experience of being part of the SNOG group, and of rhizomic learning, was particularly significant in rescuing him from a downward spiral of misbehaviour and exclusion. He described himself as having been out of control, often getting into trouble in the playground for fighting and being regularly excluded. Prior to joining SNOG, he had become a buddy to a disabled child and being responsible for someone else had made him alter his own behaviour. He described how: 'I used to be, like, really really bad. I used to fight everybody, but now I've calmed down because I've got a responsibility to look after them.' His membership of SNOG had, by his own account, transformed him into someone else, someone who had to have regard for others, and had allowed him to escape his deviant identity. It was a dramatic line of flight:

> Well, when I started to know [disabled students] I was, like, I need to show them I want to be good, 'cos I used to get into fights and stupid things like that but when I started to get to know them and got into the SNOG group I started my behaviour; I wanted to start again and be good . . . I didn't want everybody to know me as Alistair the bad boy. I want to be good now. So that's what I was trying to do when I went into the SNOG group . . . sometimes I'm amazing' (Allan and I'Anson, 2005, p. 133).

Of all the SNOG group members, Alistair seemed to have the most sophisticated understanding of disabling barriers and this, too, had undergone a dramatic shift in which he came to see the damaging effects of pity:

> I just wanted to have [disabled students] 'cos I thought they looked amazing. I just wanted to be with them . . . I thought they looked so cute and things like that. But everybody feels sorry for them but they're just the same as us so they should just be treated the same. 'Cos they don't like being felt sorry for – just because they have disabilities doesn't mean they should be treated differently. That's what the group's all about – to make sure people don't treat each other differently because they look different. So that's what we've been doing' (ibid).

He had transformed himself, but recognised that he had to police his own newly formed identity and occasionally he lapsed:

> I get into a fight or I get angry because it didn't happen. If I didn't get to sit beside my friends I start to get angry. I just want to be a good boy now. As everybody says "good boy." That's what I want to be – I want to prove them all wrong. They all think I [can't] behave but I want to prove them all wrong that I can behave . . . some people just know me as "there's Alistair – stay away from him." But I'm to prove them all wrong – that I'm good. I'm going to be good. I just want to be good now. But I was bad a couple of weeks ago . . . I was shouting at a teacher. I said something to him really bad and I had to get taken home . . . At the time I was all angry and I just shouted, but afterwards I regretted it 'cos I knew I'd done wrong, but you can't change the past but you can make sure the future's better (ibid, p. 134).

The teacher he had sworn at was mortally offended and initially refused to accept his written apology, but eventually relented, under pressure from the headteacher. Clearly such opportunities for escape would not be available to, or responded to, by every student with a label of behavioural difficulties. It is, nevertheless, a heartening transformation which delighted all with whom Alistair was connected – the headteacher, the teachers, the janitor, Alistair's mother, and us, the researchers. Most impressed of all was Alistair himself who came to know himself as 'amazing'.

SUBVERTING, SUBTRACTING, INVENTING?

The propositions offered here in relation to teachers and children are not easy ones. They require significant changes in the way teachers and children engage with each other, the school spaces and the ways in which children are asked to learn and behave. These changes could be achieved by refocusing the resources and energies which exist within schools towards more productive ends. In order to achieve this, however, better support for beginning and established teachers – for their *becomings* – is necessary and it is to this that I now turn.

8. NOMADIC LEARNING TO TEACH: RECOGNITION, RUPTURE AND REPAIR

Those calling for moves in teacher education towards greater inclusiveness have made it clear that radical structural and cultural reform of HEIs is necessary (Ballard, 2003a; Booth et al, 2003a) and that the domination of special education needs to be challenged (Slee, 2001b). The first aporia to emerge here is that this radical reform has to be undertaken alongside the standards and accountability agendas which appear to work against inclusion. Whilst it is important to try to challenge these, and I will say more about this in the final chapter, it is also necessary to be realistic about their power and longevity. So if we assume that standards and accountability are here to stay, are there ways in which teacher education for inclusion can be pursued differently and more effectively – as education? Are there ways of producing teachers who are positively oriented towards inclusion and who are keen to participate in the *struggle*? The philosophers of difference are, once again, of practical use and this chapter considers the possibilities of using the ideas of Deleuze and Guattari, Derrida and Foucault to remake teacher education along more inclusive lines. This involves a *recognition* of the double-edged and contradictory nature of inclusive teacher education; *rupture* of conventional approaches to learning to teach and attempts to *repair* the profession of teaching and teachers' own selves.

EXPOSING APORIAS AND DECONSTRUCTING DOGMA

The most significant challenge for teacher educators is accepting that the aspiration to be inclusive creates a number of responsibilities which pull them in different directions. These 'aporias' create tensions because they are assumed to be resolvable or reducible to one choice (Allan, 2003a):

1. How can student teachers be helped to acquire and demonstrate the necessary competences to qualify as a teacher *and* to understand themselves as in an inconclusive process of learning about others? (Gregoriou 2001).
2. How can student teachers develop as autonomous professionals *and* learn to depend on others for support and collaboration?

3. How can student teachers be supported in maximising student achievement *and* ensuring inclusivity?
4. How can student teachers be helped to understand the features of particular impairments *and* avoid disabling individual students with that knowledge?
5. What assistance can be given to student teachers to enable them to deal with the exclusionary pressures they encounter *and* avoid becoming embittered or closed to possibilities for inclusivity in the future? (Allan, 2003a, p. 143).

If these aporias were accepted as an inevitable element of teacher education for inclusion and if the pressure to choose between the double contradictory imperatives was resisted, there would be less confusion, frustration, guilt and exhaustion. Student teachers could be alerted to these ambivalences and contradictions, rather than simply being exposed to, and confused by, them. Uncertainty, the greatest torment for the student teacher, could become an acceptable part of the process, with the moments of undecidability being where they learn to do their most inclusive teaching. Exposing these aporias within teacher education, rather than being disruptive and negative, could prove to be an effective form of deterritorialization, by smoothing out some of the spaces where adjudication between imperatives has previously created chasms and impasses. The revelation of these aporias forces us to invent new ways of pursuing inclusion within teacher education which always involve at least two ways.

Deconstruction could enable teachers to achieve explicit recognition of the aporias which they face in their working lives and which force them into the repetition of exclusion. Acknowledgement of the impossibilities they face could go some way to according them respect for how they manage the struggle for inclusion. The aporias contained within educational policy more generally could be revealed to teachers through deconstruction. They may be more willing and able to connect with other teachers and other professionals if they can read playfully those texts which simultaneously urge them to undertake joined up working and fragment their practice and their sense of professionalism. Deconstruction may also help professionals to acquire a more realistic sense of their responsibilities than is conveyed in policy discourses.

Deconstruction of the policy and legislation relation to inclusion could expose the exclusionary pressures inscribed within them (Slee and Allan, 2001). It could unpeel the 'anxiety and compulsion to stamp and seal the truth' (Derrida, 1988, p. 31) about inclusion and find other possible inventions. Deconstruction offers scope for engaging with the texts of the special educationists, which have denounced inclusive education and have closed down avenues for debate with their tactics of ideological handbagging. Deconstruction opens possibilities for unravelling some of their arguments and turning the language of pathology back on itself. So if we cannot talk to them, perhaps we can play with their texts.

The process of preparing student teachers to meet the Professional Standards for teaching might be undertaken in a way which still ensures these are achieved, but also alerts them to some of the limitations of these kinds of frameworks. Student teachers could be encouraged to wander through the Standards, reading them in terms of the kind of performances they command, to enact these reflexively and critique their own identity work in achieving the required levels of competence. They might be guided towards a deconstruction of the Standards in which they give texts an (im)plausible reading (Honan, 2004) and identify their blind spots and the way in which they contradict themselves. I have underlined the difficulty of setting out a method for deconstruction, but a deconstructive ethos could enable student teachers to be playful and naïve in their reading of the Standards. Alternatively, students might be encouraged to treat texts as a rhizome, to look for the middles of texts (Honan, 2004) and to discover their 'scrupulous and plausible misreadings' (Spivak, 1996, p. 45).

More generally, if students are encouraged to deconstruct (or interrogate the rhizomic qualities of) inclusion policies, rather than absorb and replicate their content, they may become aware of the contradictions and inconsistencies inherent in them and recognise how aporias are disavowed and closed down. Students would then be alerted to the way in which policies 'write the teacher' (Cormack and Comber, 1996, p. 119) in ways that are contradictory and oppositional (Honan, 2004) and which constrain teachers' actions:

> Such documents and their associated technologies, written for and about the teacher, construct authorised versions of the curriculum subject, teacher and student. These statements officially 'write' the teacher and the student – who they should be, what they are to do and say and when and how they must do or say it (Cormack and Comber, 1996, p. 119).

Teachers might also be alerted to the ways in which research has constructed teachers as recipients of policy, assuming no capacity to do anything other than adjust and absorb:

> Generally, we have failed to research, analyse and conceptualize this underlife, the 'secondary adjustments' which relate teachers to policy and to the state in different ways. We tend to begin by assuming the adjustment of teachers and context to policy but not of policy to context. There is a privileging of the policymaker's reality (Ball, 1994, p. 19).

Readings of policy texts as rhizomatic could help to disrupt some of the assumptions about the relationships between teachers, policies and context and may make student teachers better placed to challenge some of the pronouncements or at the very least understand how policy texts seek to produce them as a teacher who is both regulated and effective (Honan, 2004). Recognition of how they are regulated, and thereby controlled, and of the process of producing an effective teacher who is 'elastic or infinitely flexible and ultimately dutiful figures who can unproblematically respond to new demands' (Cormack and Comber, 1996, p. 121), may make the passage towards full teacher status less of an ordeal. They may also be more able to question the nature of current trends and issues in inclusion, such as the 'epidemic' of ADHD and the plethora of dyslexic children among the school population.

FROM CONTENT TO EXPRESSION:
DETERRITORIALIZING TEACHER EDUCATION

The rigid content driven programmes of teacher education, with their special education orientation, could be replaced through the process of deterritorialization. The four strands of this activity, developed by Deleuze and Guattari (1987), could be undertaken as a collective task within HEIs or by individuals. The first of these, becoming foreigners in our own tongue, would involve scrutiny of the language used in lectures and materials, keeping an eye for where the language of special needs is prevalent and creating stutterings over words and expressions which have hitherto been familiar. Colleagues at my own HEI developed a game of 'bullshit bingo' in an effort to pick up and subvert jargon in their written work. A similar exercise could be usefully undertaken with the teaching materials used with students.

The refusal of essences or signifieds is an important second strand of deterritorialization which could be undertaken within teacher education programmes. Instead of attempting, in lectures and materials, to define inclusion, we could point to who is included and who is not. We might also ask not what inclusion is but what inclusion does. This might take us closer to elaborating some of the consequences of inclusion for children and young people and their parents. We would then perhaps begin to understand how inclusion is experienced rather than how it is represented.

Creative subtraction would involve identifying what not to do within the curriculum. Instead of responding to the latest government imperatives to insert more content by looking to see where it can be squeezed in, there could be a search for what might be removed or reduced. An invitation to lose aspects of what we currently do in the name of inclusion and in education, in order to put some other things in, could be attractive. This, of course, will not be easy as there will be opposition from those who insist that the items proposed for shedding should remain purely because they have always been there and are precious to the individuals who put them there in the first place.

The acceptance that there is no-one behind expression, the final strand of deterritorialization, is a refusal to attribute blame or responsibility for content to any individuals and to encourage the contribution of new and untried ideas. Greater use of brainstorming sessions – or thought showers, as the new nomenclature goes – could enable staff in HEIs to roam through the kind of teacher education that they really want to do, rather than what they feel constrained to do, then to ask themselves 'why not'. The ruptures provided by deterritorialization may create opportunities for more productive learning.

STUDENT TEACHERS' EMPIRICAL WANDERINGS

Adopting the rhizome as the means for learning to be a teacher ruptures the interpretation of theory (Deleuze, 1995) and privileges experimentation and experience, taking the student teachers on, in Derrida's (1992a) terms, an 'empirical wandering'

(p. 7). The rhizome allows student teachers to invent themselves as the kind of teachers they want to become and instead of absorbing, and later replicating, content, student teachers would be involved in:

> experimenting with pedagogy and recreating its own curricular place, identity, and content; expanding its syllabi and diversify its reading lists; *supplementing* educational discourse with other theories; deterritorializing theory of education from course based to interdisciplinary directions (Gregoriou, 2002, p. 231; original emphasis).

These rhizomic wanderings could help to disrupt conventional knowledge about teaching and learning. It could also interrupt the dominant knowledge of *special needs* and enable student teachers instead to experiment with responding to difference in ways which are meaningful to the young people. This would force the student teachers to question what they know themselves, to 'ask what determinations and intensities [they] are prepared to countenance' (Roy, 2003, p. 91) and to abandon ways of working that seem unreasonable:

Student teachers' knowledge and understanding might be fashioned as a series of maps, 'entirely oriented toward an experimentation in contact with the real' (Deleuze and Guattari, 1987, p. 12). These maps do not replicate knowledge, but perform and create new knowledge:

> The map is open and connectable in all of its dimensions; it is detachable, reversible, susceptible to constant modification. It can be torn, reversed, adapted to any kind of mounting, reworked by an individual, group or social formation. It can be drawn on a wall, conceived as a work of art, constructed as a political action or as a mediation (p. 12).

Reflexivity, which students are often demanded to practise but are rarely given guidance on how to, could be directed towards producing maps of their journeys as becoming teachers. Maps of their school contexts could also be created by student teachers during their teaching practice. These could detail the exclusionary points in the school as a whole, in lessons they observe and in their own classrooms.

Learning to be a teacher through the rhizome is not a journey towards a fixed end, as denoted by the standards, but wanderings along a 'moving horizon' (Deleuze, 2004, p. xix) which are documented visually. As well as creating new knowledge, these wanderings provide opportunities for student teachers to establish, in Rose's (1996) terms, new assemblages and new selves, as teachers:

> A rhizome, a burrow, yes – but not an ivory tower. A line of escape, yes – but not a refuge (Deleuze and Guattari, 1987, p. 41).

Students' wanderings need to be supported and responded to in a way which does not entrench further their novice and incompetent identity and they need to be supported within the schools in which they carry out their teaching. As Lather (1991) reminds us, the undecidable is experienced by students as an ordeal and sustained as evidence of non-mastery and Gregoriou (2004) warns that the rhizome might come to signify a sense of loss for students and produce anxiety:

> I'm confused, how does this fit in now, how is this going to be useful in my teaching, how do all these fit together . . . why do we keep shifting from subject to subject . . . why do we keep criticizing things . . . ? Whose book is this rhizome of anxious quests? Is it less authoritative than any other text-book? (p. 238).

Yet Deleuze and Guattari contend that 'it is through loss rather than acquisition that one progresses and picks up speed' (as cited in Roy, 2003, p. 56). Student teachers' 'creative stammerings' (Deleuze and Guattari, 1987, p. 98), questions and searches for links would be engaged with, rather than closed down as indicative of their failure to grasp content. It is in these spaces or schisms where complex thinking would take place and where 'a new experiment in thought could be inserted . . . that might help teachers get an insight into the generative possibilities of the situation' (Roy, 2003, p. 2). The function of the teacher educator, in Deleuzian terms, is to create pedagogical spaces which are open and smooth, in contrast with the closed and striated spaces of conventional approaches. Student teachers could, within these smooth spaces, read the scripts of teaching with an eye on their implausibility; they could also scrutinise their own knowledge of disability and where this came from (Ware, 2003a; Slee, 2005).

There is a danger that student teachers' wanderings may simply take them *all over the place* without any clear focus. Gregoriou (2004) describes a concern expressed by a University colleague to this effect:

> I have a student who has been trying to formulate the thematic for a paper for almost a semester now. She comes early in the semester with a very tidy and 'tight' proposal. Her heart is tight too, bound by stress and confusion. We discuss different options, different ways to go, various connections and inquiries to attempt. She starts to map various directions. She sounds exhilarated . . . She comes back the next week with a completely different theme. She talks about ways to expand, settles down at a new thematic. I suggest a preliminary bibliography. She comes back, again excited to discover this new author . . . She drifts again. Is this what following a 'line of flight' means? Is this rhizomatics? Is this growth? Am I going to grade this mapping of disparate things? (pp. 237–238).

This particular example relates to written work rather than to the practice of teaching, but it highlights a major difficulty: how far should students be allowed to wander before being reigned in and made to focus? The answer to this possibly depends on the nerve of the educators and their capacity to respond effectively to the students' wanderings – that is by staying with them. It also requires them to have a strong resolve and to resist the pressures of the 'marketable skills and anxious college graduates searching for that educational supplement that will bestow to them a competitive advantage' (Gregoriou, 2004, p. 238). Finally they need to be persuasive and assure their worried students that if they 'invest in encounters with ideas where novelty escapes codification, ownership and repetition' (p. 238), the returns will be rich. As Gregoriou suggests students are more likely to complain about any perceived lack of utility of what they are asked to learn than about its anti-foundational nature. The possibility of active experimentation being a better – or at least more affirmative – route to both the standards and to the kind of teacher they want to become might be enough of a temptation.

DOING DIFFERENCE AND DESIRE

Teacher education has traditionally packaged difference for the student teacher in the form of lists of deficits, their causes and their cures. Even if this is done with the caveat 'no two children are alike' and a discouragement of categorisation, it still facilitates a recognition of 'types' of failings in children and what they might expect from them. A rupture in this typing could be achieved by asking students to turn the gaze back on themselves and on the schools in which they do their teaching placements. The refusal to explain children's pathologies to student teachers could provoke wails of protest from them, but the reasons for this refusal could be set out along with a exposition of the consequences of pathologies for those at whom they are directed. Having outlawed pathologies of children, student teachers' energies could be directed instead to the pathologising of schools, teachers and themselves. They could be invited to question the nature of the categories offered to describe particular students and then to try an alternative – social model – reading of students' difficulties which identifies the environmental, structural and attitudinal barriers. We ask our own student teachers to undertake this task and although they struggle to engage with the social model at first, they eventually become skilled in reading difficulties in this way and in recognising the damaging nature of deficit thinking. Platitudes, derived from policies and the standards for teaching, which talk about celebrating difference could be refused and students' attention drawn to their patronising consequences for those identified as different. Student teachers could be encouraged to engage with difference *in itself*, as opposed to in relation to, identity and in comparison with the normal. They could undertake the task of finding out about individual children's 'conditions', but could investigate how this description has been arrived at and by whom. Student teachers might also scrutinise their own fears about responding to individuals effectively and share these with more experienced teachers or with fellow students. They might be encouraged to think of their anxieties about responding to the other as where inclusion and justice becomes a possibility:

> As soon as you address the other, as soon as you are open to the future, as soon as you have a temporal experience of waiting for the future, of waiting for someone to come: that is the opening of the experience. Someone is to come, is *now* to come. Justice and peace will have to do with this coming of the other with the promise (Derrida, 1997a, p. 22).

This desire for and openness to the other privileges relationships over the delivery of content and makes knowledge of children's *needs* less important than knowing the children themselves. I have suggested before that a concern for difference in terms of *needs* could be replaced with an attention to the children and young person's *desires* (Allan, 1999). This is not excessive but simply involves asking the child or young person for guidance on the kind of support he or she is most comfortable with.

The students' own desires could be foregrounded as part of their identity as becoming teachers. Instead of their status representing a lack of competence, they could be encouraged to articulate their trajectory – emotional as well as in terms of their acquisition of skills – towards the kind of teacher they want to become. The narratives of experienced teachers could be a valuable resource in helping student teachers to understand the fractured, partial and embodied process of becoming a teacher and the centrality of desire. Student teachers could be encouraged to offer and compare reflections on the intensities of their experiences and their 'percepts' and 'affects' (Deleuze, 1995, p. 164), the way they come to think and live as teachers.

Difference could also be investigated by student teachers in the context of community. This could be presented as a construct that is problematic, because of its tendency to privilege an impossible consensus and unity, and its essence or signified could be refused. So, instead of trying to define what a community is, students could be encouraged to consider the multiple and fragmented nature of communities, and to read their schools as communities. They could be asked to think about how they could help to build communities in their schools and invited to explore possibilities for communities in which difference is affirmed. Ballard (2003a) makes it clear that students need to be helped to be critical about how exclusion is created around difference and the responsibilities for teacher educators are to ensure there is a mutual sharing of assumptions, values and ideological positions:

> We will need to be explicit with our students in examining the assumptions and ideological positions on which our analysis of social issues is grounded. Our values, and theirs, will need to be identified and discussed in this critical context. Discomfort and uncertainty may need to be acknowledged together with an awareness that history teaches us that our best-intentioned insights and beliefs may be shown, in time, to be false or problematic for social justice (Ballard, 2003a, p. 60).

Visiting these difficult areas will clearly not make for an easy relationship between teacher educators and student teachers, but student teachers need to understand how exclusion is produced, perhaps even in these very relationships, if they are to find ways of becoming inclusive teachers.

LEARNING FROM THE EXPERTS

I suggested a number of shifts in the relationships between teachers and students which could produce more inclusiveness and some of the attempts to do this have illustrated children's capabilities and their grasp of the features of inclusive practice. Their expertise could be further utilised for teacher education and they could be invited to offer feedback to student teachers on how they have experienced their teaching. This could be set up in a non-threatening and non-personal way, ensuring that the focus is on the impact of the teaching on the children's learning and that the feedback is constructive. It is something we have tentatively introduced in my own institution and in spite of much nervousness on the part of staff of the schools where the student teachers were placed, the feedback was generally informative and helpful. Fears that the students would be 'silly' or negative were unfounded. More specifically, as I have argued, students have clear ideas about inclusion and their feedback to noice teachers could extend to guidance on how to teach more inclusively.

An experiment in rhizomic learning was carried out within our own teacher education course, facilitated by a colleague John I'Anson. Open Space Technology (openspaceworld, n.d) was used as a way of getting young people and student teachers to talk to one another about learning and teaching. The technique involves allowing the learners to determine the issues they consider to be important and which they wish to discuss further. They write their issues on post-it notes and stick them on a wall and by doing so indicate that they would be willing to lead a discussion on this topic. The entire group then decides which of the issues that have been posted are of most importance and those with the most 'votes' are selected. People are free to wander in and out of discussions as their interests dictate and discussion groups may grow or peter out, depending on the movement of the participants. The meeting between a group of secondary school students and student teachers was held in the macrobert, the University arts centre which had involved young people in its design and which was chosen as a less formal, less striated space than other parts of the University. The topics of interest and those that were selected for discussion came equally from students and student teachers. These included individuality; respect; teachers' attitudes; support for pupils; pupil involvement; particular subjects and what pupils should learn. It was an extremely unsettling process to observe; the lack of structure and the possibility that the participants would perceive the exercise as meaningless and refuse to participate provoked anxiety for us. Yet the level of engagement was intense and both students and student teachers agreed it was a powerful way to learn about the other.

The students saw themselves as having had a powerful impact on the student teachers:

> The tables were turned because our views were the main focus of the event. Our opinions were listened to and noted, which made us realise just how important our education is. We helped the student teachers to become mentors, not teachers, and showed them how to concentrate on a pupil's individual needs. They saw our side of the story and therefore how to understand us better (Allan and I'Anson, 2004, p. 25).

The student teachers, for their part, were surprised at how much they could learn by 'listening and talking to pupils' (Allan and I'Anson, 2004, p. 25) and felt that the conversation had 'closed the gap . . . and enlightened' (p. 25). One young person asked immediately after the event: 'is this another day of talk or will we see a day of action', which provoked us to ask the student teachers how they were going to change. They promised to:

- Be more aware of, and responsive to, pupils' perspectives
- Use more interactive teaching – such as groupwork and discussion
- Be more consistent and cautious with regard to discipline
- Admit when they are in the wrong
- Discuss subject choices with pupils
- Be aware of the significance of teachers' and pupils' expectations
- Treat pupils with respect and as pupils
- Listen, listen, listen (ibid).

These personal directives from the student teachers seemed to reflect a positive regard for the other and a desire for a more positive orientation towards students in their practice. The repeated nature of their enjoinder to listen seems to give particular grounds for optimism, and I will return to this point in the final chapter.

Parents of disabled children and young people are a valuable, yet largely untapped, resource. Where they have been invited into schools to inform staff about their own child's needs, this has been greatly appreciated. For example, one parent and her disabled child rewrote her Individualised Educational Plan, replacing the bland descriptions with details of her interests, desires and the kind of support which was most useful to the child. This parent has also visited the school and advised the staff on various aspects of teaching. Parents could also play a significant role within teacher education, recounting their experiences of inclusion or exclusion and of engaging with a system which does not always treat parents with respect. Parents evenings can be enormously instructive for student teachers by enabling them to watch how experienced teachers manage this process. Where student teachers have followed a parent as he or she talks to different teachers, this has been especially enlightening.

REPAIRING THE PROFESSION, PREPARING OURSELVES

Foucault's framework of ethics could be used by teacher educators to try to interrupt the machinary of special education and create more inclusive practices. Determining the ethical substance, or the part the self to be worked upon, might be undertaken by looking at disabled writers' account of the 'damage' done by the practices of special education (Barnes, 1996; Oliver, 1992, 1999) and analysing the extent to which these practices exist within the teacher education programme. Brantlinger (2004b) makes it clear that teacher educators must identify the damage they do in their own practices:

> We educators are entangled in complex and sometimes disturbing practices
> that may not benefit those we claim to serve. I ask not only that we think hard
> about practices that harm but also that we turn to a morality of social reci-
> procity and distributive justice, in which the school and life circumstances of
> the most vulnerable are considered first (p. 497).

Linton (1998) also urges that the limitations of the knowledge that teacher educators impart to students, caused by failing to take account of disabled people's perspectives, be addressed:

> New scholars of all stripes must recognize their moral and intellectual obligation to evaluate gaps and faults in the knowledge base they disseminate to students that result from the missing voices of disabled people (p. 142).

Identifying the mode of subjection might involve considering questions of ideology in inclusion and unpacking the rules and discursive regimes which govern conduct within institutions. Self practice or ethical work could be directed at teaching, looking for ways of exemplifying inclusiveness in the relationships with student teachers and contributing to debates about inclusive education. As Ballard (2003a) urges, however, it is also necessary to challenge discrimination and exclusion within our own establishments:

> Who is represented on our staff; who gets appointed (and who does not); and how we may actively recruit and support people in minority backgrounds. How might we change our educational environment to make it appropriate and safe for a diversity of staff. We should also strive to build a climate of trust (Malin, 1999) in which issues of social justice and injustice may be addressed by students and staff (p. 73).

Finally, the telos, the overall goal, could be considered by those involved in 'delivering' teacher education, asking 'what do we want to achieve and why'? Alternatively, teacher educators might start with the telos and work backwards.

This kind of ethical work could also be undertaken by student teachers by, first of all, identifying the part of themselves as teachers which they wished to work on (determining the ethical substance). The second ethical dimension, the mode of subjection, could come from examining the rules which operate within schools or within the HEI and which create barriers to inclusion. Self practice or ethical work, the third dimension, could be directed towards their professional conduct and attempts to be inclusive. This might necessitate identifying the way in which their own teaching practices and actions, carried out *in the best interests* of children, creates barriers to inclusion and modifying these. Finally, students could be invited to work out the overall goal, the telos, and they may need guidance on this from children and young people and their families. They could be asked to articulate the purpose of inclusion, that is what it should do for them, and how we might recognise good, rather than effective, inclusion when we saw it. The ethical project of inclusion is one which we undertake and practise upon ourselves, but on which we can seek advice from those who hold the greatest expertise and who are likely to know what their own best interests are.

Foucault's framework of ethics could provide a structure for staff development, helping teachers to attend to the work they wish to do on themselves in order to be more inclusive. Staff development for practising teachers, instead of being a content driven attempt to skill them up in response to the latest government imperative, could provide a smooth space for teachers to pause, think and repair some of the damage they feel has been done to them. Inclusion starts with ourselves (Ballard, 2003b) and with a 'suspicion of ourselves' (MacIntyre, 1999, p. 4) and requires that we all work to remove the barriers to inclusion in our own practice, but it is important also to take account of exclusionary aspects of the contexts in which we work and of the things that cause concern. Teachers might be given an opportunity within staff development sessions to examine the way in which the system they work in creates exclusionary pressures for them. They could do some of this work collectively and come to recognise the struggle for inclusion as something which is constant, shared and, as my enlightened student pointed out, is necessarily inconclusive. Determining the ethical substance, the part of teachers' selves and their schools to be worked on, could be done as a group activity, perhaps starting in confessional mode in which participants revealed some aspect of their practice which had led to exclusion. The mode of subjection could be identified by examining their own school context and their experiences of exclusion and regulation. Teachers' self practice or ethical work could be focused on making their classroom practice more inclusive but also on trying to tackle some of the barriers they themselves encounter. Finally they could be encouraged to think about the overall goal, the telos, for both inclusion and for themselves as teachers. Again, children and young people and their families could offer guidance on inclusion. Other teachers could share in the process of enunciating personal teaching goals in the wider context of discussions about teacher professionalism.

COLLABORATION AND COLLUSION

Despite the abundance of calls to undertake collaboration and joined up working (Makareth and Turner, 2002; Milne, 2005), we know very little about how this should be 'done' and are even less clear about how it is experienced by children and young people and by their parents. The language used in policy – joined up working, the 'whole' child and initiatives being rolled out – the last of which, as Daniels (2005) suggests conjures up notions of laying carpets and ensuring all the bumps are ironed out, privileges consensus and creates closure. The agreement reached following the McCrone Report, *Teaching for the 21st Century* (Scottish Executive, 2001b) for example, talks of clarity, commitment, harmonisation, all of which seeks to erode differences between practitioners. Collaboration among teachers and with other professionals is a complex knot of relationships which has to be learned and worked at. It cannot be assumed that by issuing an enjoinder to collaborate, and by placing people together, that the outcomes will be positive. Research by Forbes (2003) illustrates how teachers and speech therapists, espousing the value of, and 'doing', collaboration, frequently talked past one another and maintained their own work practice boundaries. In research on the New Community Schools initiative (Remedios and Allan, 2004), professionals from education, health and social work described a prolonged period of fighting for resources for their own service or school, before they learned to make decisions collectively which would achieve the goals of, among other things, inclusion.

Pre-service training is an obvious place to initiate professionals into collaborative working across boundaries, by providing spaces, for example, for teachers, health professionals and social workers to learn and engage together. CPD could enable this mutual learning and engagement to continue, with support for collaborative practices; whilst some CPD does this at present, it could be more explicitly focused on the development of inter-disciplinary working practices and joint projects. It is essential also that evidence of what 'good', rather than effective, collaborative practice looks like is documented and used to inform training and professional development. This involves finding out from the people who experience inclusion or exclusion what it means to them.

Collaboration, as well as possibly improving practice, may offer teachers support in the form of rhizomic inter-dependency and this could be particularly valuable in relation to behavioural problems. If these were addressed collectively, with an expectation that they are too difficult to be managed by any one teacher, there might be less of a sense that including troublesome pupils is an impossibility. The networks formed by teachers with colleagues and with other professionals could provide new smooth spaces for engagement and much needed solidarity to subvert the structures and regimes which control them and create barriers to inclusion – their own and that of students in their class. This kind of collective transgression does not imply major revolt against the system, but finding creative ways of resisting pressures to do things in a certain way, making what Honan (2004) calls 'agentic choices' (p. 278) and making the language used within their own school contexts stammer. The 'crisis' in inclusion, with teachers expressing serious doubts about whether it can ever be achieved, could be addressed through collaborative action research projects, in which teachers and other professionals investigate what has made inclusion such an impossibility and find ways of removing barriers and new ways of connecting with each other. Ainscow and Tweddle (2003) have facilitated a process of 'collaborative inquiry' (p. 167) in which the practitioners and academics work together to identify solutions to problems in practice. They argue that this has succeeded in closing the gap between research and practice and has created a shared understanding of inclusion. Teacher stress might be a chasm to be investigated and ameliorated through creative subtraction, asking what could be removed from teachers working lives in order to remove or reduce stress. This 'condition', instead of being a malady which reduces the capacity of the profession, could become the material for collaboration because its mammoth proportions and spread across the professions requires a collective response.

Change in the conditions within schools, as Roy (2003) reminds us, is unlikely to be achieved through 'grand plans' (p. 147), but through 'combat' (p. 147), 'looking out for microfissures through which life leaks: 'Imperceptible rupture, not signifying breaks,' (Deleuze and Guattari, 1987, p. 24) create new possibilities 'as stammerings, murmurs, decodings, and disorientations' (Roy, 2003, p.147). In other words, teachers and other professionals may find ways forward in those moments of undecidability when a new thought or a new kind of experiment emerges. These are unlikely to be new in the sense of never having been seen before, but 'uncanny . . . a thing known returning in a different form . . . a revenant' (Banville, 2005, p. 10).

RECOGNITION, RUPTURE AND REPAIR?

The pressures on teachers has eroded their souls and turned their role into that of a 'producer' (Ballard, 2004, p. 8), who must struggle to retain their own humanity and dignity. Not surprisingly, this has made some teachers unsympathetic to inclusion, particularly of certain 'types' of students. Student teachers have apprehended some of these sentiments and have generated their own wariness about inclusion and a fear of particular children. I have suggested a number of ruptures in conventional approaches to teacher education which could help student teachers to see inclusion as a much more complex and aporetic practice – a puzzle – and to recognise their own development as teachers as full of double contradictory imperatives, many of which produce exclusion. I have also identified possibilities for existing teachers to use staff development and collaborative practice to repair their fractured professionalism and their damaged selves. There is, however, a limit to what teachers can be asked to do and they need to feel that they belong to an education system that recognises their valuable contribution to the lives of children and young people and the pressures they face. If this can be achieved, they may feel more able to participate in the struggle for inclusion. This struggle is a highly political one and the politics of inclusion are considered in the final chapter. The next chapter examines the inclusive potential of the arts.

9.   PERFORMING INCLUSION: INSTRUCTIVE ARTS EXPERIENCES

> We are in a tenor of relaxation – I am speaking of the tenor of the times. Everywhere we are being urged to give up experimentation, in the arts and elsewhere
>
> (Lyotard, 1993, p. 1).

Susan Sontag, the US writer and thinker approached Bosnia and offered her services in anything that might be useful – teaching, office work, as a paramedic or directing a play. The Bosnians indicated that they needed to restore their dignity and asked her to direct a play. They saw the arts as having an important role in relation to Bosnian humanity and it is easy to imagine the contribution Sontag would make in this regard. More generally, the arts have come to be seen as a vehicle for social inclusion, and even, as the UK culture, media and sport minister, Tessa Jowell (2002), contended, a way of preventing crime. This chapter examines the emergence of the idea of the arts as a means of promoting social inclusion and considers the basis on which claims are made about the efficacy of the arts. It then goes on to explore how the arts have, in some cases, become misused and have, once again, been recruited into the play of pathologies, as a form of medicine, targeted at disabled, and other so called vulnerable, people. Inevitably, this has led to the repetition of exclusion for the targeted individuals. There is, however, a more political strand of arts activity, disability arts, which can work upon the mainstream to good effect. This genre is deliberately transgressive, sets out to expose and transform exclusionary attitudes and practices and puts itself in the face of able-bodied people, confronting them with their own banality and prejudice. The political nature and impact of disability arts is examined and its inclusive potential is considered. The opportunities for embodied and rhizomic learning which the arts could offer to children and young people, and their potential contribution to inclusion and social justice, are also explored.

SOCIAL INCLUSION: WHY THE ARTS?

The arts have long been proclaimed as having life enhancing properties, from being a food substitute, according to William Shakespeare, and of having great capacities, as Robert Browning contended, to speak the truth. For Deleuze and Guattari (1987),

131

the arts have an important disruptive role in cutting through people's defences, even though the effect may be temporary:

> People are constantly putting up an umbrella that shelters them and on the underside of which they draw a firmament and write their conventions and opinions. But poets, artists, make a slit in the umbrella, they tear open the fimament itself, to let in a bit of free and windy chaos, and to frame in a sudden light a vision that appears through the vent – Wordsworth's spring or Cezanne's apple, the silhouettes of Macbeth or Ahab. Then come the crowd of imitators who repair the umbrella with something vaguely resembling the vision, and a crowd of commentators who patch over the vent with opinions (pp. 203–204).

The essences of particular art forms are such that they escape conventional structures and forms. Music, for example, is seen as prophetic (Attali, 1985), able to explore possibilities much faster than other forms of enquiry, and 'a little bit subversive' (Said, as cited by Barenboim, 2006). Its open structure both permeates and is permeated by the world and is machinic and rhythmical rather than mechanical and mathematical. Music, for Deleuze (1981):

> Deeply traverses our bodies and puts an ear in our belly, in our lungs etc . . . it rids bodies of their inertia, of the materiality of their presence. It *disincarnates* bodies . . . it gives the most mental entities a disincarnated, dematerialized body (p. 38).

This provides greater scope for connectivity with individuals and for more embodied experiences. Visual art also requires such connectivity and embodied engagement from individuals in order to produce. The artist Paul Klee (1961) describes the period just before art is made as a 'nowhere existent something' or 'a somewhere existent nothing' (p. 4), which, once established by the artist, leaps into a new order. In Cezanne's account of making art, he depicts an assemblage of himself and the world to be painted and from which there needs to be some emergence:

> At this moment I am one with my canvas. We are an iridescent chaos. I come before my motif, I lose myself there . . . We germinate (Doran, 1976 p. 150).

Dance, the most obviously embodied form, requires individuals to form new relationships with space and with other dancers, which may lead to the formation of new identities. The moving image, according to film director Anthony Minghella (2004), helps to interrupt and punctuate the drone of the voice. Each of these art forms has particular dimensions which make them more or less engaging for different people as participants and as spectators and generalising these as the 'arts', as Deleuze and Guattari (1987) point out, is inappropriate. Nevertheless, the arts can collectively be seen to take people into new and different places and to effect the kind of deterritorialization which Deleuze and Guattari depicted. There is also a common problem, as Deleuze (1981) notes, of harnessing forces for producing arts and this is caused, in part, by the very exclusionary and elitist nature of the arts themselves. In music, for example, McLary (1985) notes how everyone, both the non-trained listeners and the trained musicians, are prevented from speaking about it:

> It is quite clear to most listeners that music moves them, that they respond deeply to music in a variety of ways, even though in our society they are told that they cannot know anything about music without having absorbed the whole theoretical apparatus necessary for music specialization. But to learn this apparatus is to learn to renounce one's responses, to discover that the musical phenomenon is to be understood mechanistically, mathematically. Thus, non-trained listeners are prevented from talking about social expressive dimensions of music (for they lack the vocabulary to refer to its parts) and so are trained musicians (for they have been taught, in learning the proper vocabulary, that music is strictly self contained structure) (p. 150).

There is something deeply paradoxical about attempting to use something as exclusionary and elitist as the arts as a vehicle for social inclusion, but this is precisely what we are seeing across the globe. In England, a Policy Action Team, PAT10 has been established to move forward thinking and practice on social exclusion, through connecting arts practice in schools with artists and arts organisations. The British Council, having previously focused on Latin America, is now working in Central and Eastern Europe and attempting to make expertise in the 'creative industries', largely from the UK, available to these countries 'as an economic driver but also as a tool for tackling issues such as social inclusion, empowerment and regeneration (British Council, n.d). The role of the arts in education more generally is being promoted and the MP, Tessa Blackstone, for example, writing in the forward to *All Our Futures: Creativity, Culture and Education* (NACCCE, 1999), proclaimed that the arts had a crucial place in education. Anthony Minghella (2004), whose plea for teachers to confound children and young people has already been mentioned, also attests to the practical value of the arts in making children better learners – and indeed better citizens – if they are able to decode the torrent of visual images they encounter. The establishment of cultural co-ordinators and creative links officers within local authorities is intended to ensure the arts are given a more central place within the curriculum and that all children benefit. At the same time, however, the withdrawal of funding for free music tuition ensures that many children are excluded from learning to play an instrument.

There is not, as yet, firm evidence that experiencing the arts can lead to greater social inclusion; this is partly because of the lack of systematic evaluation, but mostly because of the slipperiness of the concept of social inclusion itself (Galloway, 1995). Nevertheless, some individuals have claimed that they have proof that participation in the arts has positive effects on self esteem, social cohesion, wellbeing and social inclusion. An international study by Matarasso (1997), for example, found benefits to individuals and communities in the form of an increase in confidence, creative skills and human growth as well as in their social lives through friendships, involvement in the community and enjoyment. Matarasso claimed particular benefits could be experienced by minority and marginalised groups and there has recently been a great deal of attention to the role of the arts in relation to those with experience of displacement (Garret, n.d). Children have been considered to derive many advantages through arts participation, with outcomes reported which include improved learning and behaviour, better relationships with parents, peers and adults, improved psychological wellbeing and improved communication skills (Kinder et al, 2000; Kendall et al, 2003). Harland et al (2000) found similar impacts on children and saw these as significant in tackling disaffection and social exclusion amongst young people. According to Comedia (Matassaro, 1987), teachers reported improvements in children's language and physical co-ordination, as well as in creativity and imagination, after participation in arts activities. Social capital, the networks, trust and forms of reciprocity that exist among groups, has also been considered to be enhanced by culture in general and by participation in specific cultural activities (Gould, 1997). Whilst such 'outcomes' have been recognised as desirable, there has also been scepticism about the quality of the evidence and the subjective indicators on which they are based (Fisher, 2002; Kinder and Harland, 2004). There has also been some questioning about whether such instrumental uses of the arts as a social inclusion tool are appropriate. The Cultural Policy Collective (2004), for example, identifies what it sees as a cynical manipulation of culture or a 'governing by culture' by New Labour whilst McEvoy (n.d) contends that such a reliance on the arts as a means of addressing social problems is inherently misplaced:

> The arts are not a cure-all for the latest social crisis – an answer to a problem.
> They are, rather, an entitlement and opportunity for individuals and communities
> to have a positive voice in a democratic society.

Furedi (2004) sees this functional use of the arts for massaging individuals' self esteem and building community as part of a more widespread phillististinism in which knowledge and ideas are viewed with suspicion and culture is spoon fed to individuals in palatable ways. This is, he contends, deeply patronising. In spite of these warnings and criticisms, the arts have come to be seen as an answer, albeit a partial one, to the 'problem' of social exclusion.

THE ARTS ARE (GOOD) FOR YOU

The targeting of minority, marginalised or vulnerable individuals and groups as potential recipients of the arts has become big business and, as Tranter and Palin (2004) observe, an art in itself. There has been a flurry of arts projects which have social inclusion as a central strand (Arts Council of England, 1999) and this is not unrelated to the tying of local authority and Arts Council funding to projects which can demonstrate this link and produce social inclusion 'outcomes' for target groups. For example, in the recent round of Scottish Council Grants for Social Inclusion Partnerships, totalling almost half a million pounds, projects were directed at young people, 'excluded members of the community,' 'people normally excluded from arts participation' or 'cross-generational concerns' (Scottish Arts Council, 2003). Whilst there may well be considerable benefits from concentrating efforts (and, of course, finite resources) this targeting approach, once again, creates a repetition of exclusion. It foregrounds, pathologises and isolates individuals and groups as *in need* and constructs arts as a kind of medicine which will do them some good. One example of an organization adopting this medicinal approach is *Project Ability*. This Scottish organisation has attempted to promote 'equality of access to the arts by supporting people of all ages and abilities to take part in innovative visual arts projects' (Video strategy leaflet, undated). The organization was initially concerned with disabled and adults, but shifted its focus more recently onto children with learning disabilities. It has been helping children and adults to make film and considers this to have been particularly successful for children with autism and Aspergers syndrome:

> through this process, they have created a film that undoubtedly improves a child's audiovisual literacy, they have learnt to plan and work as a group and have improved their organisational skills.

These outcomes are placed alongside what is seen as a deeply pleasurable sense of achievement for the young people who are involved: 'It can only be imagined the amount of pleasure a young person experiences showing this film to family and friends' (ibid).

Escape Artists also adopt a medicinal approach, offering a 'signposted route for clients enabling them to move from the margins to the mainstream' (Escape artists, n.d.). Their 'clients' are prisoners, young people, those 'at risk', the homeless, ex-offenders and mental health service users' and they are taken on 'a journey across the Bridge' and into the culture industries – the mainstream – collecting a 'stronger sense of pride and achievement' on the way. If necessary, individuals can be offered a 'bespoke programme,' tailored to their own needs and one-to-one tuition. In order to go on this bridge crossing, clients have to qualify by 'showing commitment to pursuing personal development through the arts' and would presumably be excluded if they failed to do this. The team of Escape Artists accompany the clients on their 'first step onto The Bridge' and offer them 'a taste' of the freedom which could lie ahead. There is no reflexivity about the language of escape and the Artists come across as valiant rescuers, promising to take people across to a safer and better place. Edward Said, speaking to an Edinburgh University audience, warned against attempts to provide bridges for learners. He argued that bridges which provided safe passage denied learners the exposure to the kind of risks which would enable them to prosper.

Without wanting to begrudge any pleasures to be had through the experiences of making art of whatever kind, it is, nevertheless, important to question the inclusive value of these kinds of activities. The process of targeting pathologises and fixes those who are to receive arts experiences and there is no attempt in the projects themselves to help youngsters to connect with others, apart from through the films they create; there is also no attempt to challenge exclusion or disabling barriers. Such activities may, therefore, do more to promote exclusion, by entrenching already marginalised identities and by leaving the status quo intact. There is, however, an altogether different kind of arts activity, initiated by disabled people, and which provides a formidable challenge to exclusion. It is to this that I now turn.

DISABILITY ARTS: UNDOING EXCLUSION

Disability arts represents a particularly creative and innovative example of Foucauldian transgression. It takes the form of both a celebration of difference and of disability, but it also works upon able-bodied people's perceptions of normality and unravels these, creating dissonance and doubt. It represents a radical shift from conventional depictions of disabled people in the arts which are negative and which perpetuate ill-formed stereotypes and reinforce prejudice (Thurber, 1980; Longmore, 1997; Mitchell and Snyder, 2001). Disabled artists provide a unique take on the body which is not available to able-bodied people:

> Disabled artists have sought to remind us that one of the primary ways that bodies come to consciousness of themselves is in the midst of breakdown, loss and limitation. They call attention to our bodies as active mediators of our interactions with self and other (Susan Nussbaum, Snyder and Mitchell, n.d.(a)).

The art produced by disabled people is particularly introspective and engages the viewer in ways that are powerful:

> While the able body is often defined by the need to enhance an otherwise dulled network of sensations, the disabled body finds itself drawing an undue amount of attention to itself. For disabled artists, the socially abhorrent body is forced to engage in an exchange. First the disabled body offers itself for consumption by audiences alienated from their own bodies. And then the artist turns that spectacle into a rearticulation of disability as a source of insight and power (Nussbaum, Snyder and Mitchell, n.d.(a)).

There is a playfulness and cheekiness about disability arts, which seeks to disrupt the commonplace and the taken-for-granted in both the art form and in everyday life. Disabled artists, involved in a range of activities including music, visual art, photography, dance, film and stand-up comedy, have used their own bodies as material, or as weapons, to undermine and subvert disabling barriers. Some of the art work portrays disabled people themselves as emboldened or empowered, while other work depicts the disabling environment in which disabled people have to live. Nussbaum contends that as a result of such work, much of it generated collectively, for example through the Chicago Coalition of Disabled Artists to which she belongs, 'the 'deviant' body radically transforms its cultural assignment as a dustbin for disavowal' (ibid). Consequently, she observes disability culture emerges alongside other powerful cultural movements, for example those involving ethnic minorities, 'in the brew of conflict and dissent' (ibid).

I have suggested elsewhere (Allan, 2005d) that much of disability arts can be read as a kind of kynicism, an ancient Greek term used by the German writer Sloterdijk (1987) to describe a form of solemn mockery which is also outrageous, 'pissing against the idealist wind' (p. 103), to achieve its disruptive goals:

> Ancient kynicism begins the process of *naked arguments* from the opposition, carried by the power that comes from below. The kynic farts, shits, pisses,

masturbates on the street, before the eyes of the Athenian market. He shows
contempt for fame, ridicules the architecture, refuses respect, parodies the stories of gods and heroes (p. 103).

Kynicism attacks the piety of seriousness through the 'physiologically irresistible
energy of laughter' (Sloterdijk, 1987, p. 110). The practitioners of disability arts
confront non-disabled people with their own banality and force them to look at themselves and the way they disable and exclude through their attitudes and behaviour
and through the structures and practices they participate in. They are made to experience the comedy and irony of these and are taken to the 'horror of the comic'
(Kundera, 1986, p. 104), where they are inside the 'guts of a joke' (ibid) and are
forced to think again about how they relate to – and exclude – disabled people.

There are many powerful examples of work within this genre and it is difficult
to do justice to them here, but some selections will, I hope, create an appetite for
further exploration. Cheryl Marie Wade, who, in her poem *I'm not one of the*
reverses beauty and ugliness, portrays herself as both a sexual object – with lace
panties – and as deformed – with a stub, and demands a presence which has hitherto been denied (Davis, 1997). In *Crip Pride,* Jessie Aaron presents herself and
her 'family' of disabled people as subjects with sexualities. She offers solidarity
and difference as a response to the rejection she and others have experienced. Both
writers assert their sexual and gendered identities in playful ways which challenge
the desexing discourses of disability (Davis, 1997). The transgression of the disabled artists, therefore, has an impact on their own identities and how they portray
these, but more importantly on those who read the poems and are forced to examine their own normalising and disabling knowledge and actions. When I have
introduced these poems to teachers, I have either read them aloud or asked a member of the group to do so. The inventiveness of the poems and the images they
create never fail to produce stutterings and a recognition of individuals own culpability in exclusion.

The *Nasty Girls* are a comedy act which formed when 'some frutstrated, bitter and
cynical Disabled/Deaf women got together to take the piss out of anything that
annoyed them' (Nasty Girls, n.d). Their material is derived from their observations of
the disabling environment they inhabit and they deliberately set out to challenge
mainstream perceptions of disabled people. They acknowledge that this makes for an
uncomfortable experience for mainstream audiences:

> A big part of our humour is playing with language and a lot of the material
> that we use is worldplay . . . but it's also about pushing the boundaries of how
> we do talk about ourselves as disabled people as well and I think some audi-
> ences can feel either very nervous around that or feel quite precious around it
> and we blow that whole thing apart really (Nasty Girls, n.d.).

They tackle some of the big issues, including euthanasia: 'So you think it's all over'
with an acerbic wit and a 'twisted view of life' (Nasty Girls). Their show includes
'A cripple's ABC' and has provoked one member of their audience to say 'that was
disgusting! This has been the worst night of my life'; (Nasty Girls, n.d.). This is

RETHINKING INCLUSIVE EDUCATION

something which they were extremely proud of: 'I mean the fact that we could actually give someone the worst, the very worst, night of their lives I think is quite an achievement' (Nasty Girls, n.d).

Artist Riva Lehrer, referred to as 'the court painter of the disability kingdom' (Siebers, Snyder & Mitchell, n.d.(b)) describes herself as being 'a monster for my people' (ibid), seeking to treat disabilities as a journey for both the disabled subject and the viewer. In her series *Circle Stories,* she has painted disabled people, many of whom are performance artists, for example Hollis Zigler, Tekki Lommicki and Bill Shannon, in backgrounds which help to convey their lives as less 'flat' (Riva Lehrer, Snyder & Mitchell, n.d.(b)) than is allowed by conventional disability iconography, with its emphasis on the 'grotesque, the sentimental and the inspirational' (Garland Thomson, Snyder & Mitchell, n.d.(b)). She often introduces Greek and biblical mythology to the sitters' backgrounds and has the sitters themselves staring directly at the viewer, apparently at ease with the chaos and complexity which surrounds them and often with sensuality. As Mitchell and Snyder (2004) note, she does not go for the shock value as other artists do, but instead 'renews our commitment to the cultivation of respect and tenderness towards embodied variation' (p. 35).

Lehrer's art creates the unusual for the viewer and in so doing generates concern and surprise. For the disabled subjects she paints, she generates a form of self preservation:

> She's helping us to solidify and build disability culture and that's helping preserve us. She shows us the commonality of our lives, of our struggles and shows us a way forward (Mark Sherry, Snyder & Mitchell, n.d.(b)).

Lehrer also, according to Eli Clare, 'sees beauty in places that not many people have seen beauty before' (Mitchell & Snyder, n.d.). One of her subjects, Tekki Lommicki, finds the portrayal of her as both realistic and surprising. Lehrer's depiction of her reinvention of herself as a performance artist had close parallels with her life as a disabled person; being painted in her underwear, with smiles and with sensuality, was unusual, since, as she pointed out, as a little person she was more used to being photographed in such a state of undress in a clinical way. She delighted in such a portrayal: 'I especially loved that Riva gave me cleavage in it'. Another subject, Eli Clare, indicated that Lehrer had captured her sexual ambiguity, having just gone through a transgender transformation, and her composure, perfectly:

> I've lived a very wilful life and I think a lot of disabled people have lived very wilful lives in terms of having to insert ourselves into various places in the world that would easily deny us access (Snyder & Mitchell, n.d.(b)).

Her own self portrait is extremely provocative and consists of only her head and her feet. These are, she says, the parts of her body which people always stare at, 'trying to assess what it is about this woman that is different, what anatomically is not computing to their sense of the norm' (Yood, 2004, pp. 27–28). The inscription of the Hebrew word Emmet, on the head of her face, with its determined expression and a just discernible smile, plays with truth and death and produces an ambiguity which catches the viewer.

The greater inclusive potential of disability arts, compared with the medicinal variety of arts activities, comes from the inherently political intent of the artists and their mission to work on the mainstream. Disability arts could be could be used within schools with children and young people as a means of challenging the conventional and stereotypical depictions of disabled people in the arts and could encourage greater literacy and a capacity to read how difference is constructed. Disability arts could also be used within teacher education and continuing professional development to help beginning and practising teachers to orient themselves to inclusion as a political task.

US scholar Linda Ware has introduced disability arts in both regular classrooms and with teachers. With teachers, she has used literature, film, audio sources and poetry to then invite teachers' own reflections on their own attitudes, beliefs and assumptions about disability. She reports that the provocative nature of the work 'all but insured a collision with the studied story of disability – education's reductionist stance towards disability' Ware (2003b, p. 128). The teachers she worked with experienced the 'confusion, contradiction, and complexity' (ibid, p. 180) as deeply unsettling, but this gradually gave way to frustration that their curriculum was devoid of knowledge of disability and 'a slow invasion of previously unquestioned assumptions about professional claims to authority' (ibid, p. 131). The teachers' mission of 'working past pity' (ibid, p. 117) was recognised by them as likely to be thwarted by the pressures within the system and the way in which disability was constructed within it. As one of the teachers joked, 'there's no box to check on the IEP for the development of disability cultural pride' (p. 129). Nevertheless, the shifts in thinking and practice were experienced by the teachers as profound. Ware expresses concern that current policy does not encompass a humanities perspective on disability, 'where complexity is a given rather than a threat' (ibid), but her successes in both classroom and teacher education contexts illustrate the capacity of this kind of work to '*disrupt* education in general and special education, in particular' (ibid, p. 121; original emphasis). The need for such disruption was made evident in the earlier chapters and underlines the political nature of inclusion.

DOING ARTS, DOING INCLUSION

Art work undertaken by children and young people could be work of experimentation, providing dynamic play and allowing them to create, what Braidotti calls 'fabulations' (Braidotti, as cited in Gough, 2004, p. 256) Work of this kind is:

> A fiction that offers us a world clearly and radically discontinuous from the
> one we know, yet returns to confront that known world in some cognitive way.

Involving children in arts activities opens them to experiences as yet unknown to them and their teachers; this is merely an extension of what children do naturally and ordinarily:

> Children never stop talking about what they are doing or trying to do:
> exploring milieus, by means of dynamic trajectories, and drawing up maps

of them . . . In its own way, art says what children say. It is made up of trajectories and becomings, and it too makes maps, both extensive and intensive (Deleuze, 1998, pp. 61–66).

Prior to mass literacy, people were visually competent and constructed maps as a necessity for living. I have argued that school learning has closed down opportunities to construct maps of these kinds, but the arts, with their newly legitimised place in the curriculum, makes such activities possible. Children and young people can be helped to understand, and become readers of, the wide and diverse tapestry that is their lives through engagement with the arts. Anthony Minghella (2004) has underlined the importance of students being helped to construct three narratives. The first of these is a conscious narrative, or what we think we're doing; the second is a secret narrative, what I know about how I'm doing; and the third is the unconscious narrative, what I don't know I'm doing. School concentrates only on the first of these, but the second and third narratives are a form of literacy which may open students' awareness to the world around them.

Attempts to expose students to arts experiences have been revelatory and have pro-voked optimism that they indeed have an inclusive potential, not in the medicinal sense, but in their capacity to work on the mainstream. As part of a research and development project, funded by the Scottish Arts Council (Lynch and Allan, 2006), a one day workshop, *Art Lab,* was set up by Heather Lynch, the development officer on the project and herself a practising visual artist. Artists from music, theatre, dance, film animation, visual art and circus were brought together to offer sessions and children and young people from a range of schools were invited to select from these. The teachers who accompanied the children and young people were encouraged to take part in whatever activities interested them. Moving and still film images were taken throughout the day, the students were talked to informally as they participated and follow up focus group discussions were held some weeks after the event. To encourage the students to express themselves, Heather had asked them to draw their ideal teacher and ideal pupil during the *Art Lab* day and when she conducted the focus groups she invited them to make a piece of art which captured their sense of the day and its impact on them. She also handed the youngsters the camera and encouraged them to 'interview' each other on the subject of good teaching and learning. The experiences provided in *Art Lab* were distinctive, in that they involved the children in embodied and rhizomic learning, and appeared to be conducive to inclusion, in that all were expected to participate, regardless of ability. Furthermore, in the theatre workshop, one of the actors engaged the youngsters in activities involving his own wheelchair in a way which was inventive and, in their words, 'cool'.

The students' experiences were embodied in the most obvious sense: 'you get to do stuff', which for them contrasted starkly with the passivity of their usual school routine. According to one group of children, 'doing stuff' was more effective because 'you think more'. The activities were deliberately presented to the students as embodied. The musician Matt (who, as will be discussed later, turned out to match many children's notion of the ideal teacher) surrounded the children with percussion instruments and told them 'You don't need a drum to make good rhythm – you've got lots of bodily surfaces' and encouraged them to explore these. He also distinguished what they were doing at *Art Lab* from their school lessons: 'This is a drumming class. And, let's face it, it's not maths. It's not chemistry. It's certainly not physics. Enjoy yourself'. The other workshops involved the students almost immediately in action, sometimes in things they had never done before, such as spinning a plate, or making a piece of animation, and sometimes in things that were familiar, such as drawing, but which was led by two adults with learning difficulties. The focus of the dance workshop was science, but not as the students normally experienced it. Here, they were required to create patterns and connections with others which simulated attraction and repulsion. So, this was physics, but on the move.

The theatre workshop was the most innovative and provocative to observe and seemed to have the greatest lasting impact on those who had participated in it. The session involved a series of activities in which the students were called upon to be inventive, using their own bodily resources – voice, expression, gesture, posture and movement. In one episode, they were asked to insert punctuation, of their own choice, into a continuous passage read by one of leaders. They came up with a short sigh for a comma, a long one for a full stop, 'ping' for a question mark and slap on the floor with both hands for an exclamation mark. In another piece, they had to find different ways to say 'I don't want to be a skydiver', and in yet another, they each had to come up with a different – and loud – exclamation and many riotous variations were produced. In one particularly rhizomic activity, the group leader, Robert Softley, an actor with the company *Birds of Paradise,* came out of his wheelchair and turned it upside down on the floor. The students were then asked to compile words or phrases and accompanying actions around the wheelchair. They chose a range of actions either directly involving the wheelchair, for example spinning wheels, or gestures towards or away from it. The sounds they produced were both musical and machinic and came together in an impressive cacophany: 'Cool, wow, wah, check it out, just weird, that's dreadful'. Robert asked them to turn up both the speed and the volume, then to bring it down again. The youngsters' 'performance' seemed to represent the productive kind of repetition through which rhythmic difference is produced (Deleuze and Guattari (1987). This kind of repetition 'has nothing to do with a reproductive measure' (Deleuze and Guattari, 1987, p. 314), of the kind which produces exclusion. Rather, it is inventive, creative and powerful for spectator and participants alike.

The inclusive nature of the *Art Lab* experience was revealed in discussions after the event, in which the students expressed delight in their active participation and their achievements. One youngster proudly boasted: 'I learned how to juggle, spin plates, drum' while another described his experience of animation as 'awesome'. The participants in the drama expressed great satisfaction with what they had produced and pleasure at 'watching other people'. There was also an interestingly matter-of-fact engagement with the disabled actor and his wheelchair in their reflections. One of the participants, for example, referred to the actor, who 'could be quite funny' and who had 'that machine thing' and no mention was made of the visual artists' learning difficulties. The students appeared to have engaged with difference as interesting rather than problematic. There was some dispute over whether what they had experienced was 'work' or not:

> You didn't have to do work. You just got to do the fun stuff. It is work, but it is fun work.

The students highlighted the contrast between the teaching they had received from the artists and that which they normally endured in school. The artists made their activities more interesting and appealing than their teachers managed, albeit, they admitted, with more intrinsically interesting subjects than those they did in school; the artists also accorded the youngsters a level of respect. This was something they did not enjoy in school, because most teachers lacked a sense of humour and often shouted or, as one person commented, 'speak down to us'. For many of the children, Matt the musician was the living embodiment of their ideal teacher. Clearly his hat and 'cool' demeanour was part of his attraction, but his main strength, as far as the youngsters were concerned, was his ability to relate to them in a respectful way and to allow them to make such great noise.

PLAYING TOGETHER: AN ORCHESTRA OF THE OTHERS

> Who the song would understand. Needs must seek the song's own land'
> (Goethe, 1819).

Music has been the vehicle for attempting to forge connections within the Arab world in a profound experiment, initiated by the writer Edward Said and the conductor and musician Daniel Barenboim. Together they founded the West-Eastern Divan, whose name was derived from Goethe's (1819) series of poems. They brought together young musicians from Israel, Palestine Syria and Egypt and as well as playing in their respective homelands, they have toured the world, demonstrating the potency of combining expression and regard for the other. There are no illusions that an orchestral perfomance can solve the problems in this troubled part of the world, but Barenboim argues that the orchestra works strategically upon ignorance by creating a respectful openness to the other.

A group of young Scottish fiddlers also provides an illustration of the inclusive potential of playing music together. The inclusive nature of the group, led by Peter Cope, was initially a reaction against the territorialized space of classically-oriented instrument tuition, which he considered exclusive and exclusionary. The leader has tried to establish a smooth deterritorialized space for learning instead. There is a focus within the group on traditional music, selection is ruled out and the pupils are lent fiddles to ensure there are no financial barriers. Other barriers, such as requiring the youngsters to read music, are removed and the leader also nails the pegs of the fiddles to prevent them going out of tune, a practice which has provoked gasps of horror from music teachers when Cope has presented his findings at music education conferences. A participatory ethos has been achieved by establishing a strong social context, subverting the performance genre by dismissing competitions and formal performances, encouraging relaxed learning and ensuring success for all, including those identified as having special needs. Perhaps the most striking feature of the youngsters' engagement is that they control their own participation and will play a tune with the group if they can. This process was regarded as unproblematic, as one of the young fiddler described:

> If there's a tune [I don't know] I just sit down until there is a tune I do know . . .
> if I know a wee bit . . . I just pluck at the strings and get the right notes' (Allan
> and Cope, 2004, p. 33).

Enabling children and young people to take control of when and how they are included does not imply a removal of responsibility from adults, but requires that they learn from, and are able to respond to, the decisions that are made.

ACTING OUT INCLUSION

> The world is an egg, but the egg is itself a theatre: a staged theatre in which
> the roles dominate the actors, the spaces dominate the roles and the ideas
> dominate the spaces (Deleuze, 1994, p. 216).

The arts enable children and young people to experiment and experience and, as such, have considerable inclusive potential. Exposing children and young people to inclusive experiences may make them more open to how exclusion is produced, and to themselves as capable of challenging this. Staging creative work in their classrooms may, however, appear daunting to teachers. Before they can do this, they may, first of all, have to do some work upon themselves, letting go and allowing themselves to be playful and inventive. Two modules on creativity for teachers, artists and youth workers have been launched within Stirling University as a result of the Scottish Arts Council project on social inclusion and the arts. The participants are given the opportunity to explore creativity and learning using arts practice and theory. Individuals engage – bodily – as audience, participant and leader and are encouraged to improve their visual and sensual literacy and identify their creative selves. Although it is too soon to determine any significant impact of such an engagement, the participants' reports of their transformation and readiness to expose children and young people to similar experiences are interesting. Exposure to the arts as part of CPD enables teachers to investigate what truths fiction can add (Ballard, 2003a), but could also open their eyes to new possibilities.

10.   INCLUSIVE RESEARCH?

Indeed he knows not how to know who knows not also how to un-know

(Richard Francis Burton, as cited in Flyvbjerg, 2002, p. 166).

Research has an important role in seeking to understand the nature of the inclusion 'problem' and in producing knowledge about the possibilities for achieving inclusion in practice. The ideas of the philosophers of difference are again potentially of value in relation to framing pertinent questions for research; altering research relations; producing insightful and productive analyses; and communicating research findings and insights to those who need to know.

ASKING THE *RIGHT* QUESTIONS

Judgements about the efficacy of educational research are based on criteria which are inappropriate and, therefore, unjust and, according to Flyvbjerg (2001), this is the case for all social science research. He argues that it is compared to research within the natural science on the basis of its *episteme* (scientific knowledge) and *techne* (technical knowledge or know how). Judgements about social science research are based on its capacity to produce explanatory and predictive theory – on its epistemic qualities. This is, he says, simply not fair, since these terms are self defeating and whilst social science research has indeed contributed little to explanatory and predictive theory it has contributed a great deal to reflexive analysis and discussion of values and interests – as *phronesis*. Flyvbjerg contends that it is social science's *phronetic* qualities – its concern for values and power – that should be evaluated and this would seem to be a more appropriate basis for judging the quality of educational research:

> The goal is to help restore social science to its classical position as a practical, intellectual activity aimed at clarifying the problems, risks, and possibilities we face as humans and societies, and at contributing to social and political praxis (Flyvbjerg, 2001, p. 4).

Phronetic research, with its central interest in values and power, appears to be the most appropriate kind of research to be undertaken in relation to inclusion.

145

Questions about how power is exercised upon individuals and its effects and how inequalities are produced may be best framed, as Foucault recommends, as contingent, rather than causal questions – how, rather than why, things happen, who decides and in whose interests. A Foucauldian perspective invites a forensic attention to power and accepts that power is bound up with knowledge. It offers considerable scope for the researcher to identify questions about the power/knowledge processes which constrain and control individuals, but I have suggested that his framework of ethics allows for an investigation of more productive uses of power and the ways in which individuals transgress. Derrida's deconstruction also implies questions of contingency, but with a particular attention to discourse and the ways in which a text performs. Maclure's (2005b) more generic deconstructive ethos involves regarding constructs such as the 'child' as not neutral. The kinds of questions afforded by a Deleuzian perspective may involve active experimentation, with the research subjects, about what the research questions should be. It is difficult to envisage how a potential research funder or an academic committee would react to a proposal which had as its research questions, the intention to ask subjects to define these, although it could perhaps be justified as a more meaningful form of user engagement. The involvement of children and young people and their families in identifying the kinds of questions which need to be asked about inclusion and exclusion could be an important first step towards providing the kind of knowledge that will be of use.

Many scholars have asserted that research on inclusion has to be alert to politics. Barton (2004), for example has argued that now, more than ever, a political analysis is necessary in order to tackle 'discrimination, both subtle and overt, that are unacceptable barriers in the struggle for inclusivity' (p. 73), while Tomlinson (2005), speaking of race, reminds us that:

> Education systems and their special subsystems are not neutral elements. The decisions that assign black children to special education or otherwise exclude them from mainstream, and nonpolicies that fail to recognise the links between race and special forms of education are a product of the residual historical beliefs that shape the values of policy-makers, professionals, and practitioners (p. 84).

Schools are terminally dysfunctional institutions, as Keir Bloomer, a senior local government official in Scotland has suggested, and are negative and punitive spaces for many students. It is important that research asks questions about the nature and extent of schools as institutions and about how power is used on and against young people.

There have been many calls to make the ideology and values within research on inclusion explicit and warnings that it is dangerous not to do so (Brantlinger, 1997; Ballard, 2005; Slee, 2005, Sikes et al, 2003). Indeed Ballard (2004) names and claims his own slogan 'only ideology matters' (p. 90), in the hope that he can persuade us to 'identify, analyse, and evaluate the ethical and social implications of the ideologies that guide our research and our actions in policy and practice' (p. 90). Ballard and McDonald also proclaim the importance of working 'with the emotions of engagement necessary for collaborative research' (1999, p. 114), asserting that research, if it is to be inclusive, requires that the researchers care passionately to know people and things. In pursuing his goal of laying ideology bare, Ballard found himself gagged by the editor of a journal. A paper which was initially accepted for publication within the journal *SET: Research Information for Teachers* with the editor's comment 'no changes suggested and publication highly recommended' (Ballard, 2004, note to the reader) was subsequently subjected to censorship. Ballard was informed that the paper had 'struck an obstacle at the last moment . . . [with] a feeling that there is rather too much emphasis on the ideology component and so a concern that this could compromise the [New Zealand Council for Educational Research's] independence' (Ballard, 2004, note to the reader). He was advised to delete the sections in which ideology was discussed and faced with the option to do this or withdraw the paper, Ballard conceded the excisions and issued his own version, containing the censored material. In an attempt to make a contribution to the debate on ideology, Roger Slee and I have undertaken a project in which we are researching the researchers (Allan and Slee, forthcoming). We have interviewed key researchers and scholars and invited them to talk through the process of research connected with a particular piece of work; we have also attempted to explore issues of ideology, power and positions with them. So far, it has proved to be a challenging piece of work, but one which we hope will provoke others to scrutinise the ideological orientation of their own work.

The impasse which exists between the so-called inclusionists and the traditional special educationists may be intractable and there may be no way through this. Attempts to promote dialogue between representatives of each side have generally been met with contempt, and while the 'head-to-head' within *Exceptionality* (2006) is a notable exception, the venomous language used by Kauffman and Sasso, special educationists, to denounce postmodernism, apparently the position held by inclusionists, is hardly likely to promote dialogue. Postmodernism is rubbished as 'intellectually bankrupt' and 'poisonous' (Kauffman and Sasso, 2006a, p. 65), leaving us 'without a moral compass' (Kauffman and Sasso, 2006a, p. 86). These special educationists foretell 'catastrophic consequences . . . for educational practices' and pronounce that 'we cannot all just get along' (p. 69). Gallagher (2006), in response, agrees that consensus between both camps is probably never likely to be a possibility but holds out for 'calm, respectful, deeply informed and reasoned discussions' (p. 92). Maintaining that she is not a postmodernist, as accused, she suggests the elision of postmodernists, critical theorists and hermeneuticists into one group is sloppy. Kauffman and Sasso, in their rejoinder to Gallagher, accuse her of engaging in 'postmodern foppery . . . arguments for follies, absurdities and vanities' (2006b, p. 109), whilst insisting this is not personal. On the basis of this exchange, there seems little prospect of proper and reasoned debate and greater likelihood that the two camps will continue to talk *past* rather than *to* each another. What might be possible instead is investigation of the exclusions and inequalities created by both sides as they trade insults. This may help beginning researchers to gain a critical understanding of the debate and of the implications of their own positioning within it for their careers.

ALTERING RESEARCH RELATIONS

The minimal, and in some cases negative, impact of research on inclusion on its subjects has often been reflected in the research relations themselves and the way in which they operate within, and perpetuate, uneven power structures. Addressing these imbalances of power and ensuring that research practices themselves are inclusive is vital and requires a high level of sensitivity to issues of power. Research ethics protocols, concerned with ensuring that no harm is done to research subjects, do not require this level of sensitivity, but researchers need to interrogate the way in which their research positions their research subjects and to find ways of flattening the hierarchy between the researcher and the researched.

The question of whether non-disabled researchers should research disability and inclusion arose initially from the anger provoked by unreflexive research which was done on, rather than with, disabled groups and which was considered parasitic on disabled people (Branfield, 1998). Similar questions have been asked in respect of research involving minority ethnic and gay and lesbian groups and have led to calls to refuse participation in research without proper representation (Nelson, 1997; SABRE, 2001). However, Shakespeare (2005) also contends that that it is not people who disable and urges that 'the focus of our rage and our action should be the structures' (p. 32). Shakespeare (2006) also argues that the field of disability studies would not have developed to the status it currently enjoys without the work of non-disabled researchers such as Gary Albrecht and Len Barton as well as that of parents of disabled people such as Dora Bjarnason and Michael Berube. One of those to whom Shakespeare paid tribute, Len Barton, contends that able bodied researchers must exploit the significant power which they enjoy in the interests of disabled people and should ask themselves the following critical questions:

> What responsibilities arise from the privileges I have as a result of my social position? How can I use my knowledge and skills to challenge, for example, the forms of oppression disabled people experience? Does my writing and speaking reproduce a system of domination or challenge that system? (Barton and Clough, 1995, p. 144).

Goodley and Moore (2000) argue that non-disabled researchers can have an important role in faciliting the involvement of disabled people in political struggle, but acknowledge that there may be tensions for researchers trying to operate in such a way:

> Our position as researchers who wish to be disabled people's allies, but who are situated within a context which requires us to contribute to the building up of a respectable discipline, presents real difficulties. We may wish to advance understanding of disability politics, but we are obliged to also maintain a definite position in the academy (p. 875).

Oliver's (2002) alternative framework for research involves researchers handing over control of the process to those being researched. It also requires removing the artificial distinction between the researcher and the researched. He argues that research must not only capture faithfully the experiences of the group being researched but must make these research accounts available and acceptable to them. Furthermore, he recommends changing the research process from investigation to production:

> Research as production requires us to engage with the world, not distance our-selves from it for ultimately we are responsible for the product of our labours and as such we must struggle to produce a world in which we can all live as truly human beings. Thus the research act is not an attempt to change the world through the process of investigation but an attempt to change the world by producing ourselves and others in differing ways from those we have pro-duced before, intentionally or not (Oliver, 2002, p. 14).

Fundamentally, this involves addressing issues of power and ensuring that research is not itself exclusionary.

Moore et al (1998) have argued for the strengthening of alliances between dis-abled and non-disabled people within a framework which 'has critical reflection on human rights at its foundation' (p. 94). These alliances could take the form of consultation groups, which work on the design of the research and participate in discussions of the findings.

New alliances may be able to assist in overcoming the 'impasse' which UK dis-ability studies (Shakespeare, 2006) appears to have reached. This is characterised by intense disagreement among disabled scholars and activists, accusations of those defending the social model of being 'inward looking and sectarian' (Shakespeare, 2005, p. 1) and of those questioning it making 'superfluous' (Oliver, 2004, p. 24) criticisms of the model 'for not being something that it has never claimed to be' (p. 24) and of betraying the disability movement (Shakespeare, 2006). International alliances may enable some of the cultural imbalances to be ironed out and some of the particular strengths, such as the strong welfare orientation of Nordic research (Gustavsson et al, 2005) and positioning of disabled people as a minority group by researchers in the US and Canada (Albrecht, 1996; Rioux and Bach, 1994), to be pooled.

Involving children and young people, as researchers, in the co-production of knowledge could be an exciting alliance. Brownlie et al, (2006) found several exam-ples of children and young people doing research, including some long term projects involving Barnardos, the Children's Research Centre at the Open University and the appointment by the Scottish Commissioner for Children and Young People of two young participation workers with a research remit. In our research on children's rights, we did not engage they young people explicitly as researchers, but we observed their 'empirical wanderings' in which they literally took children's rights for a walk. The sophisticated level of their analysis of disabling barriers within their school convinced us of the value of working with young people in this way and of extending their involvement in research processes. The involvement of children and young people as researchers requires careful management and training to ensure that they do not engage in practices which are exclusionary and to help them understand their own positioning in the research processes. The training of the children and young people would have to attend to issues of power but could be an extremely worthwhile educational experience. Researchers might also establish alliances with parents of disabled children to undertake research on inclusion and exclusion and to initiate debate with policymakers and professionals.

ANALYSES WITH A DIFFERENCE

The kinds of analyses produced when the philosophers of difference are implicated are, on the one hand, messy and complex and, on the other hand, deep and pervasive. This presents a significant challenge for the researcher in holding his or her nerve with the 'undecidable' (Derrida, 1988, p. 116) during the process of analysis and in its representation. The researcher also has to provide some means of countering challenges about the validity of the research or pre-empting accusations of 'postmodern foppery' (Kauffman and Sasso, 2006b, p. 109), by foregrounding its phronetic qualities and its concern for values and power. This means both undermining the traditional epistemic criteria used to judge research and having a credible means of accounting for the validity of the research.

The philosophers of difference can be implicated in research in both 'top down' or theory testing and 'bottom up' or theory building. More significantly, they also provoke an alternative kind of research practice and a different ethics of research and each of these processes may go on in any one piece of research. I am representing this somewhat crudely and simplistically, but endeavouring to be explicit about how and where the ideas of the philosophers might do their work. A top down analysis would involve examining one's data to see if some of the key concepts, such as Deleuze and Guattari's rhizome, deterritorialization, difference and becoming, Derrida's undecidability and differance and Foucault's mechanisms of surveillance and transgression can be observed and if so, in what form. A bottom up analysis might identify themes and issues emerging from the data and look to some of these concepts to further explore them. The act of analysing the data could be more profoundly affected by the implication of the philosophers of difference by altering how the data are examined and thought about. The rhizome is the most important example of this and a rhizomic analysis is one which is non-linear and, non-hierarchical and which instead wanders, looking for 'things' rather than 'themes'. Data categories or thematic content become less interesting than routes and connections, breaks and fissures. Deconstruction also necessitates radical changes in the analytical process. I have suggested that deconstruction is a two handed job, which is challenging enough, but the process of analysis is also disturbing – in both senses. It sets out to disturb the commonplace and the taken for granted, but this can also be unsettling for the researcher who may begin to mistrust even the most benign statements and who may find that even the cornflake box at breakfast does not escape scrutiny.

Questions about the validity of research which implicate the philosophers of difference will, no doubt, arise and, whilst some of the contemptuous disavowal by the likes of Kauffman and Sasso (2006a & b) is inevitable, it is important to have an account which pre-empts some of the more reasonable potential charges. It is also necessary to try to set out what research of this kind is trying to do and to underline what it is not doing. Validity, as it is conventionally understood to mean the 'truth' of the research, is an inappropriate means of judging research done within a poststructural or postmodern framework because of the arborescent or hierarchical structure of knowledge which it implies. However, it is not enough simply to dismiss questions of validity as irrelevant and so other means of assuring the integrity of the research have to be found. Lather (1993) suggests an alternative framework for accounting for the validity of poststructural research and identifies a number of 'scandalous categories' (p. 685) which attempt to 'unsettle conventional notions of the real' (p. 685). 'Ironic validity' (p. 685) identifies problems with the real and acknowledges the problems of representation. 'Paralogical validity' (p. 686) highlights differences and heterogeneity and is concerned with the undecidables, oppositions and interruptions. 'Rhizomic validity' (p. 686) pursues an unsettlement from within the analysis and establishes open-ended proliferation of ideas rather than categories. Lather's final kind of validity is described as 'voluptuous' (p. 686) and involves 'leaky, runaway, risky practice', creating what she calls a 'questioning text that is bounded and unbounded, closed and opened' (p. 687). These elements of validity work as 'counter-practices of authority' (p. 687) which force the researcher to 'occupy the place of the impossible' (Althusser, 1990, p. 209) and, as well as making thought possible, highlight the researcher's implication in the knowledge production. Shacklock and Thorp (2005) suggest that the research subjects can have a part to play in making validity judgements. This would require, not verifying data as 'true', in the conventional sense, but in co-producing, with the researcher, 'curves of visibility and enunciation' (Deleuze, 1992b, p. 160).

GETTING THE MESSAGE ACROSS: COMMUNICATING RESEARCH

Davis (2002), asserting that 'all of us will have to do much more to educate' (p. 143) society about the causes of exclusion, offers some practical suggestions of where to start, including writing articles for newspapers, creating radio and television documentaries and challenging legal cases. Apple (2001) also calls on academics to make public challenges by writing to newspapers, publishing material on the web and using other forms of media. He describes how the Educational Policy Project has been successful in mounting challenges to the conservative agenda in the US and urges others to establish similar formations. It is only in this way, he argues, can the mighty weight of the hegemonic right be challenged.

For researchers working in Universities, there is considerable pressure not to spend time and effort on writing of this kind and to concentrate on the more weighty 'outputs' in academic journals. Evans (2004) talks of how the new 'ecology in the universities' (p. 134) has privileged particular kinds of writing over others:

> Publication was everywhere, and it became, after the first British Resarch Assessment Exercise (RAE), a matter of first necessity and then compulsion that academics should write. Stakhanov had arrived from Stalin's Russia in the British academy and with him – or his reincarnation – came the demand that every academic in the land should, over a five-year period, produce four

pieces of written work . . . The term 'prestigious journal' was bandied about
to impress upon would-be authors that their offerings only 'really' counted if
they were released to the world in those 'rigorously peer reviewed' journals
which became the sacred place of assessors (p. 134).

As Evans points out, four publications in five years is not a great deal to expect, but
her objection is to the same quota being in existence for everyone and the restrictions
it places on what and where people write. However, whilst researchers may receive
little credit, in formal terms, for more journalistic types of writing, there is little to
stop them pursuing this on top of their quota.

Writing for policymakers is perhaps the biggest challenge for researchers. The
research report, typically brief, with an even briefer 'executive summary' and a list
of 'recommendations', will fulfil policymakers' expectations of epistemic – predictive and explanatory – research and will point them to the way ahead. It will not,
however, invite them to question issues of values and power, or their understanding
of fundamental concepts, such as inclusion or education, unless the researcher can
find ways of inserting such questions in the discussion of the findings or in the recommendations and more generally orienting the research process towards *phronesis*.
I have suggested that the findings of deconstruction could be presented to policymakers as a series of aporias, so instead of recommendations, they are faced with a
number of contradictory double imperatives, such as raising achievement *and* being
inclusive. Discussions with policymakers about how they respond effectively to both
demands could be very productive. This, of course, assumes that policymakers will
be remotely interested in writing which does not conform to expectations;
researchers may have to become skilled in delivering a 'pitch' for their work which
enables them to gain policymakers' attention.

11.   THE POLITICS OF INCLUSION

Please do not shoot the pianist. He is doing his best. (Oscar Wilde, 1883)

The only thing to do, if you want to contribute to culture, or politics, or music, or whatever, is to utilize your own persona rather than just music. The best way to do this is to diversify and become a nuisance everywhere. (David Bowie, 1976, p. 338)

The hostility to inclusion has arisen, I have suggested, from confusion about what is involved, frustration at the climate of accountability within which inclusion is supposed to take place, guilt at what hasn't been achieved and exhaustion from efforts which have seemed futile. It is little wonder that inclusion has been viewed as an impossibility, a step too far for teachers. During 'Inclusion Week' in 2002, my gloomy reflections on the prospects for inclusion in the *Times Educational Supplement* (Allan, 2002) were met with an angry response from a teacher:

> INCLUSION. Inclusion. Inclusion. It seems you can hardly turn a corner these days without encountering the word. However "experts" such as Julie Allan . . . are constantly turning a blind eye to the complaints of teachers that this ideology, great on paper, simply does not work We are fobbed off with platitudes such as "this is a challenging issue" and "more will be done to support teachers/learners" . . . Senior management, keen to keep exclusion figures down, turn a blind eye to the outrageous behaviour of pupils. In what other profession (except, maybe, nursing) would anyone be expected to put up with such treatment? Surely our human rights are being infringed. Isn't it about time we stood up as a profession and said "No more"? The education system will keep functioning without . . . Allan. It cannot cope without teachers (*Times Educational Supplement*, 2002).

So why bother with inclusion? Why try to rescue a project which appears to be associated with such pain and disillusionment? Is Warnock right in saying that inclusion is 'disastrous' (2005, p. 22), creating 'casualties' (ibid, p. 14) of children? Should we try to go on with inclusion? Many of us who write about inclusion and try to foster inclusive practice among our student teachers have few problems in making our

153

positions as advocates of inclusion clear and indeed would argue that this is necessary in making the call to others to rebel or challenge exclusionary practices (Brantlinger, 2006b). But if we do not offer some consideration of why we should include, might we merely risk closure or further annoyance? And who is the 'we' here?

> Why have we kept our own names? Out of habit, purely out of habit. To make ourselves unrecognizable in turn. To render imperceptible, not ourselves, but what makes us act, feel and think . . . To reach, not the point where one no longer says I, but the point where it is no longer of any importance whether one says I. We are no longer ourselves. Each will know his own. We have been aided, inspired, multiplied (Deleuze and Guattari, 1987, p. 3).

Those of us who have taken on the task of promoting inclusion may have inadvertently descended into emotivism, which the philosopher Alasdair MacIntyre (1984) describes as a confusion between two kinds of reply to the question 'why should I do . . .?' The first reply takes the form of 'because I wish it' and is confined to the personal context of the utterance and the characteristics of the speaker. The second reply is unconditional and independent of who utters it, taking the form of 'because it is your duty'. MacIntyre suggests that the second reply is often used to mean 'I like it and urge it on or recommend it to you' (Hernstein Smith, 1992). Inclusion, in this respect, is urged and pressed on people under the guise of a well argued and moral evaluation. Emotivism, according to MacIntyre, is a widespread phenomenon, but it leaves an overwhelming sense of confusion and of having been duped:

> Now people still say 'It is good' and *think* they mean 'It is good', but, without knowing, they are really doing only what people used to do when they said 'I like it' or I want it,' namely expressing their own feelings and trying to get other people to feel, do, or believe certain things. And everyone is deceived: listeners are deceived about what speakers are doing; speakers are self-deceived about what they themselves are doing; and moral philosophers are either deceived, complacent, or complicitous' (Hernestein Smith, 1992, pp. 213–214).

Returning to the question of why we should include, and in an attempt to stammer towards an answer, we need to be reminded that the point of inclusion – is inclusion, as these young people indicated in a letter to Tony Blair:

> Dear Mr Blair,
> We are a group of disabled and non-disabled young people and supporters who believe we should all have the right to go to our local mainstream school. We feel that children in special schools miss out on a decent academic and social education and those in mainstream schools, who hardly ever see disabled people, miss out on the opportunity to learn about and appreciate differences, rather than only seeing disabled people through the patronising view of the media.
> We feel we deserve each other's friendship and that the segregated education system denies us the chance to be together and see each other for what we really are. We are asking you to put an end to compulsory segregation by changing the law. We want to be together!

Yours sincerely, the Young People of Great Britain, c/o Young and Powerful
(Shaw, 2002).

One parent highlighted the main reason for inclusion as being a basic desire among
young people to belong: 'our children just want to be cool, to be one of the group and
to be treated the same as everyone else' (EENET, n.d). Another parent, describing
her son as a 'pioneer' (EENET, n.d), offered the argument that the experience of inclusion was a learning curve for the whole school which led to a dramatic change in
attitudes (EENET, n.d).

We might also be guided by Oliver and Barnes' (1998) vision of what an inclusive world might look like:

> It will be a very different world from the one in which we now live. It will be
> a world that is truly democratic, characterised by genuine and meaningful
> equality of opportunity, with far greater equity in terms of wealth and income,
> with enhanced choice and freedom and with a proper regard for environmen-
> tal and social continuity (p. 102).

It is worth noting the caution urged by some commentators about the promotion of
full inclusion, especially in relation to employment, and both Abberley (2001) and
Henley (2001) point out that employment is not a realistic option for everyone, while
Hunt (1966) argues that individuals can contribute to society in ways other than
through work. MacIntyre (1999) highlights the inevitability and desirability of a
society in which there is some degree of dependence:

> A form of political society in which it is taken for granted that disability and
> dependence on others are something that all of us experience at certain times
> in our lives and this to unpredictable degrees, and that consequently our inter-
> est in how the needs of the disabled are adequately voiced and met is not a
> special interest, the interest of one particular group rather than of others, but
> rather the interest of the whole political society, an interest that is integral to
> their conception of their common good (p. 130).

This implies a kind of inclusive practice which does not attempt to create a level
playing field (Shakespeare, 2006), but which involves a redistribution of resources
in relation to variable levels of need.

KNOWING THE UNKNOWNS

The lack of knowledge about what inclusion looks like and feels like to children and
young people and their families is a serious omission which must be addressed with
urgency and I have suggested a number of strategic shifts which will help to privilege their voices. There is, however, some merit in the collective recognition of the
many unknowns which surround inclusion:

> There are known knowns. There are things we know that we know. There are
> known unknowns. That is to say, there are things that we know we don't know.
> But there are also unknown unknowns. There are things we don't we don't
> know (Rumsfeld, as cited in Zizek, 2005, p. 23).

Zizek (2005), rather than adding to the gleeful contempt with which Rumsfeld's stammering admission was greeted, suggested that he'd missed a fourth term 'the unknown knowns' (p. 23), things we don't know that we know, 'the disavowed beliefs, suppositions and obscene practices we pretend not to know about' (p. 23) and argued that the function of academics or 'intellectuals' was to unearth these. Much of the work needed involves undoing current ways of thinking and practice, seeking to understand the role of misunderstanding within educational processes and attempting to unravel much of what we think we know (Biesta, 2001). Oliver (1996) shares Zizek's (2005) suspicion of the:

> prattling classes, academics and journalists with no specialist education, usu-
> ally working in humanities with some vague French postmodern leanings,
> specialists in everything, prone to verbal radicalism, in love with paradoxical
> formulations that flatly contradict the obvious' (Zizek, 2005, p. 23).

Perhaps a more positive regard would be acquired if academics were to be more honest about their own lack of knowledge and to position themselves as curious, rather than as experts and 'to complicate rather than explicate' (Taylor, 1995, p. 7). Furthermore, it might be more propitious to avoid a quest for understanding and to look instead, for what lies between, or 'interstanding' (1995, p. 6):

> When depth gives way to surface, under-standing becomes inter-standing. To
> comprehend is no longer to grasp what lies beneath but to glimpse what lies
> between . . . Understanding is no longer possible because nothing stands
> under . . . Interstanding has become unavoidable because everything stands
> between (Taylor and Saarinen 1994, pp. 2–3).

The pursuit of interstanding involves risking the personal (Ware, 2002) because it requires individuals to tolerate the diminishment of the borders which define their identities and their sense of place and much of the knowledge which is used as warrants for action. These ambivalences, however, could give rise to more positive ways of being in, and engaging with, the world and Anzaldua (1987) suggests the model for such existence could be found among those of mixed ethnicity:

> The new mestiza [person of mixed ancestry] . . . copes by developing a tolerance
> for contradictions, a tolerance for ambiguity. She learns to be an Indian in
> Mexican culture, to be Mexican from an Anglo point of view. She learns to
> juggle cultures. She has a plural personality, she operates in a pluralistic mode –
> nothing is thrust out, the good the bad and the ugly, nothing rejected, nothing
> abandoned. Not only does she sustain contradictions, she turns the ambivalence
> into something else (Anzaldua 1987, p. 79).

Such tolerance of contradictions and ambiguity may be something which can be sought and practised in the pursuit of the 'something else' of inclusion.

INCLUSION *IS* POLITICAL

There have been many calls for inclusion to be undertaken as a political project. Slee (2003), for example, has called for disability and inclusion to be re-envisioned as cultural politics, while Ballard (2003a) argues that we may need to be not just overtly ideological but also overtly political in our analysis and actions. Inclusion, according to Corbett and Slee (2000), is a 'distinctly political, "in your face" activity' (p. 136) and, as Barton (2003) notes 'this is both a disturbing and challenging activity which is an essential feature of the struggle for change' (p. 12). Others have called for politics to be brought back into education more generally (Gewirtz, 2000; Ozga, 2002), seeing it as crucial in enabling teachers to resist the 'imperative of modernisation' (Ozga, 2002, p. 681). For disabled activists, such pronouncements must seem odd, since the disability movement has never been anything but political, concerned with a process of struggle (Oliver, 1996) for inclusion. As Davis (1996) notes, 'over time, disabled people have moved from acquiescence to uncertainty, discontent and, in recent years, to outright anger' (p. 124). However, as Barton (2004) contends, this anger is often dissipated and rendered neutral:

> The importance of anger, rage, and deeply felt commitment against the offensive, damaging aspects of an unjust system and our daily complicity have become sanitised, inhibited, and displaced into other less important and depoliticised endeavours (p. 67).

Disabled activists have, however, recognised the tensions between the individual and social action and the potential for allies – intellectuals – to become enemies:

> Disabled people, for our sins, encounter a whole range of people throughout our lives; parents, carers, brothers, sisters, professionals like doctors, nurses, OTs, social workers – even celebrities who sometimes 'adopt us'. Are they our allies? Many will think so and some will be surprised to find out that, not only are they not our allies, but, in fact, are the beast itself (Holdsworth, 1993, p. 4; original emphasis).

For academics concerned with inclusion, adopting a more political stance requires resisting the temptation to engage in reified debates, asking what particular disciplines, including the emergent disability studies in education, can do to foster inclusion. It is also necessary to avoid proselytising:

> The role of the intellectual does not consist in telling others what they must do. What right would they have to do that? And remember all prophecies, promises, injunctions, and programs that the intellectuals have managed to formulate in the course of the last two centuries. The job of an intellectual does not consist in moulding the political will of others. It is a matter of performing analyses in his or her own fields, of interrogating anew the evidence and postulates, of shaking up habits, ways of acting and thinking, of dispelling commonplace beliefs, of taking a new measure of rules and institutions . . . it is a matter of participating in the formation of a political will, where [the intellectual] is called to perform a role as citizen (Foucault, 1991, pp. 11–12).

Whilst the political nature of inclusion can be accepted, finding the politics with which one can engage may be a challenge, since, as Gates (1992) notes, 'it's in the gap between "is" and "ought" that politics hides out' (p. 330). On a basic level, academics might ask 'what can we do?' I have suggested that what is required is an ontological shift towards inclusion as an ethical project, using the framework offered by Foucault, in which oneself – and one's capacity to act – is considered part of the material on which work has to be done. Barton (2005) contends that it also requires placing hope at the centre of the centre of the struggle for inclusion:

> Hope involves an informed recognition of the offensive nature of current conditions and relations and a belief that the possibilities of change are not foreclosed (p. 23).

Academics may find it difficult to act politically within their own institutions, but there are multiple ways in which they might oppose institutional practices which create exclusion (Booth, 2003; Brantlinger, 2006b) and foster inclusion by 'communication across a multiplicity of cultures, identities and ways of thinking' (Booth, 2003, p. 55). More generally, academics might 'resist and reject language that carries the ideology of exclusion' (Ballard, 2004, p. 103) and challenge the appropriation of inclusive education by special education (Slee, 2003). Apple (1996) recommends that we face up to the dynamics of power in unromantic ways and promotes the use of subversive tactics to challenge the hegemonic order, including tactical and counterhegemonic alliances and heretical thought. He also suggests that while we might recapture our past to see what is possible, it is important not to romanticise dreams about the future. Corbett and Slee's (2000) depiction of academics as 'cultural vigilantes' (p. 134) is a useful starting point and the language of enmity is appropriate as a *casus belli*, an occasion of war for which there is just cause.

The role of the academic within Universities has become increasingly been constrained by the 'audit culture' (Strathearn, 1997, p. 309) and I have already noted how what is written and where it is published is now more closely circumscribed. Several commentators have expressed concern about the negative impact of the audit culture on academics' capacity to have an influence on society. Halsey (1992) bemoans the 'decline of the donnish dominion' (p. 258), while Furedi (2004) wonders 'where have all the intellectuals gone?' (p. vii). The undermining of academic culture and autonomy is a concern expressed by Paterson, (2003) and Evans (2004) sees the regulatory practices within universities as 'producing fear and little else' (p. 63) and provoking the title of her book 'killing thinking'. Said (1994) argues that the intellectual is bound by the limitations and constraints of professionalism which encourage conformity rather than critique:

> The particular threat to the intellectual today, whether in the West or the non-Western world, is not the academy, nor the suburbs, not the appalling commercialism of journalism and publishing houses, but rather an attitude that I will call professionalism. By professionalism I mean thinking of your work as an intellectual as something you do for a living, between the hours of nine and five with one eye on the clock, and another cocked at what is considered to be

proper, professional behaviour – not rocking the boat, not straying outside the accepted paradigms or limits, making yourself marketable and above all presentable, hence uncontroversial and unpolitical and 'objective' (p. 55; original emphasis).

The civic duty which was behind the creation of universities in Scotland, other parts of Europe and the US, in what was known as 'democratic intellectualism' (Paterson, 2003, p. 69), appears to have been lost. E. P. Thompson (1970), however, is rather more damming of those who inhabit the universities:

> I have never ceased to be astounded when observing the preening and mating habits of fully grown specimens of the species *Academicus Superciliosis*. The behaviour patterns of one of the true members of the species are unmistakable. He is inflated with self-esteem and perpetually self-congratulatory as to the high vocation of the university teacher; but he knows almost nothing about any other vocation, and he will lie down and let himself be walked over if anyone enters from the outer world who has money or power or even a tough line in realist talk . . . *Superciliosis* is the most divisible and reliable creature in this country, being so intent upon crafty calculations of short-term advantages – this favour for his department, that a colleague who, next week, at the next committee, has promised to run a log for him, that he has never even tried to imagine the wood out of which his timber rolls. He can scurry furiously and self-importantly around in his committees, like a white mouse running in a wheel, while his master is carrying him, cage and all, to be sold at the local pet-shop (p. 154).

Although Thompson's observations pertain to an earlier period, the simultaneous self-importance and willingness to be bought are sinister features of contemporary academic life. What might it take for academics to regain control, rediscover their civic duty and, in Bourdieu's (1998) terms, to be able to 'play seriously' (p.128)? Bourdieu suggests that what is required, above all, is for academics to be protected from imperatives arising within their work contexts:

> *Homo scholasticus* or *homo academicus* is someone who can play seriously because his or her state (or State) assures her the means to do so, that is, free time, outside the urgency of a practical situation (p. 128).

As Evans (2004) argues, academics' time is no longer 'free' because of the urgency which we know to be associated with the audit culture, and she suggests the kind of refusal of institutional power evoked by Virginia Woolf in *The three Guineas* which amounts to an 'attitude of complete indifference' (p. 309). Woolf envisaged this as a war against the 'pompous and self important' (Evans, 2004, p. 76) behaviour of males, but Evans suggests that this kind of resistance could be effective within universities and could lead to a different kind of politics, not of inclusion, but 'about, and in favour of, exclusion from those practices and processes which increasingly deform much of academic life' (Evans, 2004, p. 102).

The involvement of academics in advisory positions within local and government positions is an increasingly regular occurrence. Allan Luke, Suzanne Carrington and

Roger Slee have all served time within the Queensland Government; Tony Booth has travelled worldwide with the *Index for Inclusion;* and Alan Dyson and Mel Ainscow have offered their wisdom to local and national governments in the UK and further afield. I have recounted my own experience of being adviser to the Scottish Parliament; I also recently had dinner with the Minister for Education, but good manners, and Chatham House Rules, prevent me from repeating anything which was said, even if it were relevant. Such opportunities to rub up against those in power are to be seized enthusiastically but must be approached with extreme caution in order to avoid slipping into patronage or, worse still, incurring the charge: 'it's imperialism, stupid' (Chomsky, 2005). The experience of Slee, as seconded Deputy Director of Education within the Queensland Government, illustrates the scope for influencing change. He achieved significant progress in having 'closed the special needs chapter' (Slee, 2003, p. 214), in spite of the tendency of the civil servants to 'dance around the politics of pragmatism while attempting to retain ethical integrity' (p. 220). Slee also demanded an end to the confrontational politics between the Government and parents and established a forum for dialogue with parents of disabled youngsters which was based on mutual respect.

While forums which enable parents to engage in dialogue with policymakers are potentially extremely valuable, parents may find more support and solidarity from establishing their own alliances. The Queensland Parents for People with a Disability found they were successful as a result of being bound and bonded by their own anger at the inequalities that they and their children had experienced and individuals were able to become 'the mouse that roared' (Barkkman, 2002, p. 96) or 'more bloody-minded' (p. 101). Equity in Education, a Scottish organisation of parents and advocates of inclusion has also provided its members with much needed support during difficult times such as starting school and transition. More significantly, it has established an inclusive Learning Network which puts parents and teachers together for training. The Scottish Education Department has recognised the value of this innovative network and has funded the development of the training materials; local authorities pay for parents and teachers to participate. Those who have undertaken the training have found themselves transformed by the mutual recognition and respect and the new knowledge that has been produced by working in this novel way (Equity in Education, 2004). Organisations such as the Independent Panel for Special Education Advice (ISPEA) and SOS!SEN (n.d), an independent helpline for special educational needs, have been particularly valuable sources of information and support.

I have argued that teachers being called upon to be inclusive needed to be given the chance to examine the inclusion and exclusion in their own professional lives, through Continuing Professional Development. Sachs (2003), in advocating an activist teaching profession, suggests encouraging teachers to create individual and collective 'professional self narratives' (p. 132). These would, she contends, act as a 'glue' (ibid) for collective self identity and as a provocation for renewing teacher professionalism. Sachs also recommends that teachers be encouraged to take control of the standards for teaching, treating these developmentally rather than in the regulatory way in which they have been used (Mahoney and Hextall, 2000). The opportunities for teachers to work collectively and to build social capital may be beneficial. Social capital, the network, norms and trust which bind people together and enable them to achieve mutual goals (Schuller et al, 2000), has been recognised as having a value for teachers and a potential to reinvigorate the profession (Gamarnikow and Green, 1999; Smyth, 2000; Catts and Ozga, 2005). Within the Schools and Social Capital Network of the Applied Educational Research Scheme in Scotland (http://www.aers.org.uk/aers/ssc_network.html), a group of researchers, policymakers and key stakeholders has been exploring the capacity of social capital as a political tool to 'offer teachers a strong conceptual and political platform for demonstrating the complexity of their work (Sachs, 2003, p. 13).

Brantlinger (2006b) acknowledges that received knowledge about inclusion is 'tenacious' (p. 244) but contends that 'humans can question and refuse to comply with socialized patterns that they perceive as not constructive' (p. 244) and this is endorsed by Gillbourn and Youdell (2000) and by Apple (2001). Gillbourn and Youdell admit that whilst the scope for subversion among teachers may be limited, they can nevertheless make a substantial difference. For beginning teachers, a first step towards activism could be the dismissal of the 'clean, unrealistic textbook portrayals of children and classrooms' (Brantlinger, 2006a, p. 70) and in so doing 'may be healthier, happier, and more prepared to teach than those who retain a nagging sense of personal inadequacy' (p. 70).

REFLECTIONS ON THINKING IN PRACTICE

The suggestions offered in this book are attempts to activate some of concepts of the philosophers of difference, such as difference (and différance), the rhizome and becoming, and their strategies, including deconstruction, deterritorialization and transgression, and to put them to work on inclusion. They are not solutions to the 'problem' of inclusion, but are intended as conceptual provocation (Bains, 2002, p. 104), speaking against the urgency to decide, act and foreclose and oriented towards the open and the new. They provide what Artaud (1970–4) defines as a series of agitations:

> Everything in the order of the written word which abandons the field of clear, orderly perception, everything which aims at reversing appearances and introduces doubt about the position of mental images and their relationship to one another, everything which provokes confusion without destroying the strength of an emergent thought, everything which disrupts the relationship between things by giving this agitated thought an even greater aspect of truth and violence (p. 92).

Artaud's preferred method was to abuse his audiences in the theatre and stage histrionic collapses (Dale, 2002); the propositions in this book are hopefully less offensive, but are nevertheless radical. They are intended to produce what Deleuze and Guattari (1987) call 'affects' (p. 400), projectiles which can be fired to create new lines of flight and new ways of seeing inclusion as a 'puzzle' rather than a problem. These weapons may be directed at those needing to see things differently, but they can also create, in Deleuze and Guattari's terms, new lines of vision for ourselves and new intensities or, in James Joyce's terms, 'epiphanies':

> The epiphany was the sudden 'revelation of the whatness of a thing, the moment in which the 'soul of the commonest object . . . seems to us radiant'. The artist, he felt, was charged with such revelations, and must look for them not among the gods but among men, in casual, unostentatious, even unpleasant moments' (Ellman, 1982, p. 83).

Taylor (1989) saw such epiphanies as having a particular significance and a capacity to enact what it unfolded:

> What I want to capture with this term is just this notion of a work of art as the locus of a manifestation which brings us into the presence of something which is otherwise inaccessible, and which is of the highest moral and spiritual significance; a manifestation, moreover, which also defines and completes something even as it reveals' (p. 419).

The propositions imply a greater responsibility upon those involved in inclusion to try to identify lines of escape and to fashion, in Lather's (1993) terms, 'a field of possibilities that is not yet' (p. 684). For this to be possible, there will need to be a certain openness to the unknown and to politics.

The process of implicating the philosophers of difference has been, for me, both an exhilarating and unsettling experience. When Len Barton asked me, after reading the draft of the manuscript of this book, to comment on my own experience of engaging with the philosophers of difference, I surprised myself by my diffidence. It became clear that this was borne out of a considerable anxiety that the attempt to put the philosophers of difference to work on inclusion would amount to no more than 'rhetorical flatulence' (Eagleton, 2006, p. 2) and that this book would be dismissed as an absurd attempt to rescue inclusion from its morbidity. Reflecting on the process of producing this book has, however, been salutary. My engagement with the philosophers of difference has provoked the kind of optimism which I hope this book will generate for others. As I have indicated, my first 'encounter' with this kind of thinking was through Foucault and was an extremely negative one, finding numerous instances of exclusion being produced through the exercise of power upon people and, worse still, the complicity of individuals in that process of subjectification. I can still remember the impact upon me of hearing accounts of resistance, for example from Raschida, a blind student who described how she dropped her long cane in a lake, because it signalled her impairment and her accounts of faking being blind drunk rather than blind. This was my epiphany and I came to understand this resistance, through Foucault and his work on ethics, as transgression. It marked the start of a slippery slope of seeing philosophical ideas as vehicles for transformation. Whilst developing a framework of inclusion as an ethical project, I looked elsewhere for inspiration for thinking about the kinds of practices which might be warranted and discovered the other philosophers of difference. Their implication in the project of inclusion is one that is, in this book, merely a beginning for others to then run with. But I believe it is a worthwhile undertaking and have become far more optimistic about the possibilities for inclusion which concepts can offer. Deleuze (2004) talks of the book of philosophy being a mixture of a detective novel and science fiction, which enable concepts 'with their zones of presence' (p. xix) to resolve local situations. This, of course, is not a book of philosophy but is an attempt to create a kind of detective's 'incident room', talking aloud about the local situations and trying to resolve, if not crimes, at least misdemeanours. I hope the book will be read both with both irritation (at what is unresolved, and unsolved) and, following Deleuze (1995), with love:

> This intensive way of reading, in contact with what's outside the book, as a flow meeting other flows, one machine among others, as a series of experiments for each reader in the midst of events that have nothing to do with books, as tearing the book into pieces, getting it to interact with other things, absolutely anything . . . is reading with love. That's exactly how you read the book (Deleuze, 1995, pp. 8–9).

Through the engagement with the philosophers of difference, I have become more secure about the role of uncertainty in the process of transformation, and more comfortable with what the poet Keats (1917) calls 'negative capability':

> I mean Negative Capability, that is when man is capable of being in uncertainties, Mysteries, doubts without any irritable reaching after fact & reason.

At the same time, I have become more cynical, at times sadistically so, about the capacity of all of us to constantly repeat exclusion through what Fairclough (1992) calls the 'technologization of discourse' (p. 239), whereby we change the words in order to continue with the same maledictory practices and at the same time to pursue the 'essential illusion of change' (Adorno, 1974, p. 135). This has fed my own confusion, frustration, guilt and exhaustion and, above all, a sense of futility. Yet the children and young people with whom I have engaged have pointed to some of the more comedic aspects of the inclusion problem and it is they who have convinced me that inclusion is worth striving for. I am comfortable in the role as dissident, a benevolent outsider, using conceptual provocations to others to tackle exclusion and imagine different kinds of practice. Whether this will happen remains to be seen.

RETHINKING INCLUSION? THE REPETITION OF YES

> In order for the yes of affirmation, assent, consent, alliance, of engagement, signature, or gift to have the value it has, it must carry the repetition within itself. It must *a priori* and immediately confirm its promise and promise its confirmation (Derrida, 1991a, p. 576).

For inclusion to be a possibility, we must be ready to say yes to it and to promise to say yes to it again; this was the directive which Derrida took from James Joyce's (1993) Molly Bloom and the insight which the student who wrote in his exam of 'inconclusive' education had. The affirmation of inclusion without a repetition amounts to a 'wait and see' a 'maybe', which can quickly retreat to the refusals that we have seen. So, if we do want inclusion to happen, we need to say yes with the confidence that it will be 'repeated in the quiet, steady beat of tomorrow and tomorrow' (Caputo, 1997, p. 188). So we can be never done with the project of inclusion and must continue to puzzle over it together with those who stand to gain most.

REFERENCES

Abberley, P. (2001). Work, disability and European social theory. In C. Barnes, M. Oliver, & L. Barton (Eds.), *Disability studies today.* Cambridge: Polity

Adorno, T. (1974). *Minima moralia.* London: NLB

Ainscow, M., Booth, T., & Dyson, A. (1999). Inclusion and exclusion in schools: Listening to some hidden voices. In K. Ballard (Ed.), *Inclusive education: International voices on disability and justice.* London: Falmer

Ainscow, M., & Tweddle, D. (2003). Understanding the changing role of English local authorities in promoting inclusion. In J. Allan (Ed.), *Inclusion, participation and democracy: What is the purpose?* Dordrecht: Kluwer

Albrecht, G. (1992). *The disability business: Rehabilitation in America.* London: Sage

Alderson, P. (1995). *Listening to children.* London: Barnardo's

Allan, J. (1996). Foucault and Special Educational Needs: A box of tools for analysising children's experiences of mainstreaming. *Disability and Society, 11*(2), 219–233

Allan, J. (1999). *Actively seeking inclusion.* London: Falmer

Allan, J. (2002). Inclusion without in blood, swead and tears. *Times Educational Supplement, Scotland,* 15 November, Retrieved September 19, 2006, from http://www.tes.co.uk/search/story/?story_id=37156

Allan, J. (2003a). Inclusion and exclusion in the University. In T. Booth, K. Nes, & M. Strmstad (Eds.), *Developing inclusive education.* London: RoutledgeFalmer

Allan, J. (Ed.) (2003b). *Inclusion, participation and democracy: What is the purpose?* Dordrecht: Kluwer

Allan, J. (2005a). Inclusion as an ethical project. In S. Tremain (Ed.), *Foucault and the government of disability.* Ann Arbor: University of Michigan Press

Allan, J. (2005b). Transgression. In G. Albrecht (Ed.), *Encyclopedia of disability.* New York: Sage

Allan, J. (2005c). Inclusive learning experiences: Learning from children and young people. In M. Nind, J. Rix, K. Sheehy, & K. Simmons (Eds.), *Curriculum and pedagogy in inclusive education: Values into practice.* Abingdon: RoutledgeFalmer

Allan, J. (2005d). The aesthetics of ideology as a productive ideology. In L. Ware (Ed.), *Ideology and the politics of (in)exclusion.* New York: Peter Lang

Allan, J., Brown, S., & Riddell, S. (1991). *Off the record: Mainstream provision for pupils with non-recorded learning difficulties in primary and secondary schools.* Edinburgh: Scottish Council for Research in Education

Allan, J., & Cope, P. (2004). If you can: Inclusion in music making. *International Journal of Inclusive Education, 8*(1), 23–36

Allan, J., Duffield, J., Morris, B., & Turner, E. (1998). *Raising achievement in S1 and S2.* Report to Stirling Council Education Services. Stirling: University of Stirling

Allan, J., & I'Anson, J. (2004). What's it like at the front of the class? Scottish opinion. *Times Educational Supplement Scotland,* 10 September, 25

165

Allan, J., & l'Anson, J. (2005). Children's rights in school: Power, assemblies and assemblages. *International Journal of Children's Rights, 12*, 123–138

Allan, J., l'Anson, J., Priestley, A., & Fisher, S. (2006). *Promising rights: Children's rights in school.* Edinburgh: Save the Children

Allan, J., & Slee, R. (forthcoming). *Doing inclusive education research.* Rotterdam: Sense

Althusser, L. (1990). *Philosophy and the spontaneous philosophy of the scientists.* London: Verso

Ansell, K. (1997). Deleuze outside/outside Deleuze: On the difference engineer. In K. A. Pearson (Ed.), *Deleuze and philosophy: The difference engineer.* London: Routledge

Anzaldua, G. (1987). *Borderlands/La Frontera.* San Francisco: Spinsters/Aunt Lute

Apple, M. (2001). *Educating the 'right' way.* New York: RoutledgeFalmer

Arcilla, R. (2002). Why aren't philosophers and educators speaking to each other? *Educational Theory, 52*(1), 1–12

Arendt, H. (1968). *Between past and future: Eight exercises in political thought.* Harmondsworth: Penguin

Arnot, M., Gray, J., James, M., Rudduck, J., & Duveen, G. (1998). *Recent research on gender and educational performance.* London: The Stationary Office

Artaud, A. (1970–4) *Collected works, vols 1–4.* (V. Corti, & trans.) London: Caulder and Byars

Artiles, A. (2004). The end of innocence: Historiography and representation in the discursive practice of LD. *Journal of Learning Disabilities, 37*(6), 550–555

Artiles, A., Trent, S., & Kuan, L. (1997). Learning disabilities empirical research on ethnic minority students: An analysis of 22 years of studies published in selected refereed journals. *Learning Disabilities Research and Practice, 12*, 82–91

Arts Council of England (1999). *Addressing social exclusion: A framework for action.* London: Arts Council of England

Attali, J. (1985). *Noise,* (B. Boone, trans.) New York: Paragon

Attridge, D. (1995). Singularities, responsibilities: Derrida, deconstruction and literary criticism. In C. Caruth, & D. Esch (Eds.), *Critical encounters: Reference and responsibility in deconstructive writing.* Brunswick: Rutgers University Press

Audit Commission. (2002). *Special educational needs: A mainstream issue.* London: Audit Commission

Bains, P. (2002). Subjectless subjectivities. In B. Massumi (Ed.), *A shock to thought: Expression after Deleuze and Guattari.* London. New York: Routledge

Baker, B. (1998). 'Childhood' in the emergence and spread of US public schools. In T. Popkewitz, & M. Brennon (Eds.), *Foucault's challenge: Discourse, knowledge and power in education.* New York/London: Teachers College Press

Baker, B. (2002). The hunt for disability: The new Eugenics and the normalization of school children. *Teachers College Record, 104*(4), 663–703

Balkin, J. (1994). Being just with deconstruction, *Social and Legal Studies 393.* Retrieved April 29, 2005, from http://www.yale.edu/lawweb/jbalkin/articles/beingjust1.htm

Ball, S. (1990a). *Politics and policy making in education.* London: Routledge

Ball, S. (1990b). Management as moral technology: A Luddite analysis. In S. Ball (Ed.), *Foucault and education: Disciplines and knowledge.* London: Routledge

Ball, S. (1994). *Education reform: A critical and post-structural approach.* Buckingham/Philadelphia: Open University Press

Ball, S. (2000). Performativities and fabrication in the education economy: Towards the performative society? *Australian Educational Researcher, 27*(2), 1–23

Ball, S. (2003). The teacher's soul and the terror of performativity. *Journal of Education Policy, 18*(2), 215–228

Ballard, K. (1999). Concluding thoughts. In K. Ballard (Ed.), *Inclusive education: International voices on disability and justice.* London: Falmer Press

Ballard, K. (2003a). The analysis of context: Some thoughts on teacher education, culture, colonisation and inequality. In T. Booth, K. Nes, & M. Strømstad (Eds.), *Developing inclusive education.* London: RoutledgeFalmer

Ballard, K. (2003b). Including ourselves: Teaching, trust, identity and community. In J. Allan (Ed.), *Participation, inclusion and identity: What is the purpose?* Dordrecht: Kluwer

Ballard, K. (2004a). Learners and outcomes: Where did all the children go? Version containing material deleted by *SET:Research Information for Teachers, 1*, 20–22

Ballard, K. (2004b). Ideology and the origins of exclusion: A case study. In L. Ware (Ed.), *Ideology and the politics of in/exclusion*. New York: Peter Lang

Ballard, K., & McDonald, T. (1999). Disability, inclusion and exclusion: Insider accounts and interpretations. In K. Ballard (Ed.), *Inclusive education: International voices on disability and justice*. London: Falmer

Banville, J. (2005). *The sea*. Basingstoke: Picador

Barenboim, D. (2006). *In the beginning was sound*. The Reith Lectures. BBC

Barkkman, J. (2002) *Daring to dream ... Stories of parent advocacy in Queensland*. Brisbane: Queensland Parents for People with a Disability Inc

Barnes, C. (1996). Theories of disability and the origins of the oppression of disabled people in Western society. In L. Barton (Ed.), *Disability and society: Emerging issues and insights*. London: Longman

Barnes, C. (1997). Disability and the myth of the independent researcher. In L. Barton & M. Oliver (Eds.), *Disability studies: Past, present and future*. Leeds: The Disability Press

Barton, L. (1997). Inclusive education: Romantic, subversive or realistic? *International Journal of Inclusive Education, 1*(3), 231–242

Barton, L. (2003). Inclusive education and teacher education: A basis for hope or a discourse of delusion. London: Institute of Education

Barton, L. (2004a). Historic influences: Disability and 'special' schooling. In L. Ware (Ed.), *Ideology and the politics of (in)exclusion*. New York: Peter Lang

Barton, L. (2004b) Politics of special education: A necessary or irrelevant approach? In L. Ware (Ed.), *Ideology and the politics of in/exclusion*. New York: Peter Lang

Barton, L. (2005). Special educational needs: An alternative look. Unpublished discussion paper

Barton, L., & Clough, P. (1995). Conclusion: Many urgent voices. In P. Clough & L. Barton (Eds.), *Making difficulties: Research and the construction of SEN*. London: Paul Chapman

Benjamin, S. (2002). *The micropolitics of inclusive education: An ethnography*. Maidenhead: Open University Press

Bernauer, J. (1999). J. Carette (Ed.), Cry of spirit: Foreword to *M. Michael Foucault Religion in culture*. Manchester: Manchester University Press

Biesta, G., (2001). Preparing for the incalculable. In G. Biesta, & D. Egéa-Kuehne (Eds.), *Derrida & education*. London: Routledge

Biesta, G., & Egéa-Kuehne, D. (Eds.), (2001). *Derrida & education*. London: Routledge

Blacker, D. (1998). Intellectuals at work and in power: Towards a Foucaultian research ethic. In T. Popekewitz & M. Brennan (Eds.), *Foucault's challenge: Discourse, knowledge and power in education*. New York: Teachers College Press

Bloor, M., & McIntosh, J. (1990). Surveillance and concealment: A comparison of techniques of client resistance in therapeutic communities and health visiting. In S. Cunningham-Burley, & N. McKeganey (Eds.), *Readings in medical sociology*. London: Routledge

Bogue, R. (2004). Search, swim and see: Deleuze's apprenticeship in signs and pedagogy of images. *Educational Philosophy and Theory, 36*(3), 327–342

Booth, T. (1991). Integration, disability and commitment: A response to Mårten Söder. *European Journal of Special Needs Education, 6*(1), 1–16

Booth, T. (1998). The poverty of special education: Theories to the rescue? In C. Clark, A. Dyson, & A. Millward (Eds.) *Theorising special education*. London: Routledge

Booth, T. (2003). Views from the institution: Overcoming barriers to inclusive education? In T. Booth, K. Nes & M Strmstad (Eds.), *Developing inclusive education*. London: RoutledgeFalmer

Booth, T., & Ainscow, M. (1998). From them to us: Setting up the study. In T. Booth & M. Ainscow (Eds.), *From them to us: An international study of inclusion in education*. London: Routledge

Booth, T., Nes, K., & Strømstad, M. (2003a). Developing inclusive education: Drawing the book together. In T. Booth, K. Nes, & M. Strømstad (Eds.), *Developing inclusive education*. London: RoutledgeFalmer

Booth, T., Nes, K., & Strømstad, M. (2003b). Developing inclusive education? Introduction. In T. Booth, K. Nes, & M. Strømstad (Eds.), *Developing inclusive education*. London: RoutledgeFalmer

Boundas, C., and Olkowski, D. (Eds.) (1994). *Gilles Deleuze and the theater of philosophy*. London: Routledge

Bourdieu, P. (1998). *Practical reason*. Cambridge: Polity

Bowie, D. (1976). Musicians on life and politics. In D. Watson (Ed.), *Chambers musical quotations*. Edinburgh: Chambers

Boyne, R. (1990). *Foucault and Derrida: The other side of reason*. London: Routledge

Branfield, F. (1998). What are you doing here? 'Non-disabled' people and the disability movement: A response to Robert F. Drake. *Disability and Society, 13*(1), 143–144

Brannigan, J. (1996). Writing determination: Reading death in(to) Irish National identity. In J. Brannigan, R. Robbins, & J. Wolfreys (Eds.), *Applying: To Derrida*. Basingstoke: Macmillan

Brantlinger, E. (1997). Using ideology: Cases of nonrecognition of the politics of research and practice in special education. *Review of Educational Research, 67*(4), 425–459

Brantlinger, E. (2004a). Ideologies discerned, values determined: Getting past the hierarchies of special education. In L. Ware (Ed.), *Ideology and the politics of in/exclusion*. New York: Peter Lang

Brantlinger, E. (2004b). Confounding the needs and confronting the norms: An extension of Reid and Valle's essay, *Journal of Learning Disabilities, 37*(6), 490–499

Brantlinger, E. (2006a). The big glossies: How textbooks structure (special) education. In E. Brantlinger (Ed.), *Who benefits from special education? Remediating (fixing) other people's children*. Mahwah, New Jersey/London: Lawrence Erlbaum Associates

Brantlinger, E. (2006b). Conclusion: Whose labels? Whose norms? Whose needs? Whose benefits? In E. Brantlinger (Ed.), *Who benefits from special education? Remediating (fixing) other people's children*. Mahwah, New Jersey/London: Lawrence Erlbaum Associates

Bredo, E. (2002). How can philosophy of education be both viable and good? *Theory of Education, 52*(3)

British Council (n.d.) *Arts creative industries*. Retrieved September 6, 2004, from http:www.britishcouncil.org/home/arts/arts-creative-economy-transitional-economies/arts-creative-economy-transitional-economies-latvia.htm

Britzman, D. (1986). Cultural myths in the making of a teacher. *Harvard Educational Review, 56*(4), 442–455

Britzman, D. (1998). *Lost subjects, contested objects: Toward a psychoanalytic inquiry of learning*. New York: SUNY Press

Britzman, D. (2002). The death of curriculum? In W. Doll & N. Gough (Eds.), *Curriculum visions*. New York: Peter Lang

Broomfield, A. (2004). *All our children belong*. Report for Parents for Inclusion's Black and Minority Ethnic Reference Group. London: Parents for Inclusion

Brownlie, J., Anderson, S., & Ormston, R. (2006). *Children as researchers*. Report to the Scottish Executive Education Department. Edinburgh: SEED

Bryce, T., & Humes, W. (1999). *Policy development in Scottish education*. Synergy for the Scottish Parliament: Perspectives on policy. Retrieved March 7, 2002 from http://www.strath.gla.ac.uk/synergy/policy/index.html

Bury, M. (1997). Disability and the myth of the independent researcher: A reply. In L. Barton, & M. Oliver (Eds.), *Disability studies: Past, present and future*. Leeds: The Disability Press

Caputo, J. (1997). *Deconstruction in a nutshell: A conversation with Jacques Derrida*. New York: Fordham University Press

Catts, R., & Ozga, J. (2004). What is social capital and how might it be used in Scotland's schools? *CES Briefing no 26*. Retrieved October 15, 2006, from http://www.ces.ed.ac.uk/PDF%20Files/Brief036.pdf

CBBC. (2001). *Ant and Dec voted 'Children's Champions'*. Retrieved May 4, 2004, from news.bbc.co.uk/cbbcnews/hi/uk/newsid_1665000/1665828.stm

Centre for Studies in Education. (2001). *Working towards inclusion*. Retrieved March 7, 2006, from http://inclusion.uwe.ac.uk/csie/may01.htm

Centre for Studies in Education. (2002). *Working towards inclusion*. Retrieved September 19, 2006, from http://inclusion.uwe.ac.uk/csie/may02.htm

Centre for Studies in Education. (2005a). *News digest, June*. Retrieved on March 3, 2006, from http://inclusion.uwe.ac.uk/csie/june05.htm

Centre for Studies in Inclusive Education (2005b) *2020 Campaign: Inclusion is working!* Retrieved September 24, 2005, from http://inclusion.uwe.ac.uk/csie/2020%20Press%20Release%20 Mar%2005.pdf#search=%22%20mark%20vaughan%20negative%20inclusion%22

Centre for Studies in Inclusive Education (2006). *Government urged to step up inclusion*. Press release. Retrieved October 15, 2006, from http://inclusion.uwe.ac.uk/csie/Response%20to%20 SelComSEN-PR-7-06.pdf

Chomsky, N. (2005). It's imperialism, stupid. *Khaleej Times,* July 4, Retrieved April 16, 2006, from http://www.khaleejtimes.com/DisplayArticle.asp?xfile=data/opinion/2005/July/opinion_July10.xml &section=opinion&col

Codd, J. (1999). Educational reform, accountability and the culture of distrust. *New Zealand Journal of Educational Studies, 34*(1), 45–53

Coffield, F. (2002). *A new strategy for learning and skill: Beyond IOI initiatives*. Newcastle: Department of Education, University of Newcastle

Cohen, A. (1996). Personal nationalism: A Scottish view of some rites, rights and wrongs. *American Ethnologist,* 23, 802–815

Cohen, D. (2006). Critiques of the 'ADHD' enterprise. In *Critical new perspectives on ADHD*. Abingdon: Routledge

Connell, R. (1993). *Schools and social justice*. Philadelphia: Temple University Press

Cooper, D. (1997). Strategies of power: Legislating worship and religious education. In M. Lloyd & A. Thacker (Eds.), *The impact of Michel Foucault on the social sciences and humanities*. Basingstoke: Macmillan Press Ltd

Corbett, J. (2001). *Supporting inclusive education: A connective pedagogy*. London: Routledge

Corbett, J., & Slee, R. (2000). An international conversation on inclusive education. In F. Armstrong, D. Armstrong, & L. Barton (Eds.), *Inclusive education: Policy, contexts and comparative education*. London: David Fulton

Corker, M. (1999). New disability discourse, the principle of optimization and social change. In M. Corker, & S. French (Eds.), *Disability discourse*. Buckingham: Open University Press

Cormack, P., & Comber, B. (1996). Writing the teacher: The South Australian junior primary English teacher, 1962–1995. In B. Green & C. Beavis (Eds.), *Teaching the English subjects: Essays on English curriculum history and Australian schooling*. Geelong: Deakin University Press

Costa, S. (2005). Of how burdens can be laid on teaching activity or how a teacher can become a donkey (or a camel). *Educação & Sociedade, 26*(93), 1257–1272

Crawford, C., & Porter, G. L. (1992). *How It happens: A look at inclusive educational practice in Canada for children and youth with disabilities*. Toronto: L'Institute Roeher Institute

Crenshaw, K. (1994). Demarginalizing the intersection of race and sex: A black feminist critique of antidiscrimination docrine, feminist theory, and antiracist politics. In A. Jagger (Ed.), *Living with contradiction: Controversies in feminst social ethics*. Boulder: Westview

Critchley, S. (1999). *The ethics of deconstruction*. Edinburgh: Edinburgh University Press

Critchley, S. (2002). Ethics, politics and radical democracy – The history of a disagreement. *Culture Machine*. Retrieved April 27, 2004, from http://culturemachine.tees.ac.uk/Cmach/Backissues/j004/ Articles/Critchley.htm

Croll, P., & Moses, D. (2000). Ideologies and utopias: Education professionals' views of inclusion. *European Journal of Special Needs Education, 15*(1), 1–12

Crow, L. (1992). Renewing the social model of disability. *Coalition, July,* 5–9

Cultural Policy Collective. (2004). Beyond social inclusion: Towards cultural democracy. Edinburgh: Cultural Policy Collective

Dale, C. (2002). Cruel: Antonin Artaud & Giles Deleuze. In B. Massumi (Ed.), *A shock to thought: Expression after Deleuze and Guattari*. London New York: Routledge

170   REFERENCES

Danforth, S. (2006). Place, profession, and program in the history of special education curriculum. In E. Brantlinger (Ed.), *Who benefits from special education: Remediating (fixing) other people's children*. Mahwah, New Jersey/London: Lawrence Erlbaum

Danforth, S., & Morris, P. (2006). Orthodoxy, heresy, and the inclusion of American students considered to have emotional/behavioral disorders. *International Journal of Inclusive Education, 10*(2,3), 135–148

Daniels, H. (2005). *Young people at risk of social exclusion: Interagency working and professional learning*. Presented at the Participation, Inclusion and Equity Research Network, Stirling, 20 June 2005

Davis, K. (1996). Disability and legislation: Rights and equality. In G. Hales (Ed.), *Beyond disability: Towards an enabling society*. London: Sage

Davis, L. (1997). *The disability studies reader*. London: Routledge

Davis, L. (2002). *Bending over backwards: Disability, dismodernism and other difficult positions*. New York London: New York University Press

Davis, J., Watson N., & Cunningham-Burley S. (2000). Lives of disabled children: A reflexive experience. In P. Christiansen, & A. James (Eds.), *Researching childhood: Perspectives and practices*. London: Falmer Press

De Landa, M. (1991). *War in the age of intelligent machines*. New York: Zone Books, MIT Press

Deleuze, G. (1981). *Francis Bacon: Logique de la sensation* (Vol. 1). Paris: Editions de la différance

Deleuze, G. (1983). *Nietzsche and philosophy*. (H. Tomlinson trans). New York: Columbia University Press

Deleuze, G. (1988). *Foucault* (S. Hand, trans.). Minneapolis: University of Minnesota Press

Deleuze, G. (1990). *The logic of sense*. New York: Columbia University Press

Deleuze, G. (1992a). Postscript on the societies of control. Retrieved October 24, 2006, from http://www.n5m.org/n5m2/media/texts/deleuze.htm

Deleuze, G. (1992b). *Michel Foucault, philosopher* (T. Armstrong, Trans.). New York: Routledge

Deleuze, G. (1994). *What is philosophy?* (H. Tomlison & G. Burchell, trans.) London: Athlone Press

Deleuze, G. (1995). *Negotiations*. Trans M Joughin. New York: Columbia University Press

Deleuze, G. (1998). *Essays critical and clinical* (D. Smith & M. Greco, Trans). London/New York: Verso

Deleuze, G. (2000). *Proust and signs: The complex text* (original work pb 1969) (R. Howard, trans). Minneapolis: University of Minnesota Press

Deleuze, G. (2004). *Difference and repetition*. London: Continuum

Deleuze, G., & Guattari, F. (1977). *Anti-oedipus: Capitalism and schizophrenia*, (R. Hurley, M. Seem & H. Lane, trans). New York: Viking Press

Deleuze, G., & Guattari, F. (1986). *Kafka: Toward a minor literature* (D. Polan, trans). Minneapolis: University of Minnesota Press

Deleuze, G., & Guattari, F. (1987). *A thousand plateaus: Capitalism and schizophrenia*. London: The Athlone Press

Deleuze, G., & Guattari, F. (1994). *What is philosophy?* H. Tomlinston & B. Habberjam, trans). New York: Columbia University Press

Deleuze, G., & Parnet, C. (1987). *Dialogues* (H. Tomlinson & B. Habberjam, trans.). New York: Columbia University Press

Department of Education and Science. (1978). *Report of the Committee of Enquiry into the Education of Handicapped Children and Young People (The Warnock Report)*. London: HMSO

Department for Education and Science. (1997). *Excellence for all children*. Retrieved January 10 , 2000, from http://www.teachernet.gov.uk/wholeschool/sen/publications/excellencegp/download/

Department for Education and Science. (2003). Report of the special schools committee working group. London: DfES

Department for Education and Science. (2005). *Higher standards, better schools for all – More choice for parents and pupils*. Schools White Paper. London: DfES

Derrida, J. (1973). *Speech and phenomena and other essays in Husserl's theory of signs*. D. Allison, trans. Evanstron: Northwestern University Press

Derrida, J. (1976). *Of grammatology* (G. Spivak, trans.). Baltimore: John Hopkins University Press

Derrida, J. (1979). Living on: Border lines. In H. Bloom, P. Deman, J. Derrida, G. Hartman, & J. Hillis Miller (Eds.), *Deconstruction and criticism*. New York: Seabury Press

Derrida, J. (1982). *Margins of philosophy* (A. Bass, trans.) Chicago: University of Chicago Press

Derrida, J. (1988). *Limited inc.* (S. Weber, trans). Evanston: Northwestern University Press

Derrida, J. (1990). *Force of law: The mystical foundation of authority* (M. Quaintance, trans.), *Cardozo Law Review, 11*, 919–1070

Derrida, J. (1991a). Ulysses gramophone: Hear say yes in Joyce. In P. Kamuf (Ed.), *A Derrida reader: Between the blinds*. New York/Chichester: Columbia University Press

Derrida, J. (1991b). Letter to a Japanese friend. In P. Kamuf (Ed.), *A Derrida reader: Between the blinds*. New York/Chichester: Columbia University Press

Derrida, J. (1991c). Psyche: Invention of the other. In P. Kamuf (Ed.), *A Derrida reader: Between the blinds*. New York/Chichester: Columbia University Press

Derrida, J. (1991d). Différance. In P. Kamuf (Ed.), *A Derrida reader: Between the blinds*. New York/Chichester: Columbia University Press

Derrida, J. (1992a). Force of law: The mystical foundation of authority (M. Quaintance, trans.). In D. Cornell, M. Rosenfield, & D. Carlson (Eds.), *Deconstruction and the possibility of justice*. New York/London: Routledge

Derrida, J. (1992b). *The other heading: Reflections on today's Europe* (P. Brault & M. Naas, trans.). Bloomington/Idianapolis: Indiana University Press

Derrida, J. (1993). *Aporias*. Stanford: Stanford University Press

Derrida, J. (1995). *Points: Interviews 1974–1994*. Standford: Standford University Press, *385–387*

Derrida, J. (1997a). The Villanova roundtable: A conversation with Jacques Derrida. In J. Caputo (Ed.), *Deconstruction in a nutshell: A conversation with Jacques Derrida*. New York: Fordham University Press

Derrida, J. (1997b). On responsibility: Jacques Derrida, an interview with Jonathan Dronsfield, Nick Midgleys: Adrian Wilding. University of Warwick, 21 May 1993. In J. Dronsfield, & N. Midgley (Eds.), Responsibilities of deconstruction, *Warwick Journal of Philosophy, 6*, pp. 19–39

Derrida, J. (1998). Specters of Marx. In Wolfreys (Ed.), *The Derrida reader: Writing performances*. Edinburgh: Edinburgh University Press

Derrida, J. (2001a). 'A certain 'madness' must watch over thinking': Jacques Derrida's interview with François Ewald. In G. Biesta, & D. Egéa-Kuehne (Eds.), *Derrida & education*. London: Routledge

Derrida, J. (2001b). Time and memory, messianicity, the name of God. In P. Patton, & T. Smith (Eds.), *Jaques Derrida: Deconstruction engaged*. The Sydney Seminars. Sydney: Power Publications

Derrida, J. (2002). *Ethics, institutions and the right to philosophy* (P. Trifonas, trans.). Maryland: Rowman and Littlefield Publishers, Inc

DisabilityResources.org (n.d) *Inclusion and parent advocacy: A resource guide*. Retrieved September 24, 2006, from http://www.disabilityresources.org/DRMincl-intro.html

Diniz, F. (2003). 'Race' and the discourse of 'inclusion'. In J. Allan (Ed.), *Inclusion, participation and democracy: What is the purpose?* Dordrecht: Kluwer

Drinkwater, C. (2005). Supported living and the production of individuals. In S. Tremain (Ed.), *Foucault and the government of disability*. Ann Arbor: University of Michigan Press

Dronsfield, & Midgley (Eds.) (1997). Responsibilities of deconstruction. *Warwick Journal of Philosophy*. Warwick: University of Warwick, 6

Duffield, J., Allan, J., Turner, E. & Morris, B. (2000). Pupils' voices on achievement: An alternative to the standards agenda. *Cambridge Journal of Education, 30*(2), 263–274

Dyson, A. (2001). Special needs in the twenty-first century: Where we've been and where we're going *British Journal of Special Education, 28*(1), 24–29

Dyson, A., Ainscow, M., & Booth, T. (2004). Inclusion and the standards agenda: Squaring the circle in the English policy context? Paper presented at Critical Analyses of Inclusive Education Policy: An International Survey, Montreal, 19–21 July

Dyson, A., Howes, A., & Roberts, B. (2002). *A systematic review of the effectiveness of school-level actions for promoting participation by all students (EPPI-Centre Review, version 1.1)*. In Research Evidence in Education Library. London: EPPI-Centre, Social Science Research Unit, Institute of Education

Dyson, A., & Millward, A. (2000). *Schools and special needs: Issues of innovation and inclusion.* London: Paul Chapman

Eagleton, T. (1993). *Literary theory: An introduction.* Oxford, Basil Blackwell

Eagleton, T. (2006). Political Beckett? *New Left Review, 40*, 67–74

Eason, G. (2004). *Teachers oppose further inclusion.* Retrieved May 12, 2005, from http://news.bbc.co.uk/1/hi/education/1286108.stm

Edgoose, J. (1997). *An ethics of hesitant learning:* The caring justice of Levinas and Derrida In: *PES Yearbook.* Retrieved April 27, 2005, from http://www.ed.uiuc.edu/EPS/PES-Yearbook/97_docs/edgoose.html

Edgoose, J. (2001). Just decide! Derrida and the ethical aporias of education. In G. Biesta, & D. Egéa Kuehne (Eds.), *Derrida & education.* London: Routledge

Edmunds, A. L. (2003). The inclusive classroom – Can teachers keep up? A comparison of Nova Scotia and Newfoundland & Labrador perspectives. *Exceptionality Education Canada, 13*(1), 29–48

Education Queensland. (2002). *Professional standards for teachers: Guidelines for professional practice.* Brisbane: Education Queensland

Elliot, J. (2001). Characteristics of performative cultures: Their central paradoxes and limitations of educational reform. In D. Gleeson, & C. Husbands (Eds.), *The performing school.* London: Routledge

Ellman, R. (1982). *James Joyce.* New York: Oxford University Press

Enabling Education Network (EENET). (undated). *Striving for inclusive education for all: Queensland Parents of People with Disabilities (QPPD), Australia.* Retrived September 28, 2006, from http://www.eenet.org.uk/parents/stories/qppd.shtml

Equity in Education. (2004). *Conference report 2004.* Peebles: Equity in Education

Escape Artists. (n.d.). *The bridge.* Retrieved August 12, 2005, from http://www.escapeartists.co.uk/bridge.htm

Evans, M. (2004). *Killing thinking: The death of the universities.* London/New York: Continuum

Fairclough, N. (1992). *Discourse and social change.* Cambridge Polity

Fairclough, N. (2000). *New Labour, new language.* London: Routledge

Farrell, P., & Ainscow, M. (Eds.) (2002). *Making special education inclusive.* London: David Fulton

Fendler, L. (1998). What is it impossible to think? A genealogy of the educated subject. In T. Popekewitz & M. Brennan (Eds.), *Foucault's challenge: Discourse, knowledge and power in education.* New York: Teachers College Press

Ferri, B. (2004). Interrupting the discourse: A response to Reid and Valle. *Journal of Learning Disabilities, 37*(6), 509–515

Fielding, M. (2001). Taking education really seriously: Four years hard labour. In M. Fielding (Ed.) *Taking education really seriously: Four years hard labour.* London: RoutledgeFalmer

Fisher, R. (1997). Social cohesion in the United Kingdom: A case report. *Canadian Journal of Communication, 27*, 161–166

Flvybjerg, B. (2001). *Making social science matter: Why social inquiry fails and how it can succeed again.* Cambridge: Cambridge University Press

Foley, P., Parton, N., Roche, J., & Tucker, S. (2003). Contradictory and convergent trends in law and policy affecting children in England. In C. Hallet, & A. Prout (Eds.), *Hearing the voices of children: Social policy for a new century.* London: RoutledgeFalmer

Forbes, J. (2003). *Teacher/therapist collaborations: Discourses, positionings and power relations at work.* Ed.D Thesis. University of Stirling

Foucault, M. (1967). *Madness and civilisation.* London: Tavistock

Foucault, M. (1972). *The archaeology of knowledge.* London: Tavistock

Foucault, M. (1973). *The birth of the clinic.* London: Routledge

Foucault, M. (1977a). *Discipline and punish: The birth of the prison.* London: Penguin

Foucault, M. (1977b). A preface to transgression. In D. Bouchard (Ed.), *Language, countermemory, practice: Selected essays and interviews by Michel Foucault.* Oxford: Basil Blackwall

Foucault, M. (1978). *The history of sexuality: An introduction.* Harmondsworth: Penguin

Foucault, M. (1982). The subject and power. In H. Dreyfus, & P. Rabinow (Eds.), *Michel Foucault: Beyond structuralism and hermeneutics*

Foucault, M. (1984). On the genealogy of ethics: An overview of work in progress. In P. Rabinow (Ed.), *The Foucault reader.* New York: Pantheon

Foucault, M. (1985). *The use of pleasure: The history of sexuality, 2* (R Hurley, trans.). Harmondsworth: Penguin

Foucault, M. (1986). *The care of the self: The history of sexuality, 3* (R. Hurley, trans.). New York: Routledge

Foucault, M. (1988), The masked philosopher. In L. D. Kritzman (Ed.), *Michael Foucault: Politics, philosophy, culture. Interviews and other writings.* London: Routledge

Foucault, M. (1991). *Remarks on marx.* New York: Semiotext(e)

Foucault, M. (1994). A Preface to Transgression. In M. Foucault (Eds.). *Aesthetics: Essential works of Foucault 1954–1984* (Vol. 2.) London: Penguin

Foucault, M. (1997a). Polemics, politics and problematizations. In P. Rabinow (Ed.), *Michel Foucault ethics: Essential works of Foucault 1954–1984.* London: Penguin

Foucault, M. (1997b). Writing the self. In: A. Davidson (Ed.), Foucault and His Interlocutors. Chicago: University of Chicago Press

Freeman, M. (2000). The future of children's rights. *Children and Society, 14*(4), 277–293

French, S. (1993). Disability, impairment or something in between. In J. Swain, S. French, C. Barnes, & C. Thomas (Eds.), *Disabling barriers, enabling environments.* London: Sage

Fuchs, D., & Fuchs, L. (1994). Inclusive schools movement and the radicalization of special education reform. *Exceptional Children, 60*(4), 294–309

Fulcher, G. (1989). *Disabling policies? A comparative approach to education policy and disability.* London: Falmer

Furedi, F. (2004). *Where have all the intellectuals gone?* London: Continuum

Galbraith, J. K. (2004). *The economies of innocent fraud: Truth for our time.* London: Allen Lane

Gallagher, D. (1998). The scientific knowledge base of special education: Do we know what we think we know? *Exceptional Children, 64*(4), 294–309

Gallagher, D. (2006). If not absolute objectivity, then what? A reply to Kauffman and Sasso. *Exceptionality, 14*(2), 91–107

Galloway, S. (1995). *Changing lives: The social impact of the arts.* Edinburgh: The Scottish Arts Council

Gamarnikow, E., & Green, T. (1999). Developing social capital: Dilemmas, possibilities and limitations in education. In A. Hayton (Ed.), *Tackling disaffection and social exclusion.* London: Kogan Page

Garcia, S., & Alban-Metcalfe, J. (2005). The need for a new model. In M. Nind, J. Rix, K. Sheehy, & K. Simmons (Eds.), *Curriculum and pedagogy in inclusive education: Values into practice.* London/NewYork: RoutledgeFalmer and The Open University

Garret, S. (u.d) *A sense of place. Celebrating participation: Arts and social inclusion special feature. E-mailout.* Retrieved September 6, 2004, from http://www/e-mailout.org/garret.htm

Gates, H. (1992). Statistical stigmata. In D. Cornell, M. Rosenfield, & D. Carlson (Eds.), *Deconstruction and the possibility of justice.* London: Routledge

General Teaching Council for Scotland. (1995). *Medical examination standard for admission to courses of initial teacher education and training in relevant institutions leading to the award of a teaching qualification and for admission to the register of teachers.* Edinburgh: GTC

General Teaching Council for Scotland. (2002a). *Standard for full registration.* Edinburgh: GTC

General Teaching Council for Scotland. (2002b). *Standard for chartered teacher.* Edinburgh: GTC

General Teaching Council for Scotland. (2004). *Teaching Scotland.* March. Edinburgh: GTC

Gewirtz, S. (2000). Bringing the politics back in: A critical analysis of quality discourses in education. *British Journal of Educational Studies, 48*(4) 352–370

Gibson, M. (2004). *Additional Support Needs Bill.* National Association of Special Educational Needs Conference, March 20

Gillborn, D., & Youdell, D. (2000). *Rationing education: Policy, practice, reform and equity.* Buckingham: Open University Press

Gloucestershire Special Schools Protection League. (2005). *The tide is turning on inclusion.* Retrieved March 3, 2005, from http://www.gsspl.org.uk/

Goethe, J. (1819). The minstrel's book, West-Eastern Divan. Retrieved on August 12, 2006, from http://www.everypoet.com/archive/poetry/goethe/goethe_contents.htm

Goodley, D., & Moore, M. (2000). Doing disability research: Activist lives and the academy. *Disability and Society, 15*(6), 861–882

Gough, N. (2004). RhizomANTically becoming-cyborg: Performing posthuman pedagogies. *Educational Philosophy and Theory, 36*(3), 253–265

Gould, H. (1997). Culture and social capital. In F. Matarasso (Ed.), *Recognising culture: A series of briefing papers on culture and development*. Stroud: Comedia

Gregoriou, Z. (2001). Does speaking of others involve receiving the 'other'? A postcolonial reading of receptivity in Derrida's deconstruction of Timaeus. In G. Biesta, & D. Egéa-Kuehne (Eds.), *Derrida & education*. London: Routledge

Gregoriou, Z. (2002). *Performing pedagogy with Deleuze: The rhizomatics of 'theory of education,'* Oxford: Philosophy of Education Society of Great Britain Conference Proceedings

Gregoriou, Z. (2004). Commencing the rhizome: Towards a minor philosophy of education. *Educational Philosophy and Theory, 36*(3), 233–251

Grumet, M. (1991). The politics of personal knowledge. In C. Witherell, & N. Noddings (Eds.), *Stories lives tell: Narrative and dialogue in education*. New York: Teachers College Press

Gustavsson, A., Sandvin, J., Traustadóttir, R., & Tøssebro, J. (2005). *Resistance, reflection and change: Nordic disability research*. Lund: Studentlitteratur

Haghighi, M. (2002). Neo-anarchism. In B. Massumi (Ed.), *A shock to thought: Expression after Deleuze and Guattari*. London/New York: Routledge

Halpin, T. (2006). Mainstream schools can't manage special needs pupils, say teachers. *Times*. Retrieved on September, 25 from http://www.timesonline.co.uk/article/0,,2-2184133,00.html

Halsey, A. (1992). *The decline of the donnish dominion*. Oxford: Clarendon

Hammersley, M. (2001). On 'systematic' reviews of research literatures: A 'narrative' response to Evans and Benfield. *British Educational Research Journal, 27*(5), 543–554

Hanko, G. (2005). Towards an inclusive school culture: The 'affective curriculum'. In M. Nind, J. Rix, K. Sheehy, & K. Simmons (Eds.), *Curriculum and pedagogy in inclusive education: Values into practice*. London/New York: RoutledgeFalmer/The Open University

Hansard (2005). *Debate on special schools and special educational needs*. 22 June, Retrieved on July 10, 2006, from http://www.publicwhip.org.ukdivision.php? date = 2005-06-228 number=17

Harklau, L., Norwood, R., & Hopson, R. (2005). Negotiating researcher roles in ethnographic program evaluation: A postmodern lens. Commentary. *Anthropology and Education Quarterly, 36*(3), 278–295

Hargreaves, D. (1996). *Teaching as a research-based profession: Possibilities and prospects*. The Teacher Training Agency Annual Lecture, April

Harland, J., Kinder K., Lord, P., Slott, A., Schagen, I., & Haynes, J. (2000). *The effects and effectiveness of arts education in School*. Slough: NFER

Harvey-Koelpin, S. (2006). The impact of reform on students with disabilities. In E. Brantlinger, (Ed.), *Who benefits from special education? Remediating (fixing) other people's children*. Mahwah, New Jersey: Lawrence Erlbaum Associates

Hawkesworth, M. (1988). *Theoretical issues in policy analysis*. Albany: State University of New York Press

Henley, C. (2001). Good intentions – Unpredictable consequences. *Disability and Society, 16*(7), 933–947

Her Majesty's Inspectorate in Education. (2002). *How good is our school?* Retrieved October 24, 2006, from http://www.hmie.gov.uk/documents/publication/HGIOS.pdf

Her Majesty's Inspectorate in Education. (2003). *Count us in: Achieving potential in Scottish schools.* Retrieved July 10, 2004, from www.hmie.gov.uk/documents/publication/cui-03.html

Her Majesty's Inspectorate in Education. (2004). *How good is our school? Quality management in education. Inclusion and equality, Part 2: Evaluating education for pupils with additional support needs in mainstream schools*. Retrieved March 10, 2006, from http://www.hmie.gov.uk/documents/publication/hgiosasnms.pdf

Hernstein Smith, B. (1992). Judgement after the fall. In D. Cornell, M. Rossenfield, & D. G. Carlson (Eds.), *Deconstruction and the possibility of justice*. London: Routledge

Hodkinson, P. (2004). Research as a form of work: Expertise, community and methodological objectivity. *British Educational Research Journal, 30*(1), 3–8

Holdsworth, A. (1993). Our allies within. *Coalition*, June, 4-10

Honan, E. (2004). (Im)plausibilities: A rhizo-textual analysis of policy texts and teachers' work. *Educational Philosophy and Theory, 36*(3) 267–281

House of Commons Education and Skills Select Committee. (2006). *Special educational needs: Third report of session 2005, 2006, Volume 1. Report, together with formal minutes.* London: The Stationary Office Limited

Howard, J. (1998). Subjectivity and space: Deleuze and Guattari's BwO in the new world order. In E. Kaufman, & K. J. Heller (Eds.), *Deleuze and Guattari: New mappings in politics, philosophy and culture.* Minneapolis/London: University of Minnesota Press

Hughes, B. (2005). What can a Foucauldian theory contribute? In S. Tremain (Ed.), *Foucault and the government of disability.* Ann Arbor: University of Michigan Press

Hunt, P. (Ed.) (1996). *Stigma.* London: Geoffrey Chapman Publishing

I'Anson, J., & Allan, J. (2006). Children's rights in practice: A study of change within a primary school. *International Journal of Children's Spirituality, 11*(2), 265–279

Independent Panel for Special Education Advice. (2005). *Submission to the Education and Skills Select Committee inquiry into special educational needs.* Woodbridge: IPSEA

Independent Panel for Special Education Advice. (n.d.). Retrieved October 23, 2006, from http:/ www.ipsea.org.uk

James, A., Jenks, C., & Prout, A. (1998). *Theorising childhood.* Oxford: Polity Press

Jowell, T. (2002). *Hansard: Written answers to questions*, House of Commons, 24 June, Column 639W. Retrieved August 13, 2005, from http://www.publications.parliament.uk/pa/cm200102/cmhansrd/vo020624/text/20624w01.htm

Joyce, J., (1993) *Ulysses.* Oxford: Oxford University Press

Kauffman, J., & Hallahan, D. (Eds.) (1995). *The illusion of full inclusion: A comprehensive critique of a current special education bandwagon.* Austin: Pro-Ed

Kauffman, J., & Sasso, G. (2006a). Toward ending cultural and cognitive relativism in special education. *Exceptionality, 14*(2), 65–90

Kauffman, J. & Sasso, G. (2006b). Rejoinder: Certainty, doubt and the reduction of uncertainty. *Exceptionality, 14*(2), 109–120

Kavale, K. & Mostert, M. (2004). *The positive side of special education: Minimizing its fads, fancies and follies.* Lanham: Scarecrow Education

Keats, J. (1817). *Letter to George and Thomas Keats, 21 December.* Retrieved October 12, 2006, from http://en.wikipedia.org/wiki/Negative_Capability

Kendall, K., Kinder, K., Halsley, K., Fletcher-Morgan, C., White, R., & Brown, C. (2003). *An evaluation of alternative education initiatives.* Research report no 403. Norwich: DfES

Kinder, K., Halsey, K., Kendall, S., Atkinson, M., Moor, H., Wilkin, A., White, R., & Rigby, W. (2000). *Working out well: Effective provision for excluded pupils.* Slough: NFER

Kinder, K., & Harland, J. (2004). The arts and social inclusion: What's the evidence? *Support for Learning, 19*(2), 52–56

Klee, P. (1961). *Notebooks* (P. Findlay trans.). London: Faber & Faber

Knowleson, J. (1996). *Dammed to fame: The life of Samuel Beckett.* London: Bloomsbury

Kundera, M. (1986). *The art of the novel.* London: Faber and Faber

Lather, P. (1991). *Getting smart: Feminist research and pedagogy within/in the postmodern.* New York: Routledge

Lather, P. (1993). Fertile obsession: Validity after poststructuralism. *The Sociological Quarterly, 34*(4), 673–693

Lather, P. (2004). Applied Derrida: (Mis) Reading the work of mourning in educational research. In P. Trifonas, & M. Peters (Ed.), *Derrida, deconstruction and education.* London: Basil Blackwell

Lather, P. (2005). *Scientism and scientificity in the rage for accountability: A feminist deconstruction.* Paper presented to the ESRC Research Capacity Building Network seminar, The Educational Future and Innovative Qualitative Research: International Perspectives. Manchester Metropolitan University, February. Retrieved October 15, 2006, from http://www.coe.ohio-state.edu/plather/2000.html

Lather, P. (2006). *(Post)feminist methodology: Getting lost OR a scientificity we can bear to learn from.* Paper presented at the research methods festival, Oxford, July. Retrieved October 22, 2006, from http://www.ccsr.ac.uk/methods/festival/programme/cfe/documents/lather.pdf

Learning and Teaching Scotland. (1999). *Financial education in Scottish schools: A statement of position.* Retrieved April 10, 2004, from http://www.ltscotland.org.uk/resources/financial_ed_position_paper.pd

Lee, N. (1999). The challenge of childhood: Distributions of childhood's ambiguity in adult institutions. *Childhood, 6*(4), 455–474

Levinas, E. (1969). *Totality and infinity* (A. Lingis, trans.). Pittsburgh: Duquesne

Linton, S. (1998). *Claiming disability: Knowledge and identity.* New York: New York University Press

Lloyd, G. (2003). Inclusion and problem groups: The story of ADHD. In J. Allan (Ed.), *Participation, inclusion and identity: What is the purpose?* Dordrecht: Kluwer

Longmore, P. (1997). Screening stereotypes: Images of disabled people in television and motion pictures. In A. Gartner, & T. Joe (Eds.), *Images of the disabled, disabling images.* New York: Praeger

Luke, A., Ladwig, J., Lingard, B., Hayes, D., & Mills, M. (1999). *Queensland school reform longtitudinal study.* St Lucia: University of Queensland

Lunt, I., & Norwich, B. (1999). *Can effective schools be inclusive schools?* London: Institute of Education, University of London

Lynch, H., & Allan, J. (2006). *Social inclusion and the arts.* Report to the Scottish Arts Council. Stirling: University of Stirling

Lyotard, J. (1993). *The postmodern explained.* Minneapolis/London: University of Minnesota Press

Macbeath, J., Galton, M., Steward, S., Macbeath, A., & Page, C. (2006). *The costs of inclusion.* Report prepared for the National Union of Teachers. Retrieved September 24, 2006, from http://www.teachers.org.uk/resources/pdf/CostsofInclusion.pdf

MacIntyre, A. (1984). *After virtue: A study in moral theory.* Notre Dame: University of Notre Dame

MacIntyre, A. (1999). *Dependent rational animals: Why human beings need the virtues.* Chicago: Open Court Press

Mackie, D. (2004). *EIS presidential address.* Retrieved March 11, 2004, from http://www.thecourier.co.uk/output/2004/06/11/newsstory6010229t0.asp

Maclure, M. (2005a). 'Clarity bordering on stupidity': Where's the quality in systematic review? *Journal of Education Policy, 20*(4), 393–416

Maclure, M. (2005b). Deconstruction. In B. Somekh, & C. Lewin (Eds.), *Research methods in the social sciences.* London: Sage

Maclure, M. (2005c). *Entertaining doubts: On frivolity as resistance.* Keynote presentation to the Discourse, Power, Resistance Conference, Plymouth, March

Macmillan, R., Meyer, M., Edmunds, A., Edmunds, G., & Feltmate, C. (2002). A survey of the impact of funding cuts on inclusion. A report to the NSTU. Halifax: Nova Scotia Teachers Union

Mahony, P., & Hextall, I. (2000). *Reconstructing teaching: Standards, performance and accountability.* London: Routledge Falmer

Makareth, C., & Turner, T. (2002). *Joined up working.* London: Health Visitors Association

Malin, M. (1999). I'm rather tired of hearing about it . . . : Challenges in instructing and effective anti-racism teacher education program. *Curriculum Perspectives, 19*(1), 1–11

Mannion, G., & I'anson, J. (2004). Beyond the Disneyesque: Children's participation, spatiality and adult-child relations. *Childhood, 11*(3), 303–318

Marshall, J. (1989). Foucault and education. *Australian Journal of Education, 33*(2), 99–113

Masson, J. (2005). Researching children's perspectives: Legal issues. In K. Sheey, M. Nind, J. Rix, & K. Simmons (Eds.), *Ethics and research in inclusive education: Values into practice.* Maidenhead: Open University Press

Massumi, B. (1992). *A user's guide to Capitalism and Schizophrenia: Deviations from Deleuze and Guattari.* Cambridge: MIT Press

Matarasso, F. (1997). *Use or ornament? The social impact of participation in the arts.* Stroud: Comedia

McEvoy, A. (n.d.). Social inclusion: Some observations. Celebrating participation: Arts and social inclusion special feature. E-mailout. Retrieved September 6, 2004, from http://www/e-mailout.org/garret.htm.

McLary, S. (1985). The politics of silence and sound. Afterword in J Attali *Noise: The political economy of music* (B. Massumi, trans.). Minneapolis: University of Minnesota Press

McLean, G. (2005). In the hood. *Guardian unlimited*. Retrieved October 24, 2006, from http://www.guardian.co.uk/g2/story/0,3604,1482816,00.html

McNary, S. (2005). *What successful teachers do in inclusive classrooms*. London: Sage

McWhorter, L. (2005). Foreword. In S. Tremain (Ed.), *Foucault and the government of disability*. Ann Arbor: University of Michigan Press

Menter, I., Muschamp, Y., Nicolls, P., Ozga, J., & Pollard, A. (1997). *Work and identity in the primary school*. Buckingham: Open University Press

Midgley, N. (1997). On responsibility: Jacques Derrida, an interview with Jonathan Dronsfield, Nick Midgley Adrian Wilding, University of Warwick, 21 May 1993. In J. Dronsfield, & N. Midgley (Eds.), *Responsibilities of deconstruction*, Warwick Journal of Philosophy, Vol 6, pp. 19–39

Miller, J. (1993). *The passion of Michel Foucault*. London: HarperCollins

Milne, V. (2005). *Joined up working in the Scottish Executive*. Edinburgh: Office of Chief Researcher, Scottish Executive Social Research

Minghella, A. (2004). *Keynote speech, 21st Century literacies – Creativity and ambition*, September 17, Macrobert, Stirling

Mitchell, D., & Snyder, S. (2001). Representations and its discontents: The uneasy home of disability in literature and film. In G. Albrecht, K. Seelman, & M. Bury (Eds.), *Handbook of disability studies*. Thousand Oaks/London/New Delhi: Sage

Mitchell, D., & Snyder, S. (2004). *Disability and embodiment: The circle stories of Riva Lehrer in Riva Lehrer: Circle stories. Exhibition catalogue*. Chicago: Gescheidle

Mittler, P. (2000). *Working towards inclusive education*. London: David Fulton

Moore, M., Beazley, S., & Maelzer, J. (1998). *Researching disability issues*. Maidenhead: Open University Press

Nasty Girls (n.d.). Nasty girls. Retrieved May 22, 2006 from http: www.nasty-girls.co.uk/index.html

National Association of Education. (2005). *Testing, inclusion on a collision course?* Retrieved August 1, 2006, from http://www.nea.org/specialed/research-specialed.html

National Association of Schoolmasters Union of Women Teachers (2001). Teachers oppose further inclusion. Retrieved April 12, 2005, from http://news.bbc.co.uk/1/hi/education/1286108.stm

National Advisory Committee on Creative and Cultural Education. (1999). *All our futures: Creativity, culture and education*. London: NACCCE

National Board for Professional Teaching Standards. (1999). *Professional teaching standards*. Washington: NBPTS

National Board for Professional Teaching Standards. (2001). *Professional teaching standards*. Washington: NBPTS

National Council on Disability. (1994). *Inclusionary education for students with disabilities: Keeping the promise*. Washington: The Council

National Council on Disability. (2000). *Back to school on civil rights*. Retrieved September 24, 2006, from http://www.ncd.gov/newsroom/publications/backtoschool_1.html

Nelson, E. (1997). *Critical essays: Gay and lesbian writers of color*. Binghamton: Haworth Press

Netto, G., Arshad, R., de Lima, P., Diniz, F., MacEwen, M., Patel, V., & Syed, R. (2001). *Audit of research on minority ethnic issues in Scotland from a 'race' perspective*. Edinburgh: Scottish Office

New Horizons for Learning. *Section 504: It is not unfunded special education*. Retrieved on September 24, 2006 from http://www.newhorizons.org/spneeds/inclusion/law/hayes3.htm

Nietzsche, F. (1968). *The will to power*. Trans W. Kaufman and R. Hollingdale. New York: Vintage

Nietzsche, F. (1983). *Untimely meditations* (R. J. Hollingdale, trans.) Cambridge: Cambridge University Press

Nietzsche, F. (1994). *On the genealogy of morality*. K. Ansell, (Ed.) (C. Diethe, trans.) Cambridge New York: Cambridge University Press

Nind, M., Wearmouth, J., Collins, J., Hall, K., Rix, J., & Sheehy, K. (2004). *A systematic review of pedagogical approaches that can effectively include children with special educational needs in mainstream classrooms with a particular focus on peer group interactive approaches*. Research

Evidence in Education Library. London: EPPI-Centre, Social Science Research Unit, Institute of Education

Nixon, J., & Sikes, P. (2003). Introduction: Reconceptualizing the debate. In P. Sikes, J. Nixon., & W. Carr (Eds.), *The moral foundations of educational research.* Maidenhead: Open University Press

Office for Standards in Education. (2004). *Special educational needs and disability: Towards inclusive schools.* London: Ofsted. Retrieved December 16, 2004, from http://image.guardian.co.uk/sys-files/Education/documents/2004/10/12/Ofsted.pdf

Oliver, M. (1992). Intellectual masturbation: A rejoinder to Söder and Booth. *European Journal of Special Needs Education, 7*(1) 20–28

Oliver, M. (1996). *Understanding disability: From theory to practice.* Basingstoke: Macmillan

Oliver, M. (1999). Final accounts and the parasite people. In M. Corker, & S. French (Eds.), *Disability discourse.* Buckingham: Open University Press

Oliver, M. (2002). *Emancipatory research: A vehicle for social transformation or policy development.* Paper presented at the Annual Disability Research Seminar, December 2, Dublin

Oliver, M. (2004). The social model in action: If I had a hammer. In C. Barnes, & G. Mercer (Eds.), *Implementing the social model of disability: Theory and research.* Leeds: The Disability Press

Oliver, M., & Barnes, C. (1998). *Disabled people and social policy: From exclusion to inclusion.* Harlow: Addison Wesley Longman

O'Neil, O. (2002). *A question of trust.* Reith Lectures, BBC Radio 4. Retrieved 12 March, 2004, from www.bbc.co.uk/radio4/reith2002/lecture3_text.shtml

Openspaceworld. (n.d.). *Open space technology.* Retrieved April 10, 2006, from http://www.openspaceworld.org/

Ozga, J. (1990). Policy research and policy theory: A comment on Fitz and Halpin. *Journal of Education Policy, 5*(4), 359–362

Ozga, J. (2002). Education governance in the United Kingdom: The modernisation project. *European Educational Research Journal, 2,* 331–341

Paterson, L. (2000a). Civil society and democratic renewal. In S. Baron, J. Field, & T. Schuller (Eds.), *Social capital: Critical perspectives.* Oxford: Oxford University Press

Paterson, L. (2000b). *Education and the Scottish Parliament.* Edinburgh: Dunedin Academic Press

Paterson, L. (2003). The survival of the democratic intellect: Academic values in Scotland and England. *Higher Education Quarterly, 57*(1), 67–93

Paterson, K., & Hughes, B. (1999). Disability studies and phenomenology: The carnal politics of every-day life. *Disability and Society, 14*(5), 597–611

Patrick, M. (1996). Assuming responsibility: Or Derrida's disclaimer. In: J. Brannigan, R. Robbins, & J. Wolfreys (Eds.), *Applying: To Derrida.* Basingstoke, Macmillan

Patton, P. (2000). *Deleuze and the political.* London: Routledge

Patton, P. (2003). Future politics. In P. Patton, & J. Protevi (Eds.), *Between Deleuze and Derrida.* London: Continuum

Patton, P., & Proveti, J. (Eds.) (2003). *Between Deleuze and Derrida.* London/New York: Continuum

Persson, B. (2006). *Inclusive education in the Nordic Welfare State: Obstacles, dilemmas and opportunities.* Paper presented at the European Conference on Educational Research, Geneva, 11–15 September

Peter, M. (1995). Trends in law: Fifteen years of education policy-making, 1979–94. In P. Potts, F. Armstrong, & M. Masterton (Eds.), *Equality and diversity in education: National and international contexts.* London/New York: Routledge and Open University

Phillips, M. (2005). *The pitiliess universe of planet Warnock.* 9 June. Retrieved on March, 3, 2006, from http://www.melaniephillips.com/articles/archives/001254.html

Pinar, W. (2002). *What is curriculum theory? Anti-intellectualism in schools of education.* Miller Lecture Series, Indiana University, September

Pratt, M. (1992). *Imperial eyes: Travel writing and transculturation.* New York: Routledge

Prout, A. (1993). *Constructing and reconstructing childhood. Contemporary issues.* London: Routledge

Purves, L. (2000). Justice shines on Summerhill, *Times Educational Supplement, 3,* 96

Quality Assurance Agency for Higher Education (1999). *Code of practice for the assurance of academic quality and standards in higher education: Students with disabilities.* Gloucester: QAA

Rajchman, J. (2001). *The Deleuze connections*. Cambridge: MIT Press

Remedios, R., & Allan, J. (2004). *Evaluation of New Community Schools in Stirling*. Report to Stirling Council Services. University of Stirling

Riddell, S. (2002). *Policy and practice in education: Special educational needs*. Edinburgh: Dunedin Academic Press

Riddell, S., & Brown, S. (1994). Special educational needs provision in the United Kingdom – The policy context. In S. Riddell, & S. Brown (Eds.), *Special educational needs policy in the 1990s*. London: Routledge

Rioux, M., & Bach, M. (Eds.) (1994). *Disability is not measles: New research paradigms in disability*. North York: L'Institut Roeher Institute

Riseborough, G. (1992). Primary headship, state policy and the challenge of the 1990s. *Journal of Education Policy, 8*(2), 123–142

Riseborough, G. (1993). Recent policy, the numbers game and the schooling of the hearing impaired: A study of one teacher's career. *European Journal of Special Needs Education, 31*(2), 134–152

Rix, J., Hall, K., Nind, M. Sheehy, K., & Wearmouth, J. (2005). *A systematic review of interactions in pedagogical approaches with reported outcomes for the academic and social inclusion of pupils with special educational needs in mainstream classrooms*. Research Evidence in Education Library. London: EPPI-Centre, Social Science Research Unit, Insitute of Education

Rizvi, F., & Kemmis, S. (1987). *Dilemmas of reform*. Geelong: Deakin Institute of Education

Rorty, R. (1989). *Contingency, irony and solidarity*. Cambridge: Cambridge University Press

Rorty, R. (1990). Foucault, Dewey, Nietzsche. *Raritan, 9*, 1–8

Rose, N. (1996). *Inventing our selves: Psychology, power and personhood*. Cambridge: Cambridge University Press

Rouse, M., & Florian, L. (1995). Inclusive practice in English secondary schools: Lessons learned. *Cambridge Journal of Education, 31*(3), 399–412

Roy, K. (2003). *Teachers in nomadic spaces: Deleuze and curriculum*. New York: Peter Lang

Roy, K. (2004). Overcoming nihilism: From communication to Deleuzian expression. *Educational Philosophy and Theory, 36*(3), 297–312

Ruddock, J., Chaplain, R., & Wallace, G. (1996). *School improvement: What can pupils tell us?* London: David Fulton

Sachs, J. (2003). *The activist teaching profession*. Maidenhead: Open University Press

Said, E. (1994). *Representations of the intellectual*. London: Vintage

Scheurich, J. (1994). Policy archaeology: A new policy studies methodology. *Journal of Education Policy, 9*(4), 297–316

Schuller, T., Baron S., & Field, J. (2000). Social capital: A review and critique. In S. Baron, J. Field, & T. Schuller (Eds.). *Social capital: Critical perspectives*. London: Routledge

Scottish Arts Council. (2003). *Social inclusion projects on the button*. News release. Retrieved May 13, 2005, from http://www.scottisharts.org.uk/1/latestnews/1000728.aspx

Scottish Association of Black Researchers. (2001). *An ethical code for researching 'race', 'racism' and 'anti-racism' in Scotland*. Retrieved May 5, 2003, from www.sabre.ukgo.com

Scottish Executive. (2001a). *Scottish ministers' response to the Education Committee's report on its enquiry into special needs*. Edinburgh: Scottish Executive

Scottish Executive. (2001b). *A teaching profession for the 21ˢᵗ century: Agreement reached following recommendations made in the McCrone report*. Edinburgh: Scottish Executive

Scottish Executive. (2003). *Consultation on Draft Education (Additional Support Needs) Bill*. Edinburgh: Scottish Executive

Scottish Executive. (2004). *A curriculum for excellence*. Retrieved October 23, 2005, from http://www.scotland.gov.uk/Publications/2004/11/20178/45862

Scottish Executive. (2005). *Supporting children's learning: The code of practice*. Edinburgh: Scottish Executive

Scottish Parliament. (2000a). *Official report*. Education, Culture and Sport Committee, 30 May

Scottish Parliament. (2000b). *Official report*. Education, Culture and Sport Committee, 14 June

Scottish Parliament. (2001a). *Official report of special needs inquiry*

Scottish Parliament. (2001b). *Official report of debate on motion SIM-1931: Special educational needs*

Scottish Parliament. (2003a). *Official report.* Education Committee, 3 December

Scottish Parliament. (2003b). *Official report.* Education Committee, 26 November

Scottish Parliament. (2003c). *Official report.* Education Committee, 12 November

Scottish Parliament. (2003d). *Official report.* Education Committee, 19 November

Scottish Science Advisory Committee. (2003). *Why science education matters.* Retrieved April 10, 2004, from http://www.scottishscience.org.uk/main_files/publications.htm

Sebba, J., & Sachdev, D. (1997). *What works in inclusive education.* London: Barnardos

Semetsky, I. (2004). Becoming-language/becoming other: Whence ethics? *Educational Philosophy and Theory, 36*(3), 313–325

Sennett, R. (1995). Sex, lies and social science: An exchange. *New York Review of Books,* May 25. Retrieved October 15, 2006, from http://www.nybooks.com/articles/1889

Shacklock, G., & Thorp, L. (2005). Live history and narrative approaches. In B. Somekh, & C. Lewin (Eds.), *Research methods in the social sciences.* London: Sage

Shakespeare, T. (2005). *For whom the school bell tolls.* BBC – Ouch! July 11. Retrieved July 11, 2006, from http://www.bbc.co.uk/ouch/columnists/tom/270605_index.shtml

Shakespeare, T. (2006). *Disability rights and wrongs.* London: Routledge

Shakespeare, T., & Watson, N. (1997). Defending the social model. *Disability and Society, 12*(2), 293–300

Shapiro, J. (1993). *No pity-people with disabilities forging a new civil rights movement.* New York: Times Books

Shaw, L. (2002). *We want to be together.* Retrieved July 22, 2003, from http://inclusion.uwe.ac.uk/inclusionweek/articles/together.htm

Sheehy, K. (2005). Introduction: Inclusive education and ethical research. In K. Sheey, M. Nind, J. Rix, & K. Simmons (Eds.), *Ethics and research in inclusive education: Values into practice.* Maidenhead: Open University Press

Shilling, C. (1993). *The body and social theory.* London: Sage

Shumway, D. (1989). *Michel Foucault.* Charlottesville: University Press of Virginia

Sikes, P., Nixon, J., & Carr, W. (Eds.) (2003). *The moral foundations of educational research.* Maidenhead: Open University Press

Simons, M., & Masschelein, J. (2005). Inclusive education for exclusive pupils: A critical analysis of the government of the exceptional. In S. Tremain (Ed.), *Foucault and the government of disability.* Ann Arbor: University of Michigan Press

Skidmore, D. (2004). *Inclusion: The dynamic of school development.* Maidenhead: Open University Press

Skrtic, T. (Ed.) (1995). *Disability and democracy: Reconstructing (special) education for postmodernity.* New York: Teachers College, Columbia University

Slee, R. (1993). The politics of integration: New sites for old practices? *Disability, Handicap and Society, 8*(4), 351–360

Slee, R. (1998). The politics of theorising special education. In C. Clark, A. Dyson, & A. Millward (Eds.), *Theorising special education.* London: Routledge

Slee, R. (2001a). Inclusion in practice: Does practice make perfect? *Educational Review, 53*(2), 113–123

Slee R. (2001b). Social justice and the changing directions in educational research: The case of inclusive education. *International Journal of Inclusive Education, 5*(2/3), 167–178

Slee, R. (2003). Teacher education, government and inclusive schooling: The politics of the Faustian waltz. In J. Allan (Ed.), *Inclusion, participation and democracy: What is the purpose?* Dordrecht: Kluwer

Slee, R. (2004). Meaning in the service of power. In L. Ware (Ed.), *Ideology and the politics of in/exclusion.* New York: Peter Lang

Slee, R. (2005). Meaning in the service of power. In L. Ware (Ed.), *Ideology and the politics of in/exclusion.* New York: Peter Lang

Slee, R. (2006). Limits to and possibilities for educational reform. *International Journal of Inclusive Education, 10*(2/3), 109–120

Slee, R., & Allan, J. (2001). Excluding the included: A reconsideration of inclusive education, *International Journal of Sociology of Education, 11*(2) 173–191

Sloterdijk, P. (1987). *Critique of cynical reason,* Minneapolis: University of Minnesota Press

Smart, B. (1998). Foucault, Levinas and the subject of responsibility. In J. Moss (Ed.) *The later Foucault.* London: Sage

Smith, D. (1998). The place of ethics in Deleuze's philosophy: Three questions of immanence. In E. Kaufman, & K. J. Heller (Eds.), *Deleuze and Guattari: New mappings in politics, philosophy and culture.* Minneapolis/London: University of Minnesota Press

Smith, T., & Noble, M. (1995). *Education divides: Poverty and schooling in the 1990s.* London: Child Poverty Action Group

Smyth, J. (2000). Reclaiming social capital through critical teaching. *Elementary School Journal, 100*(5), 491–511

Smyth, J. (2001). Managing the myth of the self-managing school as an international educational reform. In *Taking education really seriously: Four years hard labour.* London: RoutledgeFalmer

Smyth, J., Dow, A., Hattam, R., Reid, A., & Shacklock, G. (2000). *Teachers' work in a globalising economy.* London: Falmer Press

Smyth, J., & Shacklock, G. (1998). *Remaking teaching: Ideology, policy and practice.* London: Routledge

Snyder, S., & Mitchell, D. (n.d.(a)). DvD: A Brace Yourselves Production

Snyder, S., & Mitchell, D. (n.d. (b)) *Self preservation: The art of Riva Lehrer.* DVD: A Brace Yourselves Production

Söder, M. (1990). Prejudice or ambivalence? Attitudes toward persons with disabilities. *Disability, Handicap & Society, 5*(3), 227–241

SOS!SEN (n.d.). *The independent helpline for special educational needs.* Retrieved October 23, 2006, from http://www.special-educational-needs.co.uk/sos!sen%20news.htm

Special Child. (undated). *Horror stories.* Retrieved on September 25, 2005 from http://www.specialchild.com/horror.html

Spinoza, B. (1985). Treatise on the emendation of the intellect. In E. Curley, trans. & Ed. *The collected works of Spinoza, vol. 1.* Princeton, NJ: Princeton University Press

Spivak, G. (1996). Explanation and culture marginalia. In D. Landry, & G. MacLean (Eds.), *The Spivak reader: Selected works of Gayatri Chakravorty Spivak.* New York: Routledge. New York: Routledge

Stead, J., Lloyd, G., & Cohen, D. (2006). Introduction: Widening our view of ADHD. In G. Lloyd, D. Cohen K. J. Stead (Eds.), *Critical new perspectives on ADHD.* Abingdon: Routledge

St. Pierre, E. (2001). Coming to theory: Finding Foucault and Deleuze. In K. Weiler (Ed.), *Feminist engagements: Reading, resisting and revisioning male theorists in education and cultural studies,* New York/London: Routledge

St. Pierre, E. (2004). Deleuzian concepts for education: The subject undone. *Educational Philosophy and Theory, 36*(3), 283–296

Strathearn, M. (1997). Improving ratings: Audit in the British university system. *European Review, 5*(3), 305–321

Strathearn, M. (2000). The tyranny of transparency. *British Journal of Educational Research, 26*(3), 309–321

Stronach, I. (2005). *On Her Majesty's disservice: The government Inspector and Summerhill.* Paper presented to the First Congress of Qualitative Inquiry, University of Illinois at Urbana-Champaign, 4–7 May

Sullivan, M. (2005). Subjected bodies: Rehabilitation and the politics of management. In S. Tremain (Ed.), *Foucault and the government of disability.* Ann Arbor: University of Michigan Press

Summerhill Press Statement. (2000). Retrieved May 11, 2006, from http://www.pathsoflearning.org/library/legal.cfm

Sunday Herald (2005) *'Inclusion has become a dogma . . . It's a mistake': Primary school teachers' discipline diaries,* January 16, 35

Swirl:Derrida (n.d). *How to astonish your friends & confound your enemies with deconstruction.* Retrieved March 15, 2005, from www.sou.edu/English/IDTC/People/derrida.HTM

Taylor, M. (1989) *Sources of the self: The making of the modern identity.* Cambridge: Cambridge University Press

Taylor, M. (1995). Rhizomic folds of interstanding. *Tekhnema 2: Technics and Finitude,* Spring. Retrieved June 27, 2003, from http://tekhnema.free.fr/2Taylor.htm.

Taylor, M., & Saarinen, E. (1994). *Imagologies: Media philosophy.* London: Routledge

Teacher Training Agency (2002). *Award of qualified teacher status and requirements for the provision of initial teacher training.* London: TTA

Thomas, G., & Glenny, G. (2005). Thinking about inclusion: Whose reason? What evidence? In K. Sheey, M. Nind, J. Rix, & K. Simmons (Eds.), *Ethics and research in inclusive education: Values into practice.* Buckingham: Open University Press

Thomas, G., & Loxley, A. (2001). *Deconstructing special education and constructing inclusion.* Buckingham: Open University Press

Thomas, G., & Vaughan, M. (2004). *Inclusive education: Readings and reflections.* Maidenhead: Open University Press

Thompson, E. P. (1970). *Warwick University Ltd.* Harmondsworth: Penguin

Thurber, S. (1980). Disability and monstrosity: A look at literary distortions of handicapping conditions. *Rehabilitation Literature, 41*(1,2), 12–15

Times Educational Supplement Scotland. (2002). *Inclusion doesn't work for outrageous behaviour.* Letters., November 22

Tomlinson, S. (2005). *Education in a post-welfare society.* Buckingham: Open University Press

Tooley, J. (1998). *Educational research: A critique.* London: Ofsted

Tranter, R., & Palin, N. (2004). Including the excluded: An art in itself. *Support for Learning, 19*(2), 88–95

Tremain, S. (2005) (Ed.), *Foucault and the government of disability.* Ann Arbor: University of Michigan Press

Troyna, B., & Vincent, C. (1996). The ideology of expertism: The framing of special education and racial equality policies in the local state. In C. Christensen, & F. Rizvi (Eds.), *Disability and the dilemmas of education and justice.* Buckingham: Open University Press

Van Manen, M. (2002). Writing in the dark. In M. van Manen (Ed.), *Writing in the dark: Phenomenological studies in interpretive inquiry.* London, Ontario: The Althouse Press

Veyne, P. (1997). The final Foucault and his critics. In A. Davidson (Ed.), *Foucault and his interlocutors.* Chicago: University of Chicago Press

Vidovitch, L., & Slee, R. (2001). Bringing universities to account? Exploring some global and local policy tensions. *Journal of Educational Policy, 16*(5), 431–453

Vincent, C. (2000). *Including parents? Education, citizenship and parental agency.* Birmingham/Philadelphia: Open University Press

Virilio, P. (1986). *Speed and politics* (M. Polizzotti, trans.). New York: Semiotext[e]

Ware, L. (2002). A moral conversation on disability: Risking the personal in educational contexts. *Hypatia, 17*(3), 143–172

Ware, L. (2003a). Understanding disability and transforming schools. In T. Booth, K. Nes, & M. Strømstad (Eds.), *Developing inclusive education.* London: RoutledgeFalmer

Ware, L. (2003b). Working past pity: What we make of disability in schools. In J. Allan (Ed.), *Inclusion, participation and democracy: What is the purpose?* Dordrecht: Kluwer

Ware, L. (2005). The politics of ideology: A pedagogy of critical hope. In L. Ware (Ed.), *Ideology and the politics of (in)exclusion.* New York: Peter Lang

Warnock, M. (2005). *Special educational needs: A new look.* Impact No.11. London: The Philosophy Society of Great Britain

Westwood, P. (2002). *Commonsense methods for children with special educational needs.* London: FalmerRoutledge

Whitty, G. (2002). *Making sense of education policy.* London: Paul Chapman Publishing

Wilde, O. (1882). *Lecture tour.* Leadville, Colorado, USA. Retrieved September 18, 2006, from http://www.neuroticpoets.com/wilde/

Wills, D. (2001). Affirmative deconstruction, inheritance, technology. In P. Patton & T. Smith (Eds.), *Jaques Derrida: Deconstruction engaged.* The Sydney Seminars. Sydney: Power Publications

Wolfreys, J. (1996). A note on a post card: Derrida, Deronda, Deguy. In J. Brannigan, R. Robbins, & J. Wolfreys (Eds.), *Applying: To Derrida.* Basingstoke: Macmillan

Wolfreys, J. (1999). Introduction: What remains unread. In J. Wolfreys. (Ed.), *Literary theories: A reader and guide*. Edinburgh: Edinburgh University Press

Wright, C., Weekes, D., & McGlaughlin, A. (2000). *'Race', class and gender in exclusion from school*. London/New York: Falmer

Yood, J. (2004). Riva Lehrer: An appreciation. In *Riva Lehrer Circle stories. Exhibition catalogue*. Chicago: Gescheidle

Young, I. (1990). *Justice and the politics of difference*. Princeton: Princeton University Press

Zizek, S. (2005). The empty wheelbarrow. *Guardian Comment, 19* February. Retrieved March 06, 2006, from http://www.guardian.co.uk/comment/story/0,3604,14 17982, 00.html

INDEX

INCLUSIVE EDUCATION: CROSS CULTURAL PERSPECTIVES

springer.com

Printed in the United States
97903LV00003B/196-240/A

9 781402 060922